Ahead of the Curve?

UN Ideas and Global Challenges

Louis Emmerij, Richard Jolly,
and Thomas G. Weiss

Indiana University Press

Bloomington and Indianapolis

This book is a publication of
Indiana University Press
601 North Morton Street
Bloomington, IN 47404-3797 USA
http://iupress.indiana.edu
Telephone orders 800-842-6796
Fax orders 812-855-7931
Orders by e-mail iuporder@indiana.edu
© 2001 by United Nations Intellectual History Project

The paper used in this publication meets the minimum requirements
of American National Standard for Information Sciences—Permanence
of Paper for Printed Library Materials, ANSIZ39.48-1984.

Manufactured in the United States of America

Library of Congress Cataloging-in-Publication Data

Emmerij, Louis.
    Ahead of the curve? : UN ideas and global challenges / Louis Emmerij,
Richard Jolly, and Thomas G. Weiss.
        p.   cm. — (United Nations intellectual history)
    Includes index.
    ISBN 0-253-33950-2 (alk. paper). —ISBN 0-253-21467-X (pbk. : alk. paper)
        1. United Nations — History.   I. Jolly, Richard.   II. Weiss, Thomas George.
III. Title.   IV. Series.
JZ4986 .E47   2001
341.23—dc21   00-054098

    1   2   3   4   5   06   05   04   03   02   01

Ahead of the Curve?

United Nations Intellectual History Project

Un livre n'est jamais terminé, seulement abandonné.

—Paul Valéry

Contents

Boxes, Tables, and Figures

Boxes

Tables

Figures

Foreword

Much has been written over the years about the United Nations and its activities, but little about its intellectual contributions and virtually nothing concerning its contributions to the world of ideas on economic and social development. Yet well over half of the organization's staff and resources have been devoted to economic and social development, and many great minds and outstanding leaders have been part of the story. With the publication of this first volume in the United Nations Intellectual History Project, a significant lacuna in twentieth-century scholarship and international relations begins to be filled.

Two aspects of this comprehensive effort are especially encouraging. First, it has strong support from a number of governments and private foundations, all of which respect the need for a project of professional independence and integrity. I urge others to join in supporting and sharing the future costs of this essential work. I would also encourage agencies and organizations of the United Nations system to bring out their own institutional histories, and to put their archives in order and at the disposition of outside researchers.

Second, the authors and directors of the project—Louis Emmerij, Richard Jolly, and Thomas G. Weiss—have been honest and hard-hitting. As independent thinkers who have inside knowledge but who write in their personal and professional capacities, they have told the story as they see it. Some people may disagree with parts of their analysis or interpretation, but I hope that everyone will respect the passion and knowledge that they bring to bear.

Ideas are a main driving force in human progress, and ideas have been among the main contributions of the United Nations from the beginning. The system and its policy research have often been attacked, sometimes rightly and often not. But at its best, the United Nations has always been rooted in powerful ideas reflecting human concerns and aspirations. The story of the organization's efforts to advance the world's development agenda—and, especially, to improve the conditions and prospects of the billions of men, women, and children living in poverty and deprivation—has never been properly documented. This book takes a huge step forward with an intriguing and insight-filled story, showing indeed how ideas "ahead of the curve" have often been among the UN's most important products.

Kofi A. Annan
Secretary-General

Acknowledgments

As the three directors of the United Nations Intellectual History Project (UNIHP), we would like to acknowledge the assistance of many people without whose helping hands and enthusiastic support this book would not have appeared in such a timely fashion.

We begin by thanking Secretary-General Kofi Annan for his unfailing support and encouragement—and that of a number of ambassadors in New York and Geneva. We also thank numerous friends and colleagues within the UN family for their interest and support, especially the UN libraries in New York and Geneva.

Our International Advisory Council is composed of eleven distinguished individuals whose guidance has been appreciable at various steps in this undertaking. A warm thanks is thus extended to Galal Amin, Margaret Joan Anstee, Lourdes Arizpe, Eveline Herfkens, Enrique Iglesias, András Inotai, Thandike Mkandawire, Gert Rosenthal, John Ruggie, Makoto Taniguchi, and Ramesh Thakur.

We would be remiss if we did not mention the late UN economist Sidney Dell, who in 1980 mapped out a twenty-volume project to document the UN's economic and social contributions. Yet he never secured the financing to complete more than one small volume before his death in 1990. We trust that he would be pleased with our efforts to follow in his footsteps.

We are extremely appreciative of the generosity of the governments of the Netherlands, the United Kingdom, and Sweden and of the Ford and Rockefeller Foundations and the Carnegie Corporation of New York. Without their support, this book and this project would have remained where it had been for too many years: on the drawing boards. Finally, we also wish to express our appreciation to the Rockefeller Brothers Fund, which made the Pocantico Conference Center available for a week in July 2000, during which time the rough draft of a manuscript took its present form.

Frédéric Lapeyre, the project's postdoctoral research fellow, was essential for compiling the tables and much of the background information. He is thorough and energetic, and we could not have finished the manuscript without him. We are extremely pleased that he will remain with the project half time when he moves to Geneva's Institut Universitaire d'Etudes du Développement later this year. He will be one of the authors of our in-depth look at international development strategies. We are proud to count him among our younger colleagues and friends.

Other research assistance was provided by Tatiana Carayannis, Kevin Ozgercin, and Richard Ponzio. Teresa Booker and Ron Nerio helped to finalize the last several drafts of the manuscript and put up with our various personality quirks and miserable handwriting. Nancy Okada, as the administrative officer, has helped to ensure the smooth running of a very complicated effort. Under the gracious guidance of Frances Degen Horowitz, The City University of New York (CUNY) Graduate Center has provided a congenial home for the secretariat. We are grateful to them all.

We also would like to thank several colleagues who set aside the time from their own busy schedules to provide comments as we rushed to put the manuscript to bed. Yves Berthelot, Dharam Ghai, Leon Gordenker, Gerry Helleiner, Benjamin Rivlin, and John Toye helped to trim the manuscript and ensure its accuracy. Alison Jolly applied her editing skills and usual good humor to improve the final product. In terms of the statistical presentations, Douglas Walker, Thomas Buettner, and Karoline Schmid have been very helpful throughout the past year.

Needless to say, we ourselves are responsible for any remaining errors in fact or interpretation.

Abbreviations

ACUNS	Academic Council on the UN System
AIDS	Acquired Immune Deficiency Syndrome
AfDB	African Development Bank
AFL-CIO	American Federation of Labor and Congress of Industrial Organizations
ADB	Asian Development Bank
CDP	Committee on Development Planning
CEA	Council of Economic Advisers
CIEC	Conference on International Economic Cooperation
CIS	Commonwealth of Independent States
COMECON	Council on Mutual Economic Assistance
CSD	Commission on Sustainable Development
DAC	Development Assistance Committee
DESA	Department for Economic and Social Affairs
EBRD	European Bank for Reconstruction and Development
EC	European Community
ECA	Economic Commission for Africa
ECE	Economic Commission for Europe
ECLA	Economic Commission for Latin America
ECOSOC	Economic and Social Council
EPTA	Expanded Program of Technical Assistance
EU	European Union
FAO	Food and Agriculture Organization

FDI	Foreign Direct Investment
G-77	Group of 77
GATT	General Agreement on Tariffs and Trade
GNP	Gross National Product
GDP	Gross Domestic Product
HDI	Human Development Index
HIPC	Highly Indebted Poor Country
HIV	Human Immunodeficiency Virus
IBRD	International Bank for Reconstruction and Development (World Bank)
IDA	International Development Association
IDB	Inter-American Development Bank
IDS	Institute of Development Studies [Sussex]
IFAD	International Fund for Agricultural Development
IFI	International Financial Institution
ILO	International Labor Organization
IMF	International Monetary Fund
INSTRAW	International Research and Training Institute for the Advancement of Women
IPC	Integrated Program for Commodities
IPPF	International Planned Parenthood Federation
ISEP	Intensified Smallpox Eradication Program
ITO	International Trade Organization
MERCOSUR	South American Common Market
NAFTA	North American Free Trade Agreement
NATO	North Atlantic Treaty Organization
NAM	Non-Aligned Movement
NGO	Non-Governmental Organization
NIEO	New International Economic Order
NTB	Nuclear Test Ban
ODA	Official Development Assistance
OECD	Organization for Economic Cooperation and Development
OPEC	Organization of Petroleum Exporting Countries
PPP$	Purchasing Power Parity

SALT	Strategic Arms Limitation Talk
SAP	Structural Adjustment Program
SDRs	Special Drawing Rights
SUNFED	Special United Nations Fund for Economic Development
TNC	Transnational Corporation
U.K.	United Kingdom of Great Britain and Northern Ireland
UN	United Nations
UNCED	United Nations Conference on Environment and Development
UNCHE	United Nations Conference on the Human Environment
UNCHS	United Nations Center for Human Settlements
UNCTAD	United Nations Conference on Trade and Development
UNDP	United Nations Development Program
UNEP	United Nations Environment Program
UNESCO	United Nations Educational, Scientific, and Cultural Organization
UNFCCC	United Nations Framework Convention for Climate Control
UNFPA	United Nations Population Fund (originally the United Nations Fund for Population Activities)
UNHCHR	United Nations High Commissioner for Human Rights
UNHCR	United Nations High Commissioner for Refugees
UNICEF	United Nations Children's Fund
UNIDO	United Nations Industrial Development Organization
UNIFEM	United Nations Development Fund for Women
UNIHP	United Nations Intellectual History Project
UNRISD	United Nations Research Institute for Social Development
UNU	United Nations University
U.S.	United States of America
USAID	United States Agency for International Development
U.S.S.R.	Union of Soviet Socialist Republics
WEP	World Employment Program
WFC	World Food Council
WHO	World Health Organization
WIDER	World Institute for Development Economics Research
WTO	World Trade Organization

Ahead of the Curve?

Introduction

- **The Project**
- **The Literature**
- **The Challenges**
- **The Approach**
- **The Book**

This is the first publication from the United Nations Intellectual History Project (UNIHP). This project was born from the conviction that after fifty years it was time to identify and trace the economic and social ideas that have been launched or nurtured by the UN family since 1945. The Cold War's end led to a substantial growth in scholarly and policy interest in the political and security activities of the world organization. There has, until now, been no such increase in the economic and social arena. It is time to begin to right the balance.

Most observers think primarily about the political and security institutions and individuals when mention is made of the UN. Nobel Peace Prizes awarded to the UN for these activities come to mind, including to Ralph Bunche, Dag Hammarskjöld, the office of the UN High Commissioner for Refugees, and UN peacekeepers.

But the UN's economic and social institutions have quietly been making an impact, often with more success than in the political and peacekeeping arenas. Indeed, two development agencies, the International Labor Organization (ILO) and the United Nations Children's Fund (UNICEF), have also been recognized with Nobel Peace Prizes. More importantly from the point of view of this intellectual history, nine Nobel Prize laureates in economics (Jan Tinbergen, Gunnar Myrdal, Wassily Leontief, James E. Meade, Arthur Lewis, Richard Stone, Lawrence Klein, Theodore W. Schultz, and Amartya Sen) have spent a substantial part of their professional lives working as UN staff members or contributing to UN ideas and activities.

We should be clear about what we mean when we speak of the "United Nations." We see the UN as an entity, for all its differences and diversity. There are common elements—including solidarity with the vulnerable, concern for universal human rights, and other common values like commitment to peace and sustainable human development. The Bretton Woods institutions are included as a counterpoint for much of our argument, and *de facto* they have considered themselves somewhat apart from the main UN system. Our assumption is that what is most needed is a history of economic and social activities coming within the purview of the main UN institutions. The work of the specialized agencies will be brought in to the extent that they are, or should be, directly related to global programs and by virtue of the coordinating responsibility of the Economic and Social Council (ECOSOC). This book, and indeed the entire UNIHP, will not provide an institutional history of the main UN organizations operating in the economic, social, and human rights arenas; rather, it will treat their contributions as and when relevant to the pursuit of ideas central to UN debates over the past half-century.

Did the big and important ideas come from within the UN system? Or did they originate outside and were then "picked up" by the world organization? Whatever their origins, what happened to ideas once they were embraced by the international civil service and within UN structures of ongoing debates and conferences? Were they debated and discarded? Were they discussed, distorted, and then adopted? And, of course, what happened once they became policy as resolutions, declarations, conventions, or treaties? Did they matter to states, corporations, non-governmental organizations (NGOs), and individuals?

The UN has no comprehensive history and no in-house historians; the archives of the UN and its specialized bodies are often in a sorry state. Brian Urquhart, one of the first recruits to the secretariat, who served for four decades, told us: "One of the troubles with the UN, which you are now rather belatedly remedying, is the fact that it never had a historical section." This is still needed. There are a few institutional histories, but no systematic overall effort has ever been made to document the UN's compelling story, especially in the area of economic and social development. Many of the early pioneers of economic and social ideas are aging or have died. There is an actuarial imperative to our efforts to help recover the institutional memory, particularly through oral histories.

Why were we driven to launch this project at the dawn of the twenty-first century? As lifelong participants in and observers of multilateral development work and diplomacy, it had struck us for some time that the UN story deserves to be better documented if it is to be better understood and appreciated. The Bretton Woods institutions in this respect are far ahead. The World Bank published two massive histories—one on the occasion of its twenty-fifth and the other (two volumes and more than 2,000 pages) of its fiftieth anniversary.[1] The International Monetary Fund (IMF) has an in-house historian who ensures the capture of its place in history with regular publications.[2]

We decided to take the plunge. Once the decision was made to fill the gaps, we opted for an *intellectual* history—a history of ideas. An institutional history is still needed, especially for those agencies and organizations that have not yet documented their own histories in sufficient depth. Institutions are, of course, a key part of the environment that helps to generate, promote, select, and discourage ideas. However, we ourselves bring in institutions insofar as a given organization at a particular moment helped launch or polish an important idea.

For instance, our discussion of international trade and finance traces the role of the United Nations Conference on Trade and Development (UNCTAD) in order to reflect the radical new ideas that challenged orthodoxy about the distribution of benefits from the international economic system. Similarly, it would be inconceivable to discuss children's rights or the environment without examining inputs from the UNICEF and the United Nations Environment Program (UNEP). In these cases, getting the history right would be impossible without an emphasis on these institutions as well as on such personalities as Raúl Prebisch, James Grant, and Maurice Strong.

Granted, there is no adequate historical study of the origins and evolution of ideas cultivated within the UN and of their impact on wider thinking and international action. "But," the reader may well ask, "why is it ideas, and not institutions, that are being analyzed?" A social scientist might query, "So what?"

Ideas and concepts have clearly been a driving force in many areas of human progress. They are arguably the most important legacy of the UN. They have set past, present, and future international agendas for the economic and social arenas. The lack of attention to the UN's role in generating or nurturing ideas is perplexing. As Oxford University political economist Ngaire Woods summarized: "In short, ideas, whether economic or not, have been left out of analyses of international relations."[3] Many political scientists, especially analysts of international political economy, as well as economic historians are rediscovering the role of ideas in international policy making. We say *re*discovering because the study of ideas, although relatively new in analyses of international politics and organizations, is common bill of fare for historians, philosophers, students of literature, and economists.

We do not worry long over the copyright for any particular idea, which is almost always futile. Observers are still arguing whether Alexander Graham Bell deserves credit for inventing the telephone because so many others were toying with the same idea at about the same time. For us, the important fact is that an idea (like the telephone) exists. The project's bottom line consists in analyzing the evolution of key ideas and concepts about international economic and social development born *or* nurtured, refined *or* applied under UN auspices. Their origins will be traced, and the motivations behind them as well as their relevance, influence, and impact will be assessed against the backdrop of the socioeconomic situations of individual countries, the global economy, and major international developments.

The Project

The UNIHP has two main components. The first is a series of commissioned books about the major economic and social ideas or concepts central to UN activity, and which in our judgment are most salient at the beginning of this century. These will be written by experts based in research institutions worldwide and will be published in the project's series with Indiana University Press. They cover the following global challenges under which pertinent ideas will be traced: human rights; international trade and finance; international development strategies; the global commons; global governance; quantifying the world; transnational corporations; development assistance; the gender revolution; human security; and development perspectives from the regional commissions.

The second component consists of some seventy-five in-depth oral history interviews with leading contributors to the development of crucial ideas and concepts within the UN system. As we go to press, we have already conducted about twenty of these, which focus on five areas. The first is primarily biographical. Here we ask about influences on an individual's educational and professional interests and career choices, as well on his or her own ideas regarding social and economic issues.

The second area explores an individual's evaluation as to whether and how particular global occurrences have affected the development of new thinking. Here we specifically refer to such major events as the UN's founding and earlier experiences by the League of Nations during the Great Depression, decolonization, the founding of the Group of 77, and the rise and fall of the Berlin Wall.

Third, we ask about how well various UN organizations, with which an individual has been affiliated throughout a career, have adapted to these global events. For instance, what ideas emerged in response to particular problems or crises? What ideas were discarded as a result of specific world events? Here we explore, for example, the link between the New International Economic Order (NIEO) and the oil price hike in 1973, or sustainable development and evidence about ecological deterioration.

Fourth, we seek to trace what happened to critical ideas within the UN system and what factors may have affected their life span and ultimate policy impact. Specifically, we are asking interview subjects for their opinions about the importance within the UN of leadership, the quality of the international civil service, the dynamics of global conferences and eminent commissions, the support or opposition of particular governments and regional groups, and of course the influence of North-South relations during the Cold War.

The fifth cluster of questions serves as a synthesis and asks individuals to identify particular UN ideas that have had an impact on international politics and why. Here we ask interviewees to express their opinions about the most crucial challenges, conceptual and operational, for the UN at the dawn of the twenty-first century.

We have quoted in this book a few insights from those whom we have already interviewed. Many more will appear in a forthcoming volume in this series containing key excerpts from interviews, tentatively titled *UN Ideas: Views from the Trenches and Turrets*. Oral history with individuals who have held key positions as staff members, consultants, researchers, or diplomats in and around the UN are especially useful in identifying ideas that never got beyond a conference room or that never made it into a document, as well as in explaining the evolution of a prominent idea that was spawned or nurtured by the world organization. We are aware of the problems in concentrating on what specialists call "elite history," but we have decided to begin with these interviews first because senior officials and diplomats have frequently been opinion-leaders, and their ideas set agendas. Except for the role of the UN secretary-general,[4] too little analytical attention has been paid to the role of leadership within international secretariats. Later, and with more resources, it would be desirable to interview other knowledgeable persons at various levels of seniority within and outside the UN. Ours is a pragmatic first attempt to help build an institutional memory about economic and social development.

The perspectives from key individuals are especially important because so few have written in detail about their own participation in and reflections on events. Their "stories" about what happened in bureaucracies and the corridors of international gatherings are an important source of knowledge and insight. As mentioned earlier, one justification for our efforts is to rectify a woeful lack of attention within international organizations to archives and to learning. Thus, the project is encouraging the establishment of international networks among archivists and researchers using UN documents, including career records of UN staff. The project's published books and oral history interviews, in an electronic form as yet to be decided upon, will be disseminated to serve as original resources for future generations of scholars and practitioners.

At the end of the present phase of the UNIHP, we have committed ourselves to drawing the lessons from the contents of commissioned books and oral histories. This synthesis volume, tentatively titled *The UN and the World of Ideas*, will capture the first five years of work by our extended research family.

But we have also decided to stick out our necks now and write this synthesis *avant la lettre*. Here we set out how the UN system has reacted with policy ideas to major global challenges, and we try to identify the areas where the UN was ahead of or behind the curve. What do we mean by this? First, an idea itself can be so unusual as to be in front of the conventional wisdom of the time or so timid as to sustain orthodoxy. For instance, decolonization was certainly ahead of its time at the Charter's signing in 1945, and this idea fired imaginations and accelerated the pace of independence. In contrast, the general UN timidity in the face of the worldwide promotion of liberalization and privatization in the early 1980s was so politically correct with the major economic powers as to be behind the curve. The UN resumed a leadership role in the 1990s in developing a more nuanced position, emphasizing human and social concerns. Second, an idea can be so far ahead of its time that it is more of an aspiration than an effective guide to policy. For instance, many of the demands contained in the mid-1970s call for a NIEO fell on deaf ears, at least among the major powers.

Moreover, when we state that the UN "succeeded" or "failed," we try to distinguish between the "two UNs" — the arena where states make decisions and the international civil service. The decision-making arena for states is more and more pluralistic. States are still the main decision-makers, and national interests have not receded as the basis for making decisions, but NGOs and the private sector are playing an ever larger role. Success or failure of this UN depends upon government perceptions of *raisons d'état* and the accompanying political will or lack thereof.

The second UN is composed of semi-independent secretariats, including outside experts, whose job descriptions include research and idea-mongering. Success or failure of this second UN is not totally independent of governments, and hence of resources and support. Nonetheless, there is more room for maneuver and autonomy, particularly in the intellectual and advocacy realms, than is often supposed. And one of our propositions is that individuals and leadership matter.

Our first attempt to determine whether or not the UN's ideas were ahead of their time follows in the pages below. We hope that readers' appetites will be sufficiently whetted to peruse the other volumes to be published by Indiana University Press over the next few years and to engage in discussions with us about this overview story, as we see it, before the research in the commissioned studies becomes available.

Early publication is not without risks. We have decided to go ahead with this volume for four main reasons. First, UN Secretary-General Kofi Annan, whose foreword graces these pages, has urged us to do so.[5] Second, the authors of the dozen books about big ideas whom we have commissioned also asked for guidance. Third, putting together this book has drawn to our attention challenges, ideas, and personalities that might otherwise have escaped us. And fourth, this first effort will, we hope, encourage readers to communicate with us to debate what we have put down and to present their own contributions.

The Literature

What, then, is an intellectual history, and how does one go about writing one? Although the term can have a variety of meanings, "intellectual history" seeks to explain the origins of particular ideas; trace their trajectories within institutions, scholarship, or discourse; and in some cases, certainly in ours, evaluate the impact of ideas on policy and action. What we seek to explain is the role of the UN as intellectual actor.

Our journey follows a stimulating yet difficult path into the theoretical literature of ideas and their policy impact.[6] The relevant literature for this project can be grouped usefully into three categories. The first is *institutionalist approaches,* such as Judith Goldstein and Robert Keohane's analyses of foreign policy[7] and Kathryn Sikkink's analysis of developmentalism in Latin America.[8] The second consists of *expert-group approaches,* which include Peter Haas's epistemic communities,[9] Peter Hall's work on analyzing the impact of Keynesian economists,[10] and Ernst B. Haas's work on knowledge[11] as well as more recent work by Sikkink on transnational networks of activists.[12] The third category consists of *constructivists* such as Alexander Wendt[13] and John Ruggie[14] and those more influenced by the Italian school of Marxism, such as Robert Cox and his followers.[15] A brief overview is in order.

Institutionalists are generally concerned with how organizations shape the policy preferences of their members. Ideas can be particularly important to the policy-making process during periods of upheaval. In thinking about the end of World War II or the Cold War, ideas provide a conceptual road map that can be used to understand changing preferences and definitions of vital interests. The institutionalist approach helps us to understand the dynamics among ideas, multilateral institutions, and national policies. It also enables us to begin thinking about how such institutions as the UN influence elite images, as well as how opinion-makers influence the world organization by themselves serving as sources of ideas. They often do this by being recruited into the world organization as staff, consultants, experts, and chairs of special commissions.

The second category of literature examines the role of intellectuals in creating ideas, of technical experts in diffusing them and making them more concrete, and of all sorts of people in influencing the positions adopted by a wide range of actors. Networks of knowledgeable experts influence a broad spectrum of international politics through their ability to interact with policy-makers irrespective of location and national boundaries. Researchers working on HIV/AIDS or climate change can have an impact on policy by clarifying an issue from which decision-makers may deduce what is in the interests of their administrations. They can help to frame the debate on a particular issue, thus narrowing the acceptable range of bargaining for international negotiations. They can introduce standards for action. These networks can help provide justifications for alternatives and often build national or international coalitions to support chosen policies and to advocate for change. In many ways this approach borrows from Thomas Kuhn's well-known work on the nature of scientific revolutions.[16]

The third body of literature, comprising the work of constructivists and critical theorists, seeks to determine the potential for individuals, their governments, and international institutions to change rather than be robots whose behavior is predetermined by material conditions. The so-called critical approach—which views the work of all organizations and their ideologies, including the UN, as given by material conditions or as instruments to maintain the status quo—is particularly pertinent. One of the reasons for this project is to examine over the past half-century how ideas about economic and social development—and here the UN system has nurtured a large number—have called into question the conventional wisdom.

The Challenges

Five questions often arise about existing approaches to the study of ideas and international organizations. We list them below, with a brief indication of how we deal with them in our own approach.

We begin with a classic: Which comes first, the chicken or the egg, the idea or the policy? Most approaches do not explain the sources of ideas, just their effects. They rarely explain how ideas emerge or change, with the exception of pointing to technological innovations. By ignoring where ideas come from and how they change, we cannot ascertain cause and effect. Do ideas shape policy? Or does policy push existing ideas forward and perhaps even generate new ideas that may emerge in response to that policy or action? Do ideas serve, after the fact, as a convenient justification for a policy or a decision? A prominent Scottish historian of political thought, Quentin Skinner, raised these issues thirty years ago: "The social context, it is said, helps to cause the formation and change of ideas; but the ideas in turn help to cause the formation and change of the social context. Thus the historian ends up presenting himself with nothing better than the time-honored puzzle about the chicken and the egg."[17]

A second question is whether ideas are mere products, or whether they have a life of their own. We trace the trajectory of ideas within the UN and examine how individual leadership, coalitions, and national and bureaucratic rivalries within it have generated, nurtured, distorted, and implemented particular ideas. At the same time, we also hope to discern how ideas, in and of themselves, have helped to shape policy outcomes at the UN.

A third and long-standing debate among intellectual historians is whether an idea should be analyzed in light of the historical and social context within which it emerged and evolved, or whether it can be understood on its own, without reference to context. We are partisans of the former school and thus assume that economic and social ideas at the UN cannot be properly understood if divorced from their historical and social context. The birth and survival of ideas in the UN—or their death and suppression—invariably reflect events and are contingent upon politics and the world economy.

We would be remiss to treat ideas merely as abstractions. Being familiar with context should enable us to understand better the constraints surrounding ideas as well as the opportunities afforded by them. For example, some come in the form of funding possibilities. Researchers who have sought support from foundations or governments have long understood that the "atmosphere" at the time of grant applications is crucial to securing adequate resources to pursue an idea. It should come as no surprise that atmospherics help to explain why certain ideas make a specific difference at a specific moment in time. They may also help to explain why ideas and their institutional sponsors may be "ahead of" or "behind" the curve in terms of their political and operational salience, whatever the intellectual attractiveness and persuasiveness of an idea.

A fourth question is when to begin tracing the trajectory of a particular idea. We can only agree with Woods that "very few ideas are very new."[18] At what point in its life or in which of its many possible incarnations should one begin to study an idea? Frederick Cooper and Randall Packard point out that postwar modernization theory aimed to transform individuals from "superstitious and status-oriented beings to rational and achievement-oriented beings."[19] But the idea of creating a new person is older than development theory. It could be traced back to the efforts of the earliest colonial missionaries, the Enlightenment, Karl Marx, or, for that matter, to God with Adam's rib in the Garden of Eden.

A related issue concerns ownership. The difficulty of identifying a single individual or institution responsible for the creation of an idea is one illustration of this problem, which is manifest in the overlapping processes of multilateral affairs. An idea often evolves and ownership becomes more widely shared through group processes, which is particularly pertinent within multilateral institutions where a multiplicity of geographic and other groupings is the only way of doing business and widespread ownership is indeed a goal of deliberations.[20] Hence, we are not undertaking the type of historical analysis pioneered by Arthur Lovejoy, who sought to trace an idea "through all the provinces of history in which it appears."[21] Rather, we pick up an idea at the time it intersects with the UN. And even within the world organization's history, there are relevant antecedents that can be treated only cursorily.

A specific project on this theme is being directed by Desmond McNeill and Morten Bøås at the University of Oslo. They are seeking to map precisely how five development ideas (the informal sector, sustainable development, governance, social capital, and local knowledge) have penetrated and been interpreted by eight intergovernmental organizations: World Bank, United Nations Development Program (UNDP), ILO, Asian Development Bank (ADB), Inter-American Development ment Bank (IDB), African Development Bank (AfDB), IMF, and World Trade Organization (WTO).[22] Their goal is to track how these ideas were adopted, adapted, distorted, or suppressed in the process. McNeill and Bøås are persuaded that "few doubt the power and influence of these institutions," but "we know next to nothing about why some particular ideas are taken up by institutions in the multilateral system."[23]

The fifth and final question relates to the influence of ideas versus that of the carriers of ideas.[24] There is little consensus about which—in our case, the ideas or the key individuals in key UN organizations or forums—are more influential. This is particularly relevant for our treatment of experts. It can be argued that the more influential the members of an expert group or the greater their access to governmental policy-makers, the greater the odds that their ideas will be adopted, irrespective of the ideas' inherent value. Ideas presuppose agents, and at the UN they cannot be divorced from agency, which is why we are documenting through oral histories the role of individuals in the evolution of international economic and social development.

Notwithstanding the methodological bumps in the road, ideas are important determinants of change. Because of their multiple uses and meanings, they are important objects of study. This project takes seriously the proposition that ideas, both good and bad, have an impact. We take our inspiration from John Maynard Keynes, who wrote of "scribblers": "The ideas of economists and political philosophers, both when they are right and when they are wrong, are more powerful than is commonly understood."[25]

The Approach

In addition, we should declare our own normative agenda, which extends beyond improving our understanding of the sources, evolution, and impact of key ideas. We seek insights in order to improve the UN's future contribution to economic and social development. More specifically, we hope to understand better the role of the UN as an intellectual actor and the processes in the multilateral marketplace of ideas, in order to identify workable strategies and tactics. The reason for this effort lies behind a comment from Jeffrey Garten, dean of Yale University's School of Management, about UN efforts to broker a pact among transnational corporations, labor associations, and watchdog NGOs. "There are just a huge number of issues that have to be addressed globally and there is no real infrastructure to do it," he said. "They can only be dealt with in partnership agreements between governments, business and non-governmental organizations."[26]

Understanding how important the UN's past role has been in disseminating and generating ideas to respond to global challenges requires responses to four questions. First, what have been the key economic and social ideas contributed by the UN? The answer to this first question is, in many ways, necessary background for the others. For us, "ideas" are defined as beliefs held by individuals that influence their attitudes and actions toward economic and social development, which, as mentioned earlier, are analyzed when they intersect with the UN.[27] In this volume we concentrate on a few of the biggest themes, which we believe have emanated from the UN and made a difference. We selected them in interactions with a host of formal and informal advisers, including our own International Advisory Council. This does not mean that our list is complete or sacrosanct. A central concern in choosing topics is that the ideas were considered, wisely or unwisely, to be relevant by those engaged in the international debates of the time. Among the many possibilities, we have given priority to those that we consider have continued relevance for public policy in the new millennium. This explains our "future-oriented history," which some have criticized as being an oxymoron, others as leading to methodological bias. We defend the choice as a pragmatic decision that allows us to proceed with ideas that have currency.

Second, we ask, What were the sources of these ideas? Were they initiated within or substantially nurtured from the UN? Were they generated by specialized agencies? Were they first articulated by eminent individuals or distinguished commissions? Were they developed within the context of lengthy preparations for global conferences, or perhaps within parallel forms organized by NGOs? If so, what portions of them about economic and social advancement were generated within the UN system? If a particular idea was developed within the UN, did a key individual bring it with him or her and subsequently lobby effectively for its organizational adoption? Or was the idea the result of ongoing group negotiating processes? Was there a two-way street, or were international secretariats more the real generators of ideas than groups of countries were?

What ideas were brought from outside the UN system and were then promoted by the UN? If an idea originated outside, did it emanate from academe or outside expert groups? What about NGOs? Did an idea emerge in response to a particular event or crisis? Did an idea originate within an elite, or was there a "mass base" reflecting widespread popular support and enthusiasm for a particular idea, as there was for the UN Charter and for the Universal Declaration of Human Rights? The inter-war period raised awareness of what was not yet labeled "interdependence," which contributed to calls for international cooperation. Did some economic and social ideas originate in the UN because of awareness from a critical mass of people about a connection between peace and development? For instance, what role was played in establishing functional agencies by the conviction that the Great Depression and severe economic dislocation and political instability should and could be mitigated? To what extent did this postwar conviction drive research, analysis, and action?

Third, what happened to particular ideas within the UN? The answer depends on tracing the trajectory of concepts, good and bad. Why was a particular idea discarded? Was it too controversial? Was it too simple or too complex? Were its backers not influential enough? Even if disputed and discarded, did the discarded idea return in another guise?

In tracing the evolution and distortion of an idea, intellectual and political leadership within UN secretariats is key. Institutional rivalries, particularly within the UN system proper and between it and the Bretton Woods institutions, are crucial variables. Tensions within and among diplomatic coalitions are still another important and under-documented factor.

Fourth and finally, what impact, if any, have particular ideas had? If so, how? There are, in our view, at least four measurable ways in which ideas can have a substantial influence on policy. These propositions will be tested throughout the UNIHP's lifetime.

The first is that they can change the nature of international public policy discourse and help states to define and redefine their interests to be more inclusive of common concerns. For example, ideas about dependency and the concept of "center-periphery," which were developed by Latin American economists within the Economic Commission for Latin America (ECLA) in the 1950s, fundamentally altered the discourse on modernization. Also, the growing emphasis on the idea of human rights in the UN reflects in part a redefinition of respect for individuals as part of the identity of responsible sovereign states.

The second type of influence is that ideas can provide a tactical guide to policy and action when norms conflict or when sequencing or priorities are disputed. The necessity to broaden the narrow orthodoxy of neo-liberalism with the requirements for a "human face" on structural adjustment is one such dispute in which ideas provided a road map to navigate between conflicting needs. Another example of a clash in norms in which ideas are useful is to override state sovereignty with military force in cases of genocide, mass murder, and displacement.

The third kind of impact is that ideas can alter prospects for forming new coalitions of political or institutional forces. For example, UNCTAD's call to take seriously the declining terms of trade and the NIEO became the glue of solidarity in the South. The common heritage of humankind provided a way to form un-usual partnerships among states and NGOs. The Integrated Program for Com-modities (IPC) provided the framework for producers and consumers, and subgroups within them, to come together in new ways.

The fourth influence is that ideas can also become embedded in institutions and thus perhaps challenge not only the founding principles of those institutions but also help in setting future agendas. The establishment of new agencies—for example, UNEP or the International Fund for Agricultural Development (IFAD) —is one manifestation, as is "mainstreaming" of issues and the creation of new units within established organizations. And as Cox notes ruefully, "Institutions take on a life of their own."[28] A better understanding of how ideas become em-bedded is essential, because this impact can be observed. In this regard, we hope to comprehend better the UN's own decision-making style and determine whether and when it has a comparative advantage in the formulation and dif-fusion of ideas. But we also need to clarify in what ways the institutionaliza-tion of ideas in the UN system has an impact on policy formulation elsewhere, particularly in governments. Strong leadership and acceptance by key institu-tions give power to ideas and impose a consensus by facilitating funding and implementation.

The Book

It is fascinating, and often amazing, how many times the UN system has been ahead of the curve. As the reader will discover in subsequent pages, this is true with respect to the early ideas on development, on international aspects of envi-ronmental problems, population and technology, women's issues, international and national development policies, and trade and finance. The League of Nations had discussed employment policies during the 1920s and 1930s, and the postwar UN contributions were pioneering. The inclusion of human rights in the Char-ter and the adoption of the Universal Declaration in 1948 appear, in retrospect, mind-boggling, or in the words of Stéphane Hessel, an early UN recruit, who sat at Eleanor Roosevelt's side in 1948 and later became Ambassadeur de France, "what makes the second half of the 20th century such an important moment of world history." And we could go on.

There have also been many instances when the UN has been behind the curve. This is true, for instance, in the case of HIV/AIDS, global income gaps, or Urquhart's candidate for the worst idea, Julian Huxley's "sex at high altitudes." In determining whether the UN system has been ahead of or behind the curve, we explore successes and failures. There is a necessity, if we wish to come to grips with the world organization's duty to swim against the tide and make room for unconventional ideas. In short, our portrait of the intellectual history of the UN includes warts and all.

We thus hope that readers now have a sense about our approach to "UN Ideas," but what do we mean by "Global Challenges" in the subtitle? These are problems that are widely perceived as sufficient threats to upset the economic and social (and eventually also the political) balance worldwide, even if a problem is circumscribed or regional. "Perception" is of the essence here, and by whom, because not everyone or even the most important governments may agree that a given problem poses a truly global threat. The time frame is also consequential. If a problem is tackled in a timely fashion, what might become a serious challenge can be postponed or even vanish. Of course, a problem may not be an immediate risk, or it may take longer to come to a head than was originally predicted; that does not make it less serious.

After this introductory discussion of the role of ideas and international institutions, this book proceeds through eight chapters in which UN ideas and global challenges are interwoven, followed by a brief chapter of conclusions. Chapter 1 analyzes the four powerful founding ideas of the UN: peace and negotiation in place of war; decolonization in place of domination; human rights in place of repression; and economic and social development in place of poverty. Chapter 2 examines the 1960s, when development became the main item on the agenda of the UN system and developing countries increasingly coalesced as a group. Chapter 3 looks into ideas to help confront the employment challenge and promote basic needs in the 1970s. Chapter 4 examines the global conferences under UN auspices of the 1970s and 1990s in which such new ideas as sustainability, gender, and habitat were placed on the international agenda. Chapter 5 analyzes the financial and social crises of the globalization era, with their intellectual criticisms and alternatives. Chapter 6 looks into the collapse of the Socialist bloc. Chapter 7 examines widening income gaps, particularly among regions and countries, and proposals to tackle this phenomenon. Chapter 8 analyzes the crises of national and global governance.

This book is somewhat different from the commissioned books and the other two overarching volumes that will follow in this series. It starts with global challenges and asks whether the UN responded with a creative framing of the issues and workable policy ideas. In future publications the ideas themselves will be the prism through which history unfolds more slowly and with far more documentation than we can permit ourselves here.

This first attempt to map the UN's intellectual history results from significant but inevitably, as yet, insufficient archival research, brainstorming, reflection, and interviews. We expect that this brief effort to sketch essential elements of the project's analytical framework will generate a lively discussion that will strengthen and sharpen our focus on the role of the UN as intellectual actor. But we underline that this book is our first rather than our final word, which will only be completed after the last book has been written. Even then, we will no doubt wonder if we could have done better.

Many observers are more than willing to regurgitate the philosopher George Santayana's incantation in *Life of Reason* that "they who cannot remember the past are condemned to repeat it." However, those who support research normally are cool toward history, even historical inquiry such as ours that has policy implications for human survival with dignity in the new millennium. We thus are extremely appreciative of the financial generosity of governments and private foundations that have made this book possible. We are grateful for their confidence. We trust that they will be satisfied with this first product. As always, we welcome comments and suggestions from our readers.

L.E.
R.J.
T.G.W.

United Nations Intellectual History Project
The CUNY Graduate Center
New York City, September 2000

1

Four Powerful Ideas and the Early Years

- **The UN's Wartime Origins**
- **San Francisco and the Charter**
- **Human Rights and Self-Determination**
- **Three Pioneering Reports on Development:**
  - **Measures for Full Employment**
  - **Measures for Economic Development**
  - **Measures for International Economic Stability**
- **Criticisms**

The United Nations (UN) was born in San Francisco in 1945, just as the deadliest and most destructive war in recorded history was coming to an end. Rising from the ashes of destruction and despair came four powerful sets of ideas.

- Peace—the idea that sovereign states could create an international organization and procedures that would replace military aggression and war by negotiations and collective security.
- Independence—the idea that peoples in all countries had rights to be politically independent and sovereign and make whatever national and international agreements that their citizens might choose.
- Development—the idea that all countries, long independent or newly so, could purposefully pursue policies of economic and social advance, which over time would rapidly improve the welfare and living standards of their populations.
- Human Rights—the boldest idea of all, namely, that every individual in every country throughout the world shared an equal claim not only to such individual civil and political rights as life, liberty, and the pursuit of happiness but also to a core of more collective economic and social freedoms.

The breathtaking nature of these four ideas was, and remains, remarkable. Each of course had predecessors including Immanuel Kant's *Perpetual Peace*, the Declaration of Independence, the New Deal, and the 1789 Declaration of the Rights of Man and of the Citizen. The gestation period for ideas, as we have underlined in the introduction, is long. The four big ideas were explicit or implicit in Woodrow Wilson's Fourteen Points at Versailles.[1]

In one or more essential respects, however, each of the four powerful sets of ideas represented important advances from historical precedents and national and international norms and institutions of the period. Even more remarkable was the political willingness to set in motion a new era based on such thinking in relationship to most thinking and expectations at the time.

At this point, it is customary for the reader to pause, sigh, and utter a deep "but." But what about the Cold War, and what about the more than 160 smaller wars around the world since 1945? But what about the egregious record of human rights violations over five decades, and the many moves to independence that ended in brutal dictatorship? But what about the failures of development that have left the world, at the opening of the new millennium, with widening gaps in wealth and income and half the global population having to survive on incomes equivalent to less than two dollars a day?

Facts are facts, failures are failures. These tragic events are part of the record. There will be no attempt to airbrush them away. But there is a positive side to the balance sheet—important successes as well as failures. Indeed, the successes are more than many people realize and certainly more than many dared hope at the time when the San Francisco Conference on International Organization was convened and during the early years of the United Nations.

Since 1945 there has been no world war. Although military spending has broken all records and tens of thousands of nuclear weapons still threaten the survival of the human race, deaths from war since 1945 have been markedly fewer than those in the first half of the twentieth century. In spite of the Cold War— indeed, because it was mostly cold rather than hot—barely a fifth of the twentieth century's 110 million war-related deaths have taken place in the fifty-five years since the UN's creation.[2]

The end of colonization and the achievement of sovereign independence came within a decade or two, although in 1945 many observers expected that the decolonization process could take up to a century. Today 189 countries belong to the United Nations, compared with the fifty-one original member states. About three-quarters of these countries now have governments chosen through multi-party elections. Only a handful had done so in 1945.

Economic and social development has been impressive in many instances. In developing countries, average life expectancy has increased to double the estimated level of the late 1930s. Child mortality has been lowered by more than three-quarters. Adult literacy has been raised to nearly three-quarters, with basic education extended to more than 85 percent of the world's children. Malnutrition has been reduced in all regions of the world except Africa. Smallpox has been eradicated (see Table 1.1), and yaws, guinea worm, and polio, a worldwide scourge in the early postwar world, have been virtually eliminated.

Progress in human rights has also been extraordinary. Action was slow at first, as was to be expected, because the Universal Declaration of Human Rights, in Stéphane Hessel's judgment, "could be only a first step in a long effort to make human rights a reality." But the original idea made inroads into policy so that, beginning in the 1980s, a surge of ratifications of human rights conventions occurred along with increasing implementation of many measures and outrage over abuses.

Table 1.1. Evolution of Selected Social Development Indicators, 1950–2000

	Life Expectancy at Birth (Years)						Under-Five Child Mortality Rate (per 1,000 Live Births)				
	1955	1965	1975	1985	1995	2000	1955	1965	1975	1985	1995
World	46	52	58	61	64	65	217	164	131	109	87
Industrialized countries	68	70	72	75	77	78	65	42	26	13	9
Eastern Europe and the CIS	61	66	68	69	70	70	131	78	53	40	32
Developing countries	43	48	53	57	60	61	245	201	162	126	101
Least developed countries	36	40	44	47	49	51	307	262	229	198	171
East Asia (excluding China)	50	57	63	67	71	72	199	121	77	52	35
China	41	50	63	67	68	70	243	149	73	61	55
Southeast Asia and the Pacific	44	50	55	59	64	66	217	165	134	104	76
South Asia (excluding India)	40	45	49	54	59	62	281	243	205	165	120
India	39	45	50	55	60	63	254	208	174	142	103
Latin America and the Caribbean	51	57	61	65	68	69	189	148	114	73	49
Sub-Saharan Africa	37	41	45	48	49	49	291	252	219	184	162
Arab states	44	49	55	61	66	67	255	205	145	95	68

Source: UN Population Division data files, 2000.

Note: Columns refer to the average life expectancy or under-five child mortality rate over the five-year period preceding the year stated at the head of the column.

Almost a hundred countries, more than half of UN member states, have now rat-ified all six major human rights instruments, and about three-quarters, the covenants on Civil and Political Rights and on Economic, Social, and Cultural Rights. More than 80 percent of countries have ratified the conventions on the elimination of all forms of racial discrimination and of all forms of discrimina-tion against women. All but two countries (Somalia and the United States) have ratified the Convention on the Rights of the Child.

The UN has of course been only part of the story. But the world organization has played a central role in bringing these ideas to fruition on the global stage — providing the occasion for their initiation, forums for their debate, means for reaching consensus, and the mechanisms for achieving decisions with interna-tional legitimacy. Through its specialized agencies and its organizations with field support, the UN has often given critical support and helped mobilize broader action.

By the standards of previous centuries, these international achievements have been numerous; many have been positive, certainly unprecedented. The rest of this chapter provides more details on the earliest years. Chapter 2 extends the analysis to the 1960s.

The UN's Wartime Origins

Whence came the ideas and the bold creativity of the United Nations? Cer-tainly, there were outstanding individuals, and one of the purposes of our ongo-ing research is to identify and document some of them and their contributions to intellectual history. But the roots of thinking about international peace and de-velopment go back centuries, gathering pace and interest over the previous hun-dred years.

The immediate preparations for the UN were taken in the early phases of the Second World War, stirred by deep reactions to the horrors that were engulfing so much of the planet. The very threats to values and democratic institutions, which the West treated as the foundations of "civilization," encouraged social and po-litical vision in preparing for postwar reconstruction. The political failure of the League of Nations, and of the Treaty of Versailles that underlay its creation, high-lighted for everyone except the most myopic a sharp awareness of the risks of fail-ing again. The Great Depression and the mass "unemployment and poverty midst affluence" of the 1930s had generated radically new ideas and approaches to eco-nomic and social policy. These were now available to be applied to the postwar world.

One of the extraordinary features of the UN's creation is how much of its foun-dation was laid during the early phases of World War II, some before the United

States had even formally entered the war. In August 1941 American President Franklin D. Roosevelt and British Prime Minister Winston Churchill agreed on common principles for their postwar policies as part of the Atlantic Charter and referred to "the establishment of a wider and permanent system of general security." Five months later, in January 1942, twenty-six governments—including China, Poland, Czechoslovakia, and a number of Latin American states—signed a Declaration of the United Nations, elaborating further these basic principles. The very name "United Nations" was a suggestion that Roosevelt proposed—and Churchill agreed to, it is recorded—while Churchill was taking a bath.[3]

By October 1943 the need for establishing "a general international organization based on the sovereign principle of the equality of all peace-loving states" had been signed by the United States, the United Kingdom, and the Soviet Union as part of the Declaration of Moscow. China joined them shortly afterward. The declaration emphasized action "at the earliest practicable date." The experience of the Peace Treaty of Versailles had shown the risks and dangers of waiting until after the war was over, when postwar ambitions and alliances might form and prevent agreement or water it down.

Planning then began in earnest. A series of important meetings was held, a year or so before the war ended. The most significant was at Dumbarton Oaks, in Washington, D.C., from August to October 1944, where the fundamental principles of the UN itself were hammered out in two parts (by the United States, United Kingdom, and Soviet Union, and then by the United States, United Kingdom, and China). The resulting proposals were put to the fifty nations that assembled in San Francisco the following April.[4]

Meanwhile, a parallel process was under way to define postwar economic and financial institutions. Beginning even earlier, in December 1940, John Maynard Keynes, arguably the most outstanding economist of the century, had put forward some initial sketches for postwar currency arrangements. He began with a pointed comment: "The authors of the Peace Treaty of Versailles made the mistake of neglecting the economic reconstruction of Europe in their preoccupation with political frontiers and safeguards. Much misfortune to all of us has followed from this neglect. The British Government is determined not to make the same mistake again."[5]

By September 1941, just after the Atlantic Charter and three months before the Declaration of the United Nations, Keynes had mapped out pioneering proposals for an International Currency Union. For the next two years these became the subject of intense discussion among a small circle of economists and government officials in Britain and the U.S. By late 1943 both the United States and the United Kingdom had draft proposals, each covering postwar international financial arrangements and a capital fund. This activity culminated in a major international gathering in Bretton Woods, New Hampshire, in July and August 1944, where forty-four governments met to formulate proposals for an International Monetary Fund "and possibly a Bank for Reconstruction and Development." Governments approved actions on both—becoming in time the IMF and the World Bank (IBRD).

There were other preparatory conferences. At Hot Springs, for instance, the Food and Agriculture Organization (FAO) was established and became the first new specialized agency to join forces with the ILO, which had been created with the League of Nations in 1919 but outlived it. International institutions that focused on technical issues had been growing steadily since the middle of the nineteenth century.[6] Also during the war, the Carnegie Endowment for International Peace sponsored a series of conferences to learn the lessons from the league's "great experiment" with creating an independent international civil service.[7] Lessons are sometimes learned (see Box 1.1).

Box 1.1. Lessons from the League of Nations

The founding of the UN and the UN's early years were greatly influenced by experiences of the League of Nations. During the 1920s and 1930s the league was more active and sometimes more successful than many remember today. Current impressions are too dominated by its failures—most dramatically, its failure to prevent the Japanese annexation of Manchuria and the Italian invasion of Ethiopia. Moreover, its efforts in a series of world conferences on economic problems and unemployment in 1920, 1927, and 1933 were increasingly seen as unsuccessful.

In fact, however, the failures of the league and of the Second World War provided a major stimulus to the founders of the UN, motivating them with strong determination not to fail again!

The early start on planning for the UN was a reaction to one mistake in the league's past. Serious negotiations on the league had begun too late—after the end of the First World War, when new alliances and new rivalries had already been formed.

Drafting of the UN's charter was helped and speeded by being able to build on the Covenant of the League, the first attempt to put forward a comprehensive constitution for a universal, all-purpose global organization.[8] Where the covenant had proved successful, sections were freely borrowed. Where it had failed or shown its weaknesses, efforts were made to incorporate improvements in the charter. The two clearest examples were replacing the unanimity clause (which required that an aggressor agreed to action against itself) with a majority vote in the Security Council (albeit with the assent of the five permanent members); and making provisions for military and economic "teeth."

The failures of the London Monetary and Economic Conference of 1933 also provided incentives for the UN, spurring action to tackle unemployment, avoid beggar-my-neighbor policies, and maintain international economic cooperation after the war. Here the world organization and the Bretton Woods institutions had Keynesian ideas on which to build. Full employment objectives were thus incorporated into the early economic activities of the UN system, including into the mandates of the Bretton Woods institutions.

Notwithstanding its failures, the league also had developed new fields and methods of work. Its work on statistics and nutrition, for example, was pioneering. This evolution was highlighted by U.S. Secretary of State Cordell Hull in 1939: "The League has been responsible for the development of mutual exchange and discussion of ideas and methods to a greater extent and in more fields of humanitarian and scientific endeavour than any other organization in the history."[9] This change of method profoundly affected the conceptions that later shaped the structure of the UN.

San Francisco and the Charter

The San Francisco Conference culminated with the signing of the UN Charter. This historic moment, taking place between the end of the wars in Europe and Asia, was a remarkable achievement. The charter established a structure of international organization that combined political, economic, and social institutions with wide mandates and that was founded on new ideas and new ideals. Most remarkable of all, the document combined the absolute prerogatives of the Westphalian state, or "We the sovereign nations," with a genuine concern for "We the peoples," the first words of the UN Charter's preamble.

The charter contained important articles relating to colonies—or, as they were termed, "non-self-governing territories." But charter article 73 committed the governing powers of these territories to "the principle that the interests of the inhabitants of these territories are paramount, and accept as a sacred trust the obligation to promote to the utmost . . . the well-being of the inhabitants . . . and to this end: to ensure their political, economic, social and educational advancement . . . to develop self government . . . to promote constructive measures of development to transmit regularly . . . statistical and other information . . . relating to economic, social, and educational conditions."

These words were the subject of intense negotiations with the colonial powers, especially the British, who were holding out for much more restrictive language and interpretations. Charles de Gaulle had held a conference with delegates from some twenty colonies in Brazzaville in 1943 to discuss possible modalities of self-rule. But article 73—which Ralph Bunche, as adviser of the U.S. delegation, helped to fashion—contained for many a revolutionary message, much more so than was realized at the time (see Box 1.2). The end of colonization was still generally thought by the colonizing powers to be decades away, if not a century or more. As to human rights for all, the language was treated by many as inspirational, in accord with high ideals but hardly a matter for immediate implementation.

Box 1.2. Ralph Bunche, Decolonization Advocate and Peacekeeping Pioneer

The Nobel Peace Prize was awarded to Ralph Bunche in 1950 for his work in bringing about an armistice between Egypt and Israel and subsequently between Israel, Jordan, Lebanon, and Syria in his role as UN acting mediator. It was the first Nobel Prize given to a UN official, and the first to an African American. Indeed, Bunche modestly tried to decline it, on the grounds that he was only doing his job, until ordered by Secretary-General Trygve Lie to accept it.

Bunche's achievement was a brilliant success in what was thought to be an impossible task: negotiating an armistice agreement to end the first Arab-Israeli war between the new state of Israel and her Arab neighbors. In fact, this success was only one of a series of remarkable contributions over Bunche's UN career, spanning a quarter of a century and ending with his death in 1971 when he was under-secretary general.

Because of Bunche's prominence as the UN's principal negotiator of international conflicts and disputes, his intellectual contributions are often not properly recognized. In fact, Bunche played an important role in drafting the articles in the Charter on Non-Self-Governing Territories and in ensuring that the UN had responsibilities for all non-self-governing peoples, not only those of trusteeship territories. In 1946 he was recruited for the Trusteeship Division because of his intimate knowledge of and experience with these issues.

Bunche brought long-standing professional expertise and commitment to this task. His prize-winning Harvard doctoral dissertation was titled *French Administration in Togoland and Dahomey in the 1930s.* He also had published *A World View on Race* before collaborating closely with Gunnar Myrdal on *The American Dilemma,* the largest and most comprehensive study that had been attempted of race relations in the United States. By the time Bunche started in the UN secretariat, he was widely known as a strong and persistent voice in the fight for racial equality and civil rights in the United States, as the leading American expert on Africa and colonial affairs, as one of the authors of the UN Charter, and as a determined advocate of decolonization.

In 1956 Bunche spearheaded the creation of the UN's first peacekeeping force following the invasion of Egypt by Israel after the nationalization of the Suez Canal. As a crucial step in achieving a cease-fire, Bunche devised the principles of UN peacekeeping: a nonviolent (that is, using force only in self-defense) but armed international military operation; with troops drawn from a wide geographical and political base; unified, as Bunche himself proposed, by wearing the common UN blue beret and without national flags. Bunche described the operation as "an experience new in history," forming "the frontline of a moral force . . . with a profound effect for future prospects for building a world order." [10]

Brian Urquhart, who worked intimately with Bunche in the crises of the 1950s and 1960s, summarized him in the following way: "Bunche was really a marvelous person, and a person of great intellectual honesty—extraordinary. Both he and Hammarskjöld were alike in that respect."

The frequent gap between rhetoric and reality was well captured in a book looking back over the UN's first twenty-five years. Edwin Tetlow, a journalist, commented on the flowery declarations of the wartime Big Three meetings attended by Roosevelt, Churchill, and Soviet Premier Joseph Stalin. The Teheran Declaration of 1943 impressively proclaimed, he noted, the support of "nations large and small, whose people in heart and mind are dedicated, as are our own peoples, to the elimination of tyranny and slavery, oppression and intolerance." To be frank, Tetlow commented, this was "plain humbug."[11] None of the three great powers could possibly claim that it was dedicated to the elimination of any of the evils mentioned except, in a literal sense, slavery.

But, as we have seen earlier and will continue to see throughout this volume, words and ideas can make a big difference, even when they run far ahead of the established wisdom or practical politics of the time.

Human Rights and Self-Determination

Notwithstanding doubts and mixed motives, the record shows that the lofty vision of the UN Charter has subsequently had more impact than either the cynics or the realists expected. Within months, major action was under way in three of the four main areas identified at the outset: decolonization, economic and social development, and human rights.

A drafting commission was established to define *human rights*, and the Universal Declaration of thirty detailed articles was agreed to in 1948. Surely this is the most subversive of the early ideas emanating from the UN system, as will be documented in a book commissioned by the United Nations Intellectual History Project.[12] The charter broke new ground and sowed the seeds in the 1940s for the recent development of intrusions into what formerly had been considered domestic affairs of sovereign states. In looking back at this period, Urquhart recalls: "The so-called realists almost always get it wrong. Partly due to the development of NGOs, human rights has become a world-class movement, a movement that is not going to stop. It is very imperfect at the moment, and all sorts of terrible things happen, but it is nothing like the kind of dead silence about human rights there was in my youth."

The Trusteeship Council was established in 1945, initially with eleven trust territories placed under its supervision. In that same year a further seventy-two territories were identified as "non-self-governing." By 1959 eight of them had become independent. Many countries argued that the charter principles were being applied too slowly. And in 1960 the General Assembly passed a Declaration on the Granting of Independence to Colonial Countries and Peoples. This called for immediate steps to be taken to transfer all powers to the peoples of non-self-governing territories, without any conditions or reservations. In the years following this declaration, a further sixty former colonial territories, with a total population exceeding 800 million people, attained independence and joined the United Nations.[13] The power of this notion to change dominant state practices is striking.[14]

Decolonization was "a change almost unparalleled in world history," stated Don Mills, a former Jamaican ambassador to the United Nations and longtime observer of multilateral organizations. "To go to the UN in 1962," he said, "for Jamaica to stand before the world and claim the right to participate and for other countries to do so, this was extraordinary." In the popular imagination, the sun finally set on the British Empire and colonialism in 1997 when Great Britain handed over Hong Kong to the Chinese. In reality, colonial rule had been delegitimized by the UN Charter and had virtually ended many decades earlier. No new colonies were formed in the last quarter of the twentieth century. And in the few instances when military action was tried, there was immediate outrage (in the case of Indonesia's occupation of East Timor in 1975) and sometimes a reaction (in the case of Iraq's occupation of Kuwait in 1990). With the disappearance of the Soviet Empire, there are few colonies left.[15] The idea of decolonization has meant, in the words of the late Tanzanian president Julius Nyerere, "that colonialism in the traditional and political sense is now almost a thing of the past."[16]

At the same time, the Cold War meant that the charter's daring objective "to save succeeding generations from the scourge of war" was placed on the back burner. New efforts to maintain international peace and security were held hostage to East-West politics. In early 1946, less than ten days after the election of Trygve Lie as the UN's first secretary-general, Stalin announced that armaments would take precedence over production for consumption in the postwar Soviet Union. The USSR, he said, had to defend itself against "all kinds of eventualities" because "no peaceful international order is possible between the Communists and the capitalist-imperialist world."[17] A month later Churchill made his famous speech in Fulton, Missouri, declaring that "an iron curtain has descended across the continent."

Confrontation between East and West polarized the work of the UN Security Council and, in turn, colored the political perspectives within which the rest of the UN's work was undertaken and viewed from the outside. The charter's vision of peace and international negotiation to resolve disputes gave way to all-consuming ideological rivalry, the arms race, the mobilization of client states, and a worldwide struggle for superiority. The two nuclear "superpowers" based their *realpolitik* on the North Atlantic Treaty Organization (NATO) and the Warsaw Pact, rather than on the UN Security Council and the UN Charter.

The Cold War also had serious repercussions for independence, development, and rights. Work to turn the Universal Declaration into a single covenant that countries could ratify was delayed and became intensely polarized. Political and civil rights became separated from economic, social, and cultural rights. The West challenged the communist bloc for their failures in political and civil rights, and the communist countries pointed fingers at the West's failures to address poverty amidst affluence and to ensure basic human needs, especially for minorities.

Less emphasized was a more fundamental failure. Human rights became separated from development.[18] To a large extent within the UN until the 1980s, human rights were an ideological football, kicked back and forth in an international game between East and West. Western players wore the colors of political and civil rights, Eastern players those of economic and social rights. The international game became a shouting match, with lots of attack and denunciation but little attention to the practical problems and issues that were often high on the domestic agendas at the time and could have benefited by sharing lessons and new approaches. Only as the Cold War was beginning to thaw, and groups concerned with the rights of women and children entered the match, did the game and playing field change.

In retrospect, we can see how the charter's language led to laying the foundation for a very different approach to the equilibrium between state sovereignty and human rights. The attempt to finesse the obvious tensions between them did not succeed, but the basis for sometimes weighing rights more heavily than sovereignty was established and has made a difference. The basic conflict was built in and has arisen many times since 1945. In recent times it has often resulted in substantial intrusions on traditional state prerogatives, including a host of humanitarian interventions in the 1990s.[19] Francis M. Deng, the UN secretary-general's special representative on internally displaced persons, has argued that implementation of rights standards is moving toward "sovereignty as responsibility."[20]

Three Pioneering Reports on Development

When the United Nations turned to issues of economic and social development in the late 1940s, the term chosen to describe the subjects was *underdeveloped* countries. In reality, so-called underdeveloped countries had rich and complex histories and cultures, economies and societies. They were economically poor rather than underdeveloped, as the pioneering UN reports to be discussed below explained. Nor was economics as underdeveloped as it appeared at the time. Adam Smith had published his *Inquiry into the Nature and Causes of the Wealth of Nations* some 170 years earlier,[21] and the nineteenth century was full of pioneering works on the early experience of development and industrialization in Europe. Robert Malthus, David Ricardo, John Stuart Mill, and Karl Marx were among the greatest, but there were many others.

However, economics as taught in the 1940s was not about development, economic or any other sort. Microeconomics was the standard bill of fare, with Keynesian analysis of unemployment the exciting frontier for both analysis and
policy.[22] Paul Samuelson's *Economics,* the classic textbook of choice, was then in
the first of its sixteen subsequent editions. It devoted fewer than three sentences
to developing countries.[23] Hans Singer was appointed to the UN as an economist to work on the problems of underdeveloped countries in 1947. During an interview he recounted how his mentor, Harvard's highly distinguished Joseph
Schumpeter, reacted to the news: "But I thought you were an economist!"

In contrast, the UN secretariat was a hothouse for ideas and early development
economists. Singer commented: "I had the feeling of being at the centre of things,
very privileged to be there. After all, the UN was the home of mankind. It was then
at the centre of international organizations, the Bank and the Fund were very
much on the periphery in those days." The silver lining to this neglect of growth
and development outside the UN was the preoccupation with unemployment and
how to prevent a 1930s-like resurgence of unemployment in the postwar world.
Both Washington and London were giving high priority to Keynesian policies in
budgetary analysis and policy.

This background—the concerns of Article 55 of the charter with promoting
conditions of economic and social progress and development, and the commitments to achieve full employment—framed the UN's early work. Fuller analysis
must await review of the archives and further interviews with some of the early
UN staff members. But an important perspective on this early work can even now
be obtained from three major UN publications, the first released in 1949 and the
latter two in 1951. These were *National and International Measures for Full Employment* (1949); *Measures for the Economic Development of Under-Developed
Countries* (1951); and *Measures for International Economic Stability* (1951).[24]

**Box 1.3. Gunnar Myrdal, Nobel Laureate in Economics
and First ECE Executive Secretary**

Gunnar Myrdal won the Nobel Prize in Economic Sciences in 1974 (shared with
Friedrich A. Hayek). Born in Gustaf's Parish, Sweden in 1898, he graduated in 1923 from
Stockholm University with a law degree and began practicing while he pursued a doctorate in economics. Until the early 1930s Myrdal emphasized theory, but his focus gradually broadened to encompass applied economics and especially social problems—
indeed, encyclopedia entries usually describe him as an economist and sociologist.

Already his first book, *The Political Element in the Development of Economic Theory* (1930), moved beyond pure economic theory. In fact, it was here that he introduced his early views on the relativity of social science, a theme that he developed continuously throughout his career.

Working at the invitation of the Carnegie Corporation of New York in 1938–1940, Myrdal explored the social and economic problems of the American Negro, which was published as *An American Dilemma: The Negro Problem and Modern Democracy* (1944). In this controversial depiction of the plight of blacks in the world's richest country, he presented his theory of cumulative causation, of poverty breeding poverty. Although the theory clearly applies to countries and regions differently than it does to social groups, it became the hallmark of his later writings on development. Rather than rich and poor countries converging, the poor might well become poorer as industrialized countries enjoyed economies of scale and poor countries relied on primary products. His best-known works in this area are *Beyond the Welfare State: Economic Planning and its International Implication* (1960) and *Asian Drama: An Inquiry into the Poverty of Nations* (1968).

Until his death in 1987, he was married to Alva Reimer Myrdal, who was awarded the Nobel Peace Prize in 1982 for her own distinguished international work, especially on disarmament.

For a decade, from 1947 to 1957, Gunnar Myrdal was executive secretary of the United Nations Economic Commission for Europe (ECE). In one of his earliest annual reports he articulated his views about the global nature of economic and social development that went far beyond the European continent:

• "While the need is urgent to subordinate the national approach to economic problems to collaboration on a European basis, this need is scarcely more compelling than that for a still broader approach to the problems of a properly functioning world economy."

• "The view is also expressed that Europe could participate, to its own advantage, in the economic development of overseas countries, not only through its exports of capital equipment but also through the provision of financing. This conclusion may encounter scepticism among those impressed by Europe's immediate difficulties and may, indeed, seem at variance with the analysis of Europe's overseas balance-of-payments problem given elsewhere in the present *Survey.* It must not be overlooked, however, that, as the study shows, Europe's industrial production and its overseas exports are already substantially higher than before the war; that Europe's balance-of-payments problem is now more clearly than ever concentrated on its relations with the dollar area; and that, even during the past several years, Europe has been supplying capital on a large scale to overseas countries, partly in the form of debt-repayment and partly in the form of new funds. While this outflow of capital from Europe has entailed some disadvantages, which the report also considers, it has unquestionably made a major an urgently needed contribution to under-developed countries abroad, many of which have faced post-war problems no less serious than those in Europe."[25]

- decisions to enable the World Bank to borrow from governments and to lend to governments for general development purposes—in other words, for the bank to start making broad-gauged program loans, rather than narrow project ones, and to have a department for general development lending to oversee them;
- an energetic expansion of the UN's technical assistance program to help underdeveloped countries in framing and operating their general development efforts; and
- new procedures to stabilize the flow of international trade, with the IMF playing a key part.

How should one react to these proposals, made in late 1949? They were bold—but no bolder than the Marshall Plan, except that they conceived of the issues within a framework of long-term world development rather than as a measure for recovery in Europe. They were forward-looking in focusing on full employment as the central goal—but that goal had already been recognized in the Full Employment Act passed by the U.S. Congress in 1946. They were intellectually pioneering and consistent, full-bloodedly Keynesian—but that was the orthodoxy of the time. Indeed, the period of Keynesian orthodoxy applied within most of the industrial countries turned out to be the best twenty-five years, economically speaking, of the twentieth century. The period 1950–1973 saw the fastest rate of economic growth in history, with lower levels of unemployment in industrialized countries and smaller fluctuations in growth and trade than ever before or since.

Keynesians would see a direct link between this outstanding economic performance and the application of their prescribed policies within most of the industrialized countries. Nonetheless, these policies were not applied internationally as guiding principles for international institutions, as the report to the UN was recommending and as Keynes himself had originally intended. If this had been the case, the broad economic success of the golden quarter-century from late 1940s to the early 1970s might have been even more shining, especially for underdeveloped countries.

But it was not to be. The financial focus of the West remained on the Marshall Plan for Europe, and the global perspective for employment policy and action remained a distant dream. World Bank lending to developing countries over the next five years remained at a very low level compared with the Marshall Plan. And developing countries had to wait until the early 1980s for the bank to introduce program loans by sector instead of merely projects. The UN was ahead of the curve in putting ideas on the table—but the industrial countries were not prepared to examine them seriously. This is one of the major points on which further research is required.

Measures for Economic Development

The second major report focused more directly on the problems of the poorer regions of the world. Although India and Pakistan had become independent in 1947, Indonesia in 1949, and most of Latin America long before, more than eighty of today's countries were still colonies or trust territories in the 1950s.[29] *Measures for the Economic Development of Under-Developed Countries* (hereafter *Measures for Economic Development*) was a truly pioneering document.[30] It broke new ground and elicited strong reactions, which we examine in some depth.

At the time, there were few contemporary books and no textbooks dealing with development in developing countries. Sir Arthur Lewis's own classic, *The Theory of Economic Growth,* was the first, but this came out in 1955.[31] Walt Rostow's *The Stages of Economic Growth: A Non-Communist Manifesto* was published in 1960, although it was preceded by an article in the *Economic Journal* in 1956.[32] Peter Bauer and Basil Yamey's classic in the Cambridge University handbook series, *The Economics of Under-Developed Countries,* emerged in 1957.[33] Myrdal's *Economic Theory and Under-Developed Regions* was also published in 1957.[34] Albert Hirschman's free-thinking inspiration, *The Strategy of Economic Development,* and Ragnar Nurkse's *Lectures on Economic Development* followed in 1958. [35] Probably the earliest development book of that period was Eugene Staley's *World Economic Development,* prepared for the ILO in 1944, which emphasized that there would be an insistent demand in many parts of the world for rapid progress in economic development after the war.[36] And there were some analyses using Keynesian concepts to develop dynamic models of economic growth along the lines of those pioneered by Roy Harrod.[37] But these were theoretical studies and not examinations of the actual process of economic development in developing countries, let alone empirical analyses reaching conclusions for national and international policy.

Measures for Economic Development filled the gap and was well ahead of the curve. It was broad-ranging and multidisciplinary in its analysis and careful but bold in its recommendations. Lewis's hand is very clearly evident (see Box 1.4), especially in the report's focus on the priority for poor countries to increase their rates of saving and investment and on the transfer of labor from low-productivity rural areas to higher-productivity urban areas as being central to the development process.

As with the two other UN reports, the starting point in *Measures for Economic Development* is unemployment and underemployment and policies to reduce them. But the report identified the rapid creation of new employment as the main part of the solution, and long-term economic development as the critical condition for achieving it.[38] This led to a wide-ranging discussion of necessary measures, mostly to be initiated by developing countries themselves. The preconditions

Box 1.4. Sir Arthur Lewis, First Third-World Nobel Prizewinner in Economics

Arthur Lewis was awarded the Nobel Prize in economics in 1979 for his contributions to economic development. Born on the Caribbean island of St. Lucia in 1915, he left school at age fourteen and went to work as a clerk in the civil service. When old enough to do so, he took the examination for a government scholarship and enrolled at the London School of Economics, where he obtained his bachelor's degree and doctorate. In 1948 he moved to Manchester University as a full professor, where he did his seminal work on development economics.

Lewis made major contributions to the UN from its earliest years, and he continued working on these issues until his death in 1991. During the 1950s and 1960s he served on expert committees, as a UN adviser in Ghana, and for eighteen months in 1958–1959 as deputy managing director of the UN Special Fund, which later became the UNDP. He was a professor at Princeton University, vice chancellor of the University of the West Indies, and from 1970 to 1974 president of the Caribbean Development Bank.

Although Lewis made important theoretical contributions, his writings were deeply grounded in both the history and the contemporary experience of development. He wrote several specialist economic publications on *Tropical Trade 1883–1965; Growth and Fluctuations 1870–1913; Economic Survey 1919–39;* and *The Evolution of the International Economic Order.*

Lewis's ideas on development were closely informed by his first-hand experience and UN service, and he emphasized the practical aspects of planning and policy making. Beginning in the mid-1940s he published a number of important articles and influential reports: "An Economic Plan for Jamaica" (1944); "Industrialization of Puerto Rico" (1949); "Industrial Development in the Caribbean" (1950); and *Report on Industrialization in the Gold Coast* (1953).

These laid the foundation for his contributions to the forward-looking UN report, *Measures for the Economic Development of Under-Developed Countries* (1951) as well as for his seminal article on "Economic Development with Unlimited Supplies of Labour" in *Manchester School of Economic and Social Studies* (1954) and his pioneering textbook, *The Theory of Economic Growth* (1955).

for economic development are spelled out—with a frank discussion of how inequalities in wealth and social structure may exclude many people who, given the chance, could contribute to raising national income. The report pointed to concentration of land ownership and discrimination within banking systems as other factors hindering the mobility of resources on which development depends.

Attention was placed also on the need for appropriate administrative and legislative action, in both the public and private sectors, recognizing nonetheless that the "proportion between public and private activity varies widely from country to country."[39] The first thing demanded of government is efficiency and honesty. Governments should ensure adequate financing for roads and communications and for education, health, and other public services. The report added an interesting emphasis on the need for ensuring market research and prospecting and agricultural research on new crops. It stressed that governments have important functions to ensure that the private sector runs efficiently and in ways that release the productive energies of populations. So land reform, tenancy legislation, and measures to ensure adequate markets at home and abroad were analyzed in some detail.

There was a chapter on technology—one of the first looks at the potential for achieving substantial increases in productivity by the use of relatively simple and inexpensive technological improvements, particularly in the field of agriculture. It should be possible, the report stated, "to increase the yield of many agricultural crops 50 per cent within two decades or less by the use of fertilizers, insecticides, better seeds and better crop rotation."[40] The technology of developed countries often must be adapted before it is suitable to the conditions of developing countries. Fertilizer trials are needed, new strains of plants and livestock must be bred, new crop rotations worked out, and manufacturing processes and equipment adjusted to local climatic and other conditions.

This led to a discussion of the problems and costs of employing too many foreign personnel at high salaries, often a cause of resentment with dubious returns on the investments in time and resources. Plans were therefore needed for rapidly expanding training institutions and for on-the-job learning. The report commented: "Men learn administration by participating in it. They therefore learn fastest in countries where self-governing institutions are most widespread, embracing central and local government, right down to the level of the village, the co-operative movement, trade unions and the hundred and one other voluntary or official groups in which free peoples love to foregather."[41]

This was in part an honest criticism of the weaknesses of colonial administrations and governments. But it was also surely an early recognition of what today would today be glorified as an example of the importance of civil society, as learning and human investment as well as a process strengthening development through positive spillovers. About the only hesitations that a modern reader might have about this paragraph drafted some fifty years ago is the reference to men instead of to women and men or just to people.

Increasing savings and domestic capital formation was a central recommendation and a central part of the report's analytical framework. Here *Measures for Economic Development* was ahead of the times and foreshadowed the evolution of thinking and research in the 1950s and 1960s.

In the early 1950s capital formation was conceived essentially as physical capital—machines and infrastructure. By the 1960s investment in education had been recognized as an even more important form of capital formation. More and more research showed that productivity rose because of a complex array of variables, including the "residual" factor—the unmeasurable items that had to be included in equations to "explain" the increases in productivity after all of the additional inputs that actually could be measured had been taken into account. Initially, this included pure technological advance, learning by doing, and other such factors.

The rapid growth of population throughout the developing world was highlighted almost two decades before governments agreed to set up the United Nations Fund for Population Activities (UNFPA), now called the UN Population Fund. In fact, fears still existed in some industrial countries about the problems of *declining* populations. *Measures for Economic Development* declared that in one or two countries the annual rate of population increase was already very near to what appeared to be the maximum probable rate: 3.5 percent annually. The report disagreed with a then prevalent view that economic development must inevitably be dissipated by rapid population growth. But the experts argued that development called for discovering ways and means, consistent with the values and culture of each of the peoples concerned, of speeding up the reduction of fertility rates.

The report dealt with many other social issues including education and health—and how the provision of these vital social services could be a productive investment, with higher returns than investment in material capital. The emphasis on education was very much on quality and relevance, rather than simple expansion. Relevance was illustrated by emphasizing the importance of agricultural extension services and of secondary and higher education with practical relevance.

The final part of the report concerned domestic policy and dealt with foreign trade and the need for development planning, especially issues of sectoral balance between agriculture and industry. On trade, the experts recognized the compelling requirement to reduce export dependence on primary products, but they also warned of the need for careful analysis in each country situation in order to tailor policy approaches rather than to have a one-size-fits-all garment.

Measures for International Economic Stability

The third report, *Measures for International Economic Stability,* arose in part from reactions to the first report and the request from ECOSOC that the secretary-general appoint another group of knowledgeable economists to explore alternative practical ways of reducing the international impact of recessions.

Another star-studded team was assembled—with James Angell of Columbia University as chair and four other economists who later would become well known in trade and development: G.D.A. Mac Dougall, Javier Marquez, Hla Myint, and Trevor W. Swan.

As with the first two reports, *Measures for International Economic Stability* began with then orthodoxy: "The major countries have both the will and the means to avoid deep and prolonged depressions. The full employment pledges embodied in the United Nations Charter, and in other national and international instruments, reflect the fact that in one decade the world has taken a long step forward in social attitudes and economic techniques." But the authors added, "We are still living in the shadow of the great depressions of the past. Full employment commitments cannot wipe out overnight the ingrained distrust of dependence upon a many-sided international system."[42]

The challenge was to propose an economic mechanism that would cushion the international impact of disturbances, even minor ones, arising in one part of the world that in turn has major negative repercussions elsewhere. The authors started with examples of catastrophic declines in imports by the United States in the pre–World War II years. But they soon moved to more contemporary problems: cycles in the movement of inventories, of outputs of crops in agriculture, and in the supply and demand of primary products which give rise to wide fluctuations in their prices. Writing in 1951, they emphasized that the problem of the hour was not recession but the reverse: economic problems arising from "the vast rearmament programmes being undertaken in the United States and elsewhere."[43] These were leading underdeveloped countries and other exporters of primary products to experience large and welcome increases in export prices, although irregular and unevenly distributed, but at the same time they were unable to import development goods because of physical shortages of capital equipment.

The 1949 report on *Measures for Full Employment* had recommended two bold measures to deal with this type of problem. The first was a scheme under which countries experiencing a decline in their exports as the result of a decline in effective demand in another country could obtain a special supplement of foreign exchange sufficient to enable them to purchase the same volume of imports from the other country as in some reference year. The report recommended a second scheme under which countries undertaking long-term investment abroad should fix for five years the annual total of their lending on public and private account and through a special account in the World Bank make good any gaps between intention and performance.

These proposals were too far ahead of the curve for the major powers to find them acceptable, which had led to the request for a further report and for alternative recommendations. No doubt they are even further from what would seem sensible today. Nonetheless, it is worth pausing to reflect that they tackled an important dimension of instability, one that still afflicts many developing countries and for which adequate solutions have not yet been devised. The Asian crisis of 1997–1999 is merely a recent reminder of the enormous impact that fluctuations in export earnings and foreign exchange can have on even the stronger and better-off developing countries — and of the cost in lost production and human well-being which most countries of the world suffer through such instabilities. Action is still required.

Measures for International Economic Stability proposed three alternative measures, more modest but still bold. These were:

- A direct and detailed attack on short-run fluctuations in the prices and terms of trade of primary products through the negotiation of international commodity agreements. The report proposed a series of commodity agreements of different types, with the World Bank participating in the financing of commodity arrangements that involve buffer stocks.[44]
- The provision by the World Bank of a substantial increase in the flow of its lending to developing countries in the event of recession, with countries able to rely upon a larger flow of capital from the bank in bad times than in good. The report suggested that the bank should have access to a more flexible source of funds than provided by the sale of its securities on the market. This led to the proposal for an increase in the proportion of the bank's capital available for making loans, for an increase in the bank's total capital, and for new arrangements for governments or central banks to repurchase World Bank securities if the need arose.
- More flexible arrangements by the IMF, including being prepared in the event of recession promptly to help overcome the temporary difficulties of its members, "even though their practices might normally be regarded as out of keeping with its long run objectives." The report added, "If the Fund has any doubt whether a member's need of assistance is temporary, it should give the member the benefit of the doubt, while at the same time reinforcing the repurchase provisions of its Articles of Agreement by asking for more specific commitments to repurchase over an agreed period."[45] Again the report recognized that this would probably require an increase in the total of the IMF's subscriptions.

These proposals focused on actions needed in the case of recession, with the direct purpose of containing any such recession from becoming catastrophic. However, they recognized that action along these lines, even taking the most hopeful of views, would not meet the special difficulties of the poorer underdeveloped countries, many of which "are dependent on a very limited range of exports, which in some cases may be left largely uncovered by such commodity agreements as it is possible to negotiate."[46] The report pointed to the danger that some poor countries have to look to the IMF and the World Bank to help them out of these difficulties but may fall between two stools. Uncertainties over their exports may cast doubt on the prospects to make early repayment, and long-run views of development may give too little attention to the pressing needs of the moment. This all underlined the need for the World Bank to be ready to increase its lending, especially in times of recession.

The report recognized that developing countries required a steady inflow of resources to maintain a steady rate of economic development. In fact, this need led the experts to highlight an interest in maintaining global stability even more than in meeting the needs of industrialized countries. Moreover, the experts recognized a *prima facie* case for expanding the rate of development in underdeveloped countries in times of recession, through foreign lending. We see shades of the Brandt Commission's plea of 1980,[47] but three decades ahead of time!

What is striking in this third report is again the boldness of its global view and analysis. Even though it proposed alternative recommendations, more cautious and from a more conservative team of economists than those of the 1949 report, the analysis and recommendations still stand out. They display a bold confidence: They analyze and tackle the issues of instability within a clear global frame; recognize how underdeveloped countries have an even greater stake in stability for their long-run development than industrialized countries have; and show how action for the underdeveloped countries could and should be combined with global action to avoid instability and recession.

What a contrast with the global failures of the 1970s and 1980s! Fluctuations in the global economy were moderated until the 1970s, when they returned with a vengeance, following the breakdown of the Bretton Woods system in 1971 and the oil-price shocks of 1973–74 and 1979. Some two decades later UNCTAD would call for a common fund to support a range of commodity agreements, much as recommended in the 1951 report. The sudden increases in oil prices in the mid- to late 1970s corrected the long-run decline since the 1950s, but they also threw the global economy into major imbalance. Gross national product (GNP) actually declined for a year or two in most industrialized countries.

Much more serious and sustained was the impact on most of the developing countries — except for the large and better-off economies including China, Korea, later India, and perhaps a dozen others, mostly in Asia. The instabilities and higher oil prices severely disrupted development in most of the weaker countries, setting up the debt overhangs and debt crises of the 1980s. The Brandt Commission recommended a global stimulus through a twenty-year Marshall Plan for developing countries. But this was not taken seriously. Instead, the one-on-one approach to adjustment in each developing country became the norm, and most in Latin America and Africa were obliged to carry the full burden of adjustment themselves, with far too little international support.

The 1980s became a lost decade for development in which most countries of sub-Saharan Africa and of Latin America and the Caribbean suffered grievous declines in per capita income. On average sub-Saharan Africa ended the decade more than 10 percent poorer in terms of per capita income than in 1980.

Let the moral not be oversimplified. Adjustment in the 1980s was in most cases necessary—even though a more human form than was usually imposed or encouraged by the heavy hand of the IMF and the World Bank. Larger and more flexible support was required in the form of foreign exchange and access to export markets freed from the risks of large commodity price fluctuations and declines. These were precisely what *Measures for International Economic Stability* had addressed. How different the situation of a third of the world's people living in poverty might have been today if the recommendations had been taken more seriously at the time—or rediscovered and implemented two or three decades later.

Criticisms

Notwithstanding the pragmatism in these reports, their boldness and proposals for market intervention aroused opposition. Peter Bauer wrote highly critically in professional journals in reaction to *Measures for Economic Development.*[48] Bauer later became a critic of almost everything done by UN economists, but at this juncture he took issue specifically with the report's emphasis on industrialization, arguing that more intensive agriculture would be a better way to bring about higher incomes. While Bauer recognized the "interesting asides on the influence of systems of land tenure" he faulted the report for its focus on the way "inequality and privilege act as major obstacles to development."[49] He even asked whether it was appropriate for an expert-group report to include such remarks as those in the section on land tenure, where the report had stated: "In many under-developed countries, the cultivators of the soil are exploited mercilessly by a landlord class which performs no useful social function. This class contrives to secure to itself the major part of any increase in agricultural yields, and is thus a millstone around the necks of the tenants, discouraging them from making improvements in agriculture and, in any case, leaving them too little income from which they might save to invest in the land. In such countries, land reform, abolishing this landlord class, is an urgent pre-requisite of agricultural progress."[50]

International reports were perhaps more frank and colorful in the early 1950s than the drab documents that came to be the standard bill of fare in later years. The 1951 World Bank Report on pre-revolutionary Cuba described the Ministry of Education as a "principal focus of political patronage and graft" and went on to quote the minister of education describing his own ministry as having been "an opprobrium and a shame and, in addition, a dangerous menace to the Cuban nation. It was a cave of entrenched bandits and of gunman and an asylum of professional robbers."[51]

Bauer also argued that "at an early stage of economic development pre-occupation with egalitarian ideas may serve to retard the growth of real income, including the real income of the poorer classes."[52] Battle lines thus were drawn in the early 1950s over trickle-down effects and whether issues of inequality and redistributive policy should be an important part of economic policy.

The battle has swung backward and forward since the 1950s, and different an-swers would have been given by different parties in each of the following decades — and, no doubt, even today. Nevertheless, half a century later the con-sensus among those working in development would surely be that issues of in-come distribution deserve policy attention from the earliest stages of development (see Chapter 3). Most would also accept that extremes of inequality are counter-productive to development, let alone to poverty reduction (see Chapter 7). And, as a particular case, reform of land tenure, although difficult, is essential. Part of the economic success of Japan, Korea, Taiwan, and China is attributed to their early land reform measures. And, in contrast, part of the slowness to reduce poverty and achieve more rapid advance in Latin America, South Asia, and Africa is widely attributed to weaknesses or failures in land reform efforts.

A second major criticism related to the alleged secular decline in the terms of trade between underdeveloped and more advanced countries. On the one hand, the report had referred to the fact that the "terms of trade between primary and manufactured commodities entering into international trade moved against pri-mary commodities for the sixty years between 1873 and 1937."[53] Bauer, on the other hand, argued that for considerable periods within this span the movement had been in the opposite direction.[54]

How old-fashioned this now seems. The subject can still stir many hours of battle and debate among economists in seminar rooms, even if there have been short upward swings (for instance, during the Korean War). Yet the facts can be traced without too much controversy to show what has actually happened over the past fifty years. The terms of trade between industrialized and developing countries deteriorated by 18 percent during the period 1950–1962. Thereafter, no significant trend was apparent in commodity prices until the early 1970s, when the dramatic increases in oil prices resulted in a small upward movement in terms of trade. From 1980 onward, however, the fall has been steep and catastrophic, with real commodity prices falling more severely than anything seen since the Great Depression. This has continued in the 1990s, albeit with a slight upward blip from 1993 to 1995.[55] By 1999 commodity prices in real terms were at their lowest level since the *Economist*'s index of industrial-commodity prices was first published a century and a half ago.[56]

Not surprisingly, the impact on poorer countries still dependent on commodities for the bulk of their export earnings has been disastrous. Quite a few of these countries are now poorer in terms of per capita income than they were thirty or forty years ago—a few of them barely above the level that they had attained when the UN report was first published. Although debt and declining aid are additional reasons why these countries lack sufficient foreign exchange, the declines in their terms of trade are a major part of the problem.

Two of the UN's recognized intellectual stalwarts, Raúl Prebisch and Hans Singer, made their professional reputations publicizing that the terms of trade between developed and developing countries would, in the long run, move against developing countries (see Chapter 2).[57] *Measures for Economic Development* can legitimately claim to be ahead of the debate that raged between North and South during the 1960s and 1970s.

A third point of dispute related to the report's calculation of the need for increased transfers of capital from developed to developing countries, largely through official (that is, government-to-government or bilateral) loans and gifts. Notwithstanding the transfers of some 2 percent of U.S. GNP to Europe under the Marshall Plan, critics balked at the idea that resources locally available in underdeveloped countries were insufficient to stimulate and sustain economic development. *Measures for Economic Development* had suggested that a minimum capital investment of approximately $19 billion a year was needed to raise per capita incomes in developing countries by 2 percent per year—and that more than $10 billion of this would have to be provided by industrialized countries.

Bauer disagreed, as did others. World Bank President Eugene Black was an opponent who throughout the 1950s "never stopped arguing for less emphasis on large-scale external assistance, and more on domestic policies and effort."[58] The bank's lending to developing countries at the time was only a few hundred million dollars per year. Stéphane Hessel, who worked on development issues within the French government and on two occasions within the UN system, recalled "the illusion that without really large transfers of capital one could achieve development. . . . I always thought that what we needed was more direct aid money and that the World Bank and even [the International Development Association] IDA were not sufficiently liberal to really help the developing countries."

In the event, the World Bank's capital doubled in 1958 and again in 1968 with the arrival of Robert McNamara to the bank's presidency. Recognizing the need for a major increase in the institution's resources for development purposes, bank lending doubled every few years after McNamara took over. During his thirteen-year tenure he transformed the World Bank into truly a development bank.

Herbert Frankel was another critic who raised doubts about whether it was reasonable, let alone proper, to envisage the rate of development being made more rapid by government action. He noted that the report reflected "current opinion, and in particular . . . the belief that development is largely a matter of social will." It is, he added, "precisely because the authors of the report see economic development primarily as an intellectual or artistic exercise by leaders and governments that they fail to do justice to their examination of existing realties in underdeveloped countries."[59]

But underlying the dispute was a more fundamental philosophical difference. Bauer ended his critique with the following sentence: "It is doubtful whether economists in their professional capacity are able to make recommendations, the acceptance of which would significantly accelerate economic development."[60]

This view of course remains in the mainstream today, perhaps more than in the 1950s. And certainly, most commentators and analysts today display more caution before immediately assuming that all governments will use their resources for accelerated development and the welfare of their peoples. Nevertheless, the UN continues to explore what government can and should do to accelerate economic development. Moreover, the record of the 1960s and the 1970s shows that rate of economic development did indeed accelerate. Arthur Lewis, in a rejoinder to Frankel, defended a growth rate of per capita income of 2 percent per annum as "not too ambitious a goal for underdeveloped countries to set themselves."[61] In the event, it was a goal more than exceeded on average and in a number of individual developing countries in the 1950s and 1960s.

2

Development Hits Its Stride in the 1960s

- **The First Development Decade**
- **UN Conference on Trade and Development**
- **Aid and Development Finance**
- **Conclusions**

By the early 1960s development in what would soon become known as the "South" was gathering steam. Decolonization had moved from controversy and sometimes conflict to practical arrangements for handing over and independence, at least for more than a score of countries in Africa — with virtually all others to follow in short order. The Non-Aligned Movement (NAM) emerged after the 1955 Bandung Conference, and UN membership had grown from fifty-one nations at the founding to 104 by 1961.[1] The Korean War seemed long past, as was the Suez invasion and the suppression of the Hungarian uprising — although the Bay of Pigs invasion of Cuba and the missile crisis of October 1962 meant that East-West relations remained tense to an extreme.

Economic and social development was high on the international agenda, because it was *the* priority for the leaders of the many countries coming to independence. The UN was providing support through the Expanded Program of Technical Assistance (EPTA), established in 1949 and picking up on President Harry Truman's Point Four, and the Special United Nations Fund for Economic Development (SUNFED), established ten years later. The World Bank had doubled its capital and shifted its focus from post–World War II reconstruction of Europe to development. In 1960 it had established the International Development Association (IDA). This provided low-interest loans on soft terms along the lines originally proposed years earlier by the UN for SUNFED — but which the bank, in line with strong U.S. resistance, had opposed root and branch.[2] But once it seemed that money would flow, the bank shifted 180 degrees to support the proposal, provided that it would be in charge. The World Bank's history notes that the IDA "carried the genes of its third world and United Nations parentage,"[3] even though Eugene Black, the World Bank's president, had pronounced less than a year before the IDA was established that it would not be a "soft lender." The bank made its first IDA development credit to Honduras in 1961.

Building on the experience of the early years described in Chapter 1, development became the preoccupation of the UN system in the 1960s. This is the story that we now tell.

The First Development Decade

With hindsight, one can see that the postwar "golden age" of development was well underway. But at the time, progress seemed "painfully slow."[4] With population growing faster than expected, economic growth per capita over the 1950s was estimated to have been less than 2 percent. Most indices of social progress suggested slow and spotty improvement, with progress uneven and unbalanced by sector and region. The number of persons "living in distress and unacceptable poverty" was thought almost certainly to have increased rather than diminished over the 1950s. In spite of efforts to stamp out illiteracy, the number of illiterate persons was thought to have risen, in part because of the relentless growth of populations.[5]

Against this background the UN took the lead in proposing a First Development Decade. According to General Assembly resolution 1710 (XVI) of December 1961, member states and their peoples would "intensify their efforts to mobilize and to sustain support for the measures required on the part of both developed and developing countries to accelerate progress towards self-sustaining growth of the economy of the individual nations and their social advancement." U.S. President John F. Kennedy launched the proposal. Addressing the 1961 General Assembly, he declared that if the United States could commit itself to put a man on the moon before the decade was over, it would certainly support the idea of improving the living standards of people in the poorest countries over the same period. Ambassador Seymour Maxwell Finger, who served in the U.S. permanent mission to the UN from 1956 to 1971, recalled that one of the "motivations was to highlight Washington's leadership in [Official Development Assistance] ODA at the time."

The main economic objective of the First Development Decade was to accelerate economic growth in developing countries and, more specifically, "to create conditions in which the national incomes of the developing countries [would] be increasing by 5 percent yearly by 1970 [and would] also continue to expand at this annual rate thereafter."[6] With population growing at an estimated rate of 2–2.5 percent per annum, the economic goal was reckoned to be sufficient to double living standards in twenty-five to thirty years—although it was recognized that if population growth accelerated to 3–3.5 percent, this doubling would take thirty-five to fifty years.

This broad goal was backed up by more specific goals for education and the "mobilization of human resources, including particular attention to the needs of children and young people, which was explicitly recognized as a matter of their basic human rights." There were quantitative targets for agriculture and industry—and broad goals also for "agriculture and the reduction of hunger and malnutrition; for natural resources, water, mineral resources and energy; for large and small scale industrial development; for health and housing, transport and communications." These sectoral programs drew heavily on supporting material provided by the UN's specialized agencies.

Looking at these goals forty years later, one finds much to praise: the vision, the range of issues covered, the freshness and subtlety of much of the drafting, the clear focus on national action and goal setting. There was also a more operational bent—the recognition of the role that the UN's country representative, the world organization's agent in each country, should and could play in this. In 1966 the UNDP was founded, and its resident representative became the coordinator for the system,[7] which by this time resembled fairly closely today's organigram (see Figure 2.1). The document warned against forgetting the end in preoccupation with the means: "Human rights may be submerged and human beings seen only as instruments of production rather than as free entities for whose welfare and cultural advance the increased production is intended. The recognition of this issue has a profound bearing upon . . . the objectives of economic development and the methods employed in attaining them."[8]

The very idea of a global framework for accelerated development was far ahead of its time. The orthodoxy at the time was a more piecemeal approach, which is one reason that a forthcoming book from this project will examine the four development decades in depth.[9] Although some said, and many still say, that the decade was no more than wishful—even dangerously misguided—thinking, in some key respects it foreshadowed mainstream international economic policy in the 1980s, although in a way not yet recognized. For a decade or more, beginning in 1981, the Bretton Woods institutions directed a major part of their efforts and resources to supporting and achieving structural adjustment in developing countries. The focus of adjustment in the 1980s was much narrower than were the goals and vision of the development decade of the 1960s. At the core of structural adjustment were international efforts led by the World Bank and the IMF to encourage and enable countries to reduce inflation, to achieve balance-of-payments equilibrium, and (at least it was always claimed) to attain a reasonable rate of economic growth. Moreover, 1980s structural adjustment was being imposed with little attention to social needs or the protests from hard-strapped governments.

Notwithstanding, as an example of coordinated international action directed to the support of individual developing countries to achieve a global economic goal, structural adjustment in the 1980s had many similarities with what the First

Figure 2.1. The United Nations System–Principal Organs of the United Nations

International Court of Justice	General Assembly	Economic and Social Council	Security Council	Trusteeship Council	Secretariat

- Main and other sessional committees
- Standing committees and ad hoc bodies
- Other subsidiary organs and related bodies

▲ **UNRWA**
United Nations Relief and Works Agency for Palestine Refugees in the Near East

■ **IAEA**
International Atomic Energy Agency

▲ **INSTRAW**
International Research and Training Institute for the Advancement of Women

▲ **ODCCP**
United Nations Office for Drug Control and Crime Prevention

▲ **OHCHR**
Office of the High Commissioner for Human Rights

▲ **WFP (UN/FAO)**
World Food Programme

▲ **ITC**
International Trade Centre
UNCTAD/WTO

- Military Staff Committee
- Standing committees and ad hoc bodies
- International Tribunal for the former Yugoslavia
- International Criminal Tribunal for Rwanda

● **UNSCOM**
United Nations Special Commission (Iraq)

■ **ILO**
International Labour Organization

■ **FAO**
Food and Agriculture Organization of the United Nations

■ **UNESCO**
United Nations Educational, Scientific and Cultural Organization

■ **WHO**
World Health Organization

OSG
Office of the Secretary-General

OIOS
Office of Internal Oversight Services

OLA
Office of Legal Affairs

DPA
Department of Political Affairs

DDA
Department for Disarmament Affairs

DPKO
Department of Peacekeeping Operations

OCHA
Office for the Coordination of Humanitarian Affairs

DESA
Department of Economic and Social Affairs

DGAACS
Department of General Assembly Affairs and Conference Services

▲ **UNCHS**
United Nations Centre for Human Settlements (Habitat)

▲ **UNCTAD**
United Nations Conference on Trade and Development

▲ **UNDP**
United Nations Development Programme
  ▶ **UNIFEM**
  United Nations Development Fund for Women
  ▶ **UNV**
  United Nations Volunteers

▲ **UNEP**
United Nations Environment Programme

▲ **UNFPA**
United Nations Population Fund

▲ **UNHCR**
Office of the United Nations High Commissioner for Refugees

▲ **UNICEF**
United Nations Children's Fund

▲ **UNICRI**
United Nations Interregional Crime and Justice Research Institute

▲ **UNIDIR**
United Nations Institute for Disarmament Research

▲ **UNITAR**
United Nations Institute for Training and Research

▲ **UNOPS**
United Nations Office for Project Services

▲ **UNU**
United Nations University

● **FUNCTIONAL COMMISSIONS**
Commission for Social Development
  ▶ United Nations Research Institute for Social Development (UNRISD)
Commission on Human Rights
Commission on Narcotic Drugs
Commission on Science and Technology for Development
Commission on Sustainable Development
Commission on the Status of Women
Commission on Population and Development
Statistical Commission

● **REGIONAL COMMISSIONS**
Economic Commission for Africa (ECA)
Economic Commission for Europe (ECE)
Economic Commission for Latin America and the Caribbean (ECLAC)
Economic and Social Commission for Asia and the Pacific (ESCAP)
Economic and Social Commission for Western Asia (ESCWA)

● **SESSIONAL AND STANDING COMMITTEES**

● **EXPERT, AD HOC AND RELATED BODIES**

WORLD BANK GROUP
■ **IBRD**
International Bank for Reconstruction and Development
■ **IDA**
International Development Association
■ **IFC**
International Finance Corporation
■ **MIGA**
Multilateral Investment Guarantee Agency

■ **IMF**
International Monetary Fund

■ **ICAO**
International Civil Aviation Organization

■ **UPU**
Universal Postal Union

■ **ITU**
International Telecommunication Union

■ **WMO**
World Meteorological Organization

■ **IMO**
International Maritime Organization

■ **WIPO**
World Intellectual Property Organization

■ **IFAD**
International Fund for Agricultural Development

■ **UNIDO**
United Nations Industrial Development Organization

■ **WTO***
World Trade Organization

DPI
Department of Public Information

DM
Department of Management

UNSECOORD
Office of the United Nations Security Coordinator

UNOG
UN Office at Geneva

UNOV
UN Office at Vienna

UNON
UN Office at Nairobi

▲ United Nations programmes and organs (representative list only)
■ Specialized agencies and other autonomous organizations within the system
● Other commissions, committees and ad hoc related bodies
* Not part of the United Nations system although has cooperating arrangements and practices with the Organization

Development Decade envisaged. Unfortunately, the goals and priorities were quite different from the comprehensive UN ones:

- economic growth *and* social progress were the critical objectives, closely linked to employment creation;
- the emphasis was on "individual nations" and on "each country setting its own target";
- international aid was calculated in relation to what was needed to enable developing countries as a group to achieve their goals; and
- emphasis was given to technology — and to disarmament as a critical way for developing countries to mobilize resources.

Two elements of the first decade's approach were also stressed, each with a contemporary ring. The "principle of partnership" between developed and developing countries was the first, at the heart of any definition of international cooperation. The second principle was also in the UN Charter but was considerably more controversial, namely that individual countries should set their own goals and targets — "ownership" in modern terms. Some other things were not mentioned. There was no reference to the need for stronger governance or of the corrosive effects of corruption. There was no hint of the informal sector — and little of the private sector, except for language that implied that a pragmatic and non-ideological approach would be best. The problem of ending malnutrition was seen mostly as a food problem, with a word on the need for attention to income distribution but no forthright emphasis on the need to ensure income and entitlements for the poor or of the dramatic potential of "new seeds" — technology that, we now know, was already on the drawing boards of Rockefeller Foundation–funded research laboratories.

As with most international documents, compromise was necessary to reach agreement on the final text. With the Cold War in full force, the document skates around the theories of development pushed by East and West. As such, the respective roles of the state and of the market in productive activities were finessed.

References to the health sector were especially bland — focusing on the need for building local intermediate, provincial, and national infrastructures for health services. Although the need for setting health targets was recognized — focused on infant mortality, communicable diseases, nutrition, and sanitation — the text is brief and lacking in specifics. No mention was made of the smallpox eradication program of the World Health Organization (WHO) in the document on the First Development Decade, even though when smallpox was eradicated in 1977, this was rightly hailed as one of the great health victories of the twentieth century (see Box 2.1).

Box 2.1. Eradicating Smallpox, and Avoiding Two Million Deaths Each Year

For more than three thousand years smallpox was a scourge of mankind, feared for its high fatality—often 10 percent of all deaths each year—and for the pockmarks which disfigured those that survived. Edward Jenner, an English country doctor, discovered a vaccine in 1796, and the spread of vaccination led to a marked decrease in the toll of small-pox in industrial countries. Yet the disease continued almost unabated in Africa, Asia, and Latin America. In the 1960s some two million people were estimated to be dying of small-pox every year.[10]

In 1953 the first director general of the World Health Organization (WHO) made an un-successful attempt to persuade the World Health Assembly to undertake a global program for smallpox eradication. Five years later, a Soviet delegate persuaded the WHO to ac-cept responsibility for a global program—but only minimal funds were provided. The WHO itself was preoccupied with a major and eventually unsuccessful effort to eradicate malaria, and many were skeptical about the feasibility of smallpox eradication, especially in Africa.

In 1966 the World Health Assembly agreed on an Intensified Smallpox Eradication Program (ISEP)—although still amid grave reservations and many doubts about its ulti-mate success. At that time, the WHO's entire global staff numbered only some 3,302 per-sons, and only about 150 professionals were available to oversee smallpox vaccination programs in more than fifty countries.

Notwithstanding, once started, the program advanced rapidly. A strategic plan con-centrated on mass vaccination campaigns, using freeze-dried vaccines whose quality was assessed by special teams. A surveillance system was set up to detect and investigate cases and contain outbreaks. Three principles were critically important. First, all countries would need to participate, with some form of regional and global coordination. Second, programs would need to be flexible and adapted to the specifics of each country. Third, ongoing research, in the field and the laboratory, would be needed to evaluate progress and solve problems as they arose.

By the early 1970s smallpox was on the retreat—although still widespread, especially in Asia and Africa. A surveillance containment strategy was developed, sending flying squad teams wherever a possible case was discovered. The squads would make a di-agnosis, identify and vaccinate all contacts, and swiftly contain the spread of infection. By 1975 the number of countries where the disease could still be found had fallen from thirty to three: India, Bangladesh, and Ethiopia. By the end of the year the last case of variola major, the most serious form of the disease, was reported in Bangladesh.

Attention then turned to Ethiopia, where the last case was reported in August—but not before nomads had carried the disease across the border into Somalia, where an epi-demic occurred in mid-1977. In October 1975 the last case was finally reported in Soma-lia. Three years later the WHO declared the disease extinct. The total cost of the eleven-year effort had been around $300 million, one-third of which came from international sources and two-thirds from the countries affected. The total cost was the equivalent at the time of the cost of three fighter-bombers. The world now saves at least $2 billion each year by avoiding the purchase of smallpox vaccine, vaccine administration, applying international health regulations, and related costs. Most of the savings have been in the budgets of industrialized countries, which have been able to avoid the up-front investment costs of vaccination and smallpox health regulations.

The eradication of polio, inspired in part by the successful experience with smallpox, is well under way. Some 150 countries have reported no case for three years or more, and the target date for eradication is 2005. Tragically, efforts to tackle HIV/AIDS have been very different (see Chapter 7).

With the First Development Decade in place, the UN during the 1960s made two major contributions to ideas and thinking on development. These were the creation of UNCTAD to focus directly on the issues of trade and development from a Third-World perspective, and sharpening the concept of development assistance and the adoption of the 0.7 percent goal. There were other important contributions in the 1960s—a series of regional conferences organized by UNESCO on education goals for the decade and the creation in 1964 of the World Food Program as a channel for food aid against hunger and food insecurity.

UN Conference on Trade and Development

From the early days of the UN, the terms on which developing countries interacted with the rest of the world were seen as crucial to their chances for accelerated development. Article 28 of the Universal Declaration of Human Rights states that "everyone is entitled to a social and international order in which the rights and freedoms set forth in this Declaration be fully realized." The three major UN reports on development issued between 1949 and 1951 (see Chapter 1) had each recognized that international trade and finance would be major mechanisms for the economic advance in underdeveloped countries.

However, important problems would need to be tackled if international trade and finance were to deliver their full potential: the special vulnerability of developing countries to economic fluctuations arising outside their borders; instability and long-run decline in commodity prices, which formed the main exports of many developing countries; and fluctuations in flows of international capital, private and public. Initially fluctuations were seen as the most important issue. But by the 1960s the long-term decline in commodity prices was being placed at the top of the list, especially after the high prices of the Korean War era. In little more than a decade the terms of trade between developing and developed countries deteriorated by 18 percent. The trade surplus of $2 billion which developing countries enjoyed in 1950 had become a deficit of $2.3 billion by 1962. Accelerated economic growth would require an increase in imports—and would widen the gap further unless some action were taken,

Thinking and research was taken forward by two of the UN's major economic thinkers, Raúl Prebisch and Hans Singer. Prebisch had been a professor of political economy in Buenos Aires from 1925 to 1948, as well for periods undersecretary of finance and first director-general of the Argentine Central Bank. In 1950 he was appointed executive secretary of the ECLA and in 1963 the first secretary-general of UNCTAD. Bernard Chidzero was later recruited by Prebisch to head the Commodities Division after having been the first black African to head a UNDP country office. He recalled that Prebisch "believed in what John Maynard Keynes had believed—to have free and effective institutions . . . and managed to give body and soul to the child of the Group of 77, namely UNCTAD."

Singer was the third economist to be appointed to the UN secretariat. In 1932 he had fled from Nazi Germany to Cambridge, where he obtained his doctorate under Keynes—having previously been taught in Bonn by Schumpeter. From 1936 to 1938 Singer had worked on a pioneering study of unemployment in Britain, *Men without Work,* living with poor and unemployed families while undertaking the research.[11] After joining the UN he wrote prolifically, almost all as anonymous contributions to official UN publications. His ideas and thinking underpinned many UN initiatives before and after he retired in 1969 to become a professorial fellow of the Institute of Development Studies at the University of Sussex in England. In recalling how he developed his analytical lenses, Singer stated: "One tries to look at the world from the viewpoint of the under-dog—of the recipient, the victim. You may get insights into the world that are not open to people who look at the world from the top down."

The Prebisch-Singer analysis sought to explain the tendency for developing countries to face persistent balance-of-payments problems. This tendency reflected the disparity between the rate of growth of earnings from their exports of primary products and their rate of imports of industrial goods, needed for investment and growth as well as for consumption. This radical proposition was much disputed at the time,[12] and the statistical bases have also continued to be debated.[13] Economic historians discuss who actually was the first to develop this idea. In a forthcoming book in the series commissioned by the UNIHP, John and Richard Toye will come down on the side of Singer. Although the primary documentation is far from complete, the authors argue that Prebisch did not independently discover that the terms of trade were secularly declining but relied on previous work by Singer. An uneven application of the UN's rules about the anonymity of authorship created the impression that the discovery was made independently.[14]

The imbalance, Prebisch and Singer argued, arose from a number of factors: the low income and price elasticity of demand for staple foodstuffs and consumer goods, compared with the demand for industrial goods and services; the concentration of technological progress in the industrial countries, resulting in the increased use of synthetics and the diminished raw-material content of finished goods; and the modernization of agriculture in industrial countries, resulting in enormous increases in agricultural production, agricultural protection and farm support policies in developed countries, and agricultural exports from developed to developing countries. The imbalances caused by these factors were compounded by their effects on the terms of trade. Commodity prices fell with the tendency of their supply to run ahead of demand, and, in contrast, the prices of industrial goods tended to rise, as manufacturers of new products could exploit monopolistic power in the market.

These tendencies were man-made, not God-given. Over the 1950s various initiatives were taken to encourage developing countries to take remedial action, some already proposed in the 1951 *Measures for International Economic Stability*. Strategies of industrialization, through import substitution and processing of primary products before exporting them, were proposed as major priorities. The so-called Haberler report was published in 1958 by the General Agreement on Tariffs and Trade (GATT), which provided a kind of imprimatur for the Prebisch-Singer explanation for the rich getting richer and the poor poorer.[15] Income from exports from developing countries failed to grow as rapidly as did those from developed countries whose tariff and other barriers had been erected against imports of products, especially manufactured goods, that were of particular interest to the South. International action was also needed—especially to remove tariff barriers and end agricultural protection.

In 1964 UNCTAD was established to explore further these issues and to act as a forum for negotiations about them. Originally an International Trade Organization (ITO) had been envisaged to play this role—indeed, to be much more than this by serving with the World Bank and the IMF as the third leg of the tripartite stool of the international system. But the ITO failed to come into existence, primarily due to the non-ratification of its charter by the United States after the 1948 Havana Conference. The resulting institutional gap was only partly filled by GATT, which itself gave way to the WTO in 1995.

Perhaps the most significant development during the two years of preparations for the first UNCTAD was the crystallization of developing countries into a single unit for the purposes of international economic negotiations. This was anything but a painless birth, especially because it so clearly aimed at changing the distribution of benefits from growth and trade.[16] What Alfred Sauvy had first characterized as the *tiers monde* (Third World) at the outset of the 1960s[17] became the Group of 77 (G-77, named after the original number of members, which has now grown to some 135). As becomes clearer throughout this book (see especially Chapter 4), the G-77 became the voice of the South and its pressure group during the series of world conferences and elsewhere.[18]

The G-77 marked the emergence of a cohesive voting coalition of developing countries, an economic extension of the momentous political gathering at Bandung, Indonesia, in 1955 that had led to the NAM. "It was the kind of meeting that no anthropologist, no sociologist, no political scientist would ever have dreamed of staging," wrote African American novelist Richard Wright. It cut "through the outer layers of disparate social and political and cultural facts down to the bare brute residues of human existence: races and religions and continents."[19] Jan Pronk, deputy secretary-general of UNCTAD throughout much of the 1980s and a contributor to development thinking as a minister in the Netherlands, recalled: "UNCTAD, of course, had a major analytical input to international thinking. . . . A little radical, but there would not have been any progress without such a challenge. It was a confrontational attitude on the basis of the Group of 77's New International Economic Order approach."

The hope of developing countries was that UNCTAD would become a forum through which they could improve their bargaining position more effectively than in other multilateral economic institutions in which the West was dominant. In fact, the "conference" became a permanent institution, although the "C" was maintained in UNCTAD's title.

With Prebisch as secretary-general, UNCTAD set forth on a pioneering program of research and negotiation. It had four principal aims:

- to promote international trade and economic development of developing countries;
- to promote trade and economic co-operation, particularly between countries at different stages of economic development and between developing countries and between countries with different economic and social systems;
- to formulate principles and policies on international trade and development; and
- to promote a more equitable international economic order, a larger voice for developing countries in decision making, and a development dimension and consensus in international institutions and policies.

The early work of UNCTAD concentrated on commodity arrangements and compensatory finance, access to developed country markets, and increased volume and terms of aid. Other issues were also explored: shipping, technology, restrictive business practices, monetary issues, and the "link" — how the creation of liquidity by the IMF in the form of Special Drawing Rights (SDRs) could be linked to new allocations of development finance to developing countries. Gamani Corea, who would later become UNCTAD's third secretary-general after being engaged in the management of Ceylon's (now Sri Lanka's) Planning Ministry and Central Bank and chaired the Committee on Development Planning (CDP), recalled: "Those days we were a hive of activity — the Common Fund, IPC, the technology code, restrictive business practices, multi-modal transport, least-developed countries. Delegates used to come and complain to me that the tempo was too much. I used to tell them, 'You are living in a comfortable city; you are having good food; you are having good places to work; and you also want a good night's sleep?'"

The high growth rates of the industrial countries in the 1960s provided the positive context for this somewhat moderate agenda. When the world economy worsened in the 1970s — especially after the United States dropped the link between gold and the dollar, the Bretton Woods system collapsed, and the Organization of Petroleum Exporting Countries (OPEC) sharply increased world oil prices — UNCTAD took on a broader and more fundamental set of issues, which included the NIEO's controversial action program (see Chapter 4).

In fact, the various committees and working groups provided a forum for challenging the whole range of orthodox approaches to development. Ideas about how to approach special groups of countries (for example, the least developed) or special problems (for example, preferential access to markets or protection of prices for raw materials) were part of ongoing research and negotiating efforts by the secretariat. Beginning in the mid-1980s UNCTAD's *Trade and Development Report* was conceived as a kind of annual riposte to the World Bank's *World Development Report*. An examination of the pages indicates skepticism about pure liberalization, arguments that debt payments were unsustainable, and predictions about the Asian crisis.

The Organization for Economic Cooperation and Development (OECD) acts as a secretariat for research and coordination of positions for the industrialized countries of the West. UNCTAD is sometimes viewed as a "Third World secretariat," and its views often dismissed. However, successive secretaries-general of the organization have always made clear its universalism. Corea, for one, stated: "UNCTAD was presenting — at least we wanted to present — problems which reflected the development dimension of issues, not the narrow interests of the developing countries." At the same time, the visceral resistance of developed countries was usually quite clear. Robert Cox, who left the ILO in the early 1970s and became a professor of international organization, recalled the West's common view: "There was the view that this Group of 77 were basically irresponsible countries and that they should not be allowed to unduly influence the direction of policy."

Aid and Development Finance

From its earliest years the UN had emphasized the need and obligation of richer countries to support development in poorer countries, an analysis that will also be the subject of in-depth treatment by the UNIHP.[20] This was partly normative and partly geopolitical. The UN's position reflected desirable actions to fulfill the Universal Declaration of Human Rights, especially the international measures to ensure "a social and international order in which the rights and freedoms set forth in this Declaration can be fully realized."

But the justification for foreign policy-makers in the West was to gain allies in the Cold War's competition. As one observer noted, there was a "Manichean view of the world, against the background of a growing number of independent countries in the developing world."[21] The "loss" of China in 1949 was followed shortly thereafter by the invasion of South Korea by North Korea with Chinese support. The battleground was Asia, where the "domino theory" was born, but competition for the newly independent countries in Africa soon entered the calculations of decision-makers, particularly in Washington and Moscow. Singer stressed this dimension in comparing the background for the Marshall Plan with the First Development Decade, which "was conceived as showing that the Western approach to development problems can get results and there's no need for communism."

The proposals for action for the First Development Decade calculated that the total flow of capital and assistance to the developing countries should reach and maintain 1 percent of the national income of the advanced countries—a level recommended by the General Assembly. Underlying this was the view that total capital formation in developing countries would need to be twice its level of the early 1960s in order to support the proposed growth rate of 5 percent or more in the national incomes of the developing countries. It was recognized that a precise calculation was not possible. The exact requirement would depend on what happens in the field of trade and on the degree of success of developing countries in mobilizing internal resources.

Over the 1960s calculations and commitments were sharpened. The chair of the newly formed CDP was Jan Tinbergen, who would later in the decade win the first Nobel Prize in the Economic Sciences (see Box 2.2). Composed of prominent development economists, the committee was originally intended to monitor progress in the development decade. Toward the end of that first decade, its functions were broadened to make recommendations for what was to become the Second Development Decade.

**Box 2.2. Jan Tinbergen, First Nobel Prizewinner in Economics
and Lifetime Visionary of the UN**

Jan Tinbergen was born in the Hague in 1903 and died in 1994, with a distinguished career spanning virtually the entire twentieth century. He studied theoretical physics at the University of Leiden and refused, as a conscientious objector, to do military service. He thus was put to work for two years in alternative service for the Bureau of Statistics. These were the years of the Great Depression, and he discovered the severity of social dislocations on the streets in the Hague and through the statistics that he handled. He was offered a job by Albert Einstein, but Tinbergen had found his destiny. He would become an economist and try to solve the economic and social problems of his day, and subsequently of his century. Like other members of the first generation of development economists who did not believe in the neoclassical scheme, he combined his economics with a sense of history as well as with geographical and temporal contingencies.

Combining his knowledge of mathematics and economics, Tinbergen pioneered econometrics—the application of quantitative techniques to economics—for which he won the first Nobel Prize in economics, together with Ragnar Frisch.

Tinbergen's career can be divided into four periods:

• The 1930s marked his first forays into econometrics. His innovations were embodied in studies of business cycle theory and practice that were commissioned by the League of Nations prior to World War II. He sought to understand the Great Depression and the possible ways to emerge from the economic morass.

• Between 1945 and 1955 his work as a founder of macroeconomic modeling took place as he served as the first director of the Central Planning Bureau of The Netherlands. This was not only a creative theoretical period but above all an eminently practical exposure to the postwar reconstruction of the Dutch economy and its path to sustained economic and social growth. Tinbergen showed in very practical terms the way from chaos to prosperity.

• The years from 1955 to 1975 marked his switch to development economics in a number of capacities—adviser to many governments in developing countries, director of the Netherlands Economic Institute in Rotterdam, and chairman of the UN's Committee on Development Planning (CDP), where he inspired the first two development decades. He concentrated on finding possible ways out of global inequalities by setting ambitious targets for developing countries and equally ambitious ones for development assistance by industrialized countries.

• His last twenty years consisted of a very active retirement and were marked by continued interest and research in the UN, development, employment, and income distribution. At the same time, he pursued his lifelong passion for peace by concentrating more so than earlier on peace economics.

What is striking about Tinbergen and other members of the first generation of development economists is their ability to be ahead of the intellectual curve by mixing a sense of history with economic analyses and stressing not only the rate of economic growth but also its pattern. In what must have been one of his last writings, Tinbergen in a two-page article reviewed many themes to which he attached the utmost importance — war and peace, the establishment of a world government, and the reform of the UN. "We must calculate the costs of the wealth destroyed, and the money value of being killed," he wrote, "or a friend or one's partner or relatives killed."[22] He remained himself until the end.

In this connection, the calculations of aid and other external flows of resources from developed to developing countries were refined. The goal for economic growth during the Second Development Decade was raised from 5 to 6 percent, as an annual average to be achieved over the ten-year period. Even with this elevated growth rate, the estimated inflow of external resources required by developing countries was still estimated to be 1 percent of the national incomes of developed countries. This 1 percent figure was also approved by the first and second UNCTAD conferences in Geneva and New Delhi in 1964 and 1968.

This target was, however, was soon to be more specifically broken down into a private and a public component. Inflows of private investment of some 30 percent of total inflows were thought possible. The remainder would need to be inflows in the form of foreign aid from the public sectors of industrialized countries. This was the basis of the famous target for aid, 0.7 percent of the national incomes of the industrialized countries. Tinbergen himself made the calculation, which was eventually approved in the resolution for the Second Development Decade in 1970. Although its basis has often been criticized, this target has stood for three decades as a rallying cry for supporters of aid for developing countries.[23] As mentioned earlier, in 1969 Tinbergen was awarded the Nobel Prize in economics, the first year it was awarded.

A substantial contribution to the debate was the first of what would become a series of reports on development issues from independent commissions. In October 1967 the then president of the World Bank, George Woods, suggested that an international group with stature should "meet together, study the consequences of twenty years of development assistance, assess the results, clarify the errors and propose the policies which will work better in the future." In August 1968 former Canadian prime minister Lester B. Pearson accepted an invitation from Robert McNamara, who had by then taken the reins at the World Bank, to form and chair such a commission. Arthur Lewis joined Pearson and six other commissioners whose voices are recorded in *Partners in Development*.[24] This report included the recommendation for the 0.7 percent target for Official Development Assistance (ODA).

Two postscripts are required to explain how the aid target was further developed on two later occasions. In 1981 and 1990 (and again in 2001), the UN organized a world conference around the special needs of the least developed countries. Governments declared that 0.15 percent of GNP should be allocated as development assistance to these poorest of poor countries.[25]

Ten years after the 1981 Paris Conference on the Least Developed Countries (see Box 4.1), "the 20/20 proposal" was floated in the *Human Development Report 1992*.[26] Under this, some 20 percent of aid was to be allocated to basic social services—as part of a partnership in which developing countries would also allocate 20 percent of their own domestic public expenditures to the same ends. It was estimated that together this would raise the finance required to ensure education for all; primary health for all; water and sanitation for all; nutrition for all; and reproductive health care services and family planning for all. It is a fitting tribute to the continuity of ideas that one of the strongest supporters of the 20/20 proposal was Pronk, then minister of development in The Netherlands, who first studied development under Tinbergen.

Have these aid targets been met? It is conventional to lament that they have not. The share of ODA in the country GNP figures of OECD countries rose in the 1970s and 1980s and thereafter has been falling continuously, from 0.33 percent in 1990 to 0.24 percent in 1998 (the share of ODA in U.S. GNP fell from 0.19 to 0.10 percent).[27] But this generalization is too simple. Focusing on individual donors shows that four countries (Norway, The Netherlands, Denmark, and Sweden) have for more than twenty years met or exceeded the 0.7 percent target, and seven (Norway, The Netherlands, Denmark, Sweden, Finland, Belgium, and Italy) have met or exceeded the 0.15 percent for least developed countries. The decline reflects reductions in the aid contributions by the largest donors.

Conclusions

To sum up what has been said so far, in 1948 the Universal Declaration of Human Rights was agreed. By the 1950s the process of decolonization proceeded apace, with clear principles having been set out earlier in the UN Charter (see Table 2.1). By 1951, the UN was well launched into development, having set a new international framework for action, more far-reaching and radical than many realized at the time or since. This framework for international development and support had been elaborated in three priority areas: employment, development strategy, and international trade and finance. The principle that each country must fashion its own development strategy in relation to its own objectives and situation was well established but with the recognition that major international assistance, both technical and financial, would also be necessary.

The significance of these earlier contributions was largely ignored at the beginning of the 1950s. The Korean War was raging. The drama of the Security Council and the UN's political debates and battles then, as now, monopolized the headlines. Moreover, the Marshall Plan, being handled outside both the UN system and the Bretton Woods institutions, meant that the big money of international assistance had become intentionally a North American–European issue instead of a global enterprise.

Part of the UN's hitting its stride involved articulating the collective demands of developing countries. In the period under review, the formulation of a global framework in the form of the First Development Decade was a critical step. This was followed by the establishment of UNCTAD, with its use of group negotiations, and the focus on the requirements for outside finance in developing countries to help break the cycle of poverty.

All of this encouraged rather than prevented the UN to be a pioneer for one other element, which over the years has continued to distinguish its work, at least its better and more forward-looking contributions. This was analysis directed to basic human objectives, for which the UN has shown a willingness to reach conclusions for action in advance of mainstream thinking. This is perhaps the most important respect in which the UN has been — and often remains — ahead of the curve. It has meant that many of the early UN reports and proposals were dismissed as idealistic, and sometimes as ideological. But whatever the immediate reactions, the UN at the beginning and over the years has continued to challenge conventional wisdom and thinking. A theme that reappears throughout these pages is how often and how soon ideas once readily dismissed became widely accepted.

Table 2.1. Decolonization and Growth in UN Membership, 1945–2000

	Year										
	1945	1950	1955	1960	1965	1970	1975	1980	1990	1995	2000
Total UN membership	51	60	76	100	118	127	143	153	160	185	189

Source: UN, United Nations Member States (New York: UN, 2000).

Notes: The first two decades of the UN are marked by the admission of new states that achieved independence in the decolonization process. In September 1960 alone seventeen newly independent states, sixteen from Africa, joined the UN. This was the biggest increase in membership since the establishment of the UN. In the late 1960s half of the member states had achieved independence since 1945, and more than one-fourth had been independent for less than five years.

In the 1990s the disintegration of the USSR, Czechoslovakia, and the Republic of Yugoslavia led to the admission of nineteen new independent states to UN membership: the eleven states of the Commonwealth of Independent States (CIS), with the membership of the Soviet Union being continued by the Russian Federation; three Baltic states (Estonia, Latvia, and Lithuania); and Bosnia and Herzegovina, Croatia, Slovenia, the former Yugoslav Republic of Macedonia, and Slovakia.

3

Employment Creation and Basic Needs

- **The Framework and the "New" Policies**
- **International Cooperation**
- **What Happened to the Ideas?**

The 1970s were a creative decade for the UN system. Many ideas were launched—sometimes controversial, normally interesting, and often ahead of the curve. In reaction to the bittersweet record of the 1960s—better-than-expected economic growth but mounting unemployment, population growth, resource scarcity, and environmental pollution—the UN became the forum for several pioneering activities and debates during the 1970s. Employment creation and poverty reduction moved to center stage. Work by the ILO on this was pathbreaking.

The world economy came roaring into the 1970s, and this included developing countries. Never in economic history had so many countries grown so fast for so long. Over the 1950s and the 1960s (and indeed over the 1970s) the average annual rate of growth for the developing countries as a whole amounted to more than 5 percent, an altogether exceptional performance (see Table 3.1).

But toward the end of the 1960s astute observers noted mounting problems in the developing world, including increased poverty, growing unemployment, grievous inequalities in income distribution, and a variety of deteriorating environmental indicators. This seemed paradoxical, although outside the neoclassical framework in the nineteenth century there had also been others who had doubted that growth was a panacea. Until the late 1960s, however, the mainstream view held—to paraphrase the Bible—that with economic growth everything else, including social advancement, would be added unto you. But this was not the case. High rates of economic growth were accompanied by worsening social and socioeconomic circumstances. Dudley Seers, who had worked for the UN in Latin America and Africa, emphasized the multidimensional character of the development process:

"without work" yet willing to work at the existing wage rate. This is the industrial countries' definition of unemployment, but it constitutes only a small component of the overall problem in developing counties, where most people cannot afford to be openly unemployed in the absence of social safety nets.

The second component is the working poor. This refers to people who are working but whose earnings in cash or in kind are below minimum needs, either because of too few working hours or (more frequently) because of low productivity combined even with long hours. The working poor are by far the most important component.

The third component is frustrated job seekers. Many of these are young people who have achieved a certain level of education and have high expectations about types of jobs and levels of remuneration. If they cannot realize these expectations immediately, they prefer to "queue" rather than to take on any other job. This small but often vocal group tends to get disproportionate attention from policymakers. The WEP christened the sum of these three components the "employment problem." And the ILO sought to address this problem by framing an appropriate development strategy.

The second discovery pioneering at the time was the existence of the informal sector. In the paradigm of modernization in the 1950s and 1960s, a strong dualism existed between modern and traditional sectors—which drew from Arthur Lewis but was developed by John Fei and Gustav Ranis.[7] An emerging modern sector was seen as the hard core of modernity, rationality, and economic dynamism. The traditional sector was archaic and characterized by low productivity. According to productivist economic logic, development was associated with industrialization. And the priority was thus to emphasize the modern sector and reduce the traditional sector to a marginal part in the economic structure of a modern society. Human and capital resources were to be transferred from one sector to the other. The "steel and glass sector," mainly in the cities, was to benefit from the transfer from the traditional and low-productivity sector, mainly in rural areas.

The discovery of the informal sector was the identification of an overlooked group in between the modern and the traditional.[8] As the modern, formal sector started to develop, more and more people in the traditional sector became attracted by the bright lights of the city and the prospects for jobs there. They flooded into urban settings in search of a prize in the job lottery—and a lottery it turned out to be. Because of the relatively high productivity and capital intensity in the modern sector, few jobs were being created. Most rural-urban migrants were disappointed. Instead of returning to their villages, however, many installed themselves on the outskirts of cities, the origin of the informal sector that is situated both economically and geographically on the margins. Governments had tended to react negatively to the murkiness of that sector, its lack of modernity, and its shameful appearances. They overlooked the wonders of small-scale innovation and economic imagination. The WEP proposed that governments start to view the informal sector positively and to help it establish links with enterprises in the modern sector.

This and many other ideas proved fertile. Research and debate on the informal sector has been lively ever since. Further work on the informal sector has revealed many more areas where it is important and active, including informal education, housing, health services, and insurance.

The third idea relates to the identification of appropriate technologies and their introduction by a shift in macro policies. There was intense debate during the 1970s about technologies — "appropriate," "labor-intensive," "intermediate," and the like.[9] The quest was for technologies that used more of the abundant and less of the scarce factors of production. In the case of developing countries, the abundant factor obviously was labor, and the scarce one capital. However, there were two catches. One was that the use of technologies should be examined sector by sector. The appropriate technology may be capital-intensive for exports, but the room for technological choice and maneuver is greater for local consumption. The second was that the identification of the most appropriate technologies is meaningless without changing the relevant macro policies that have prevented their introduction in the first place. Entrepreneurs are not fools. If they use more capital-intensive technologies, it is often because incentives point in that direction. In other words, exchange rates, fiscal systems, and tax policies should be adapted if a change in the use of technology is desirable.

The fourth idea concerned the crucial role of education in any economic policy, but particularly in a more employment-intensive development strategy. At the beginning of the WEP, the renaissance of the economics of education was already ten years old. It was, therefore, already clear that education was not only a consumption good — to be afforded after a certain level of income was achieved — but also an investment and a prerequisite to achieving higher levels of income.[10] This was an important rediscovery. Equally important, however, was the necessity to reduce the gap between the school and the labor market. As it was then — and to a large extent still is today — the education system was characterized by "cannibalistic" tendencies. Primary school prepared for secondary school, which prepared for the university, rather than for the outside world. Since only a very small percentage made it to the top of the educational pyramid, this meant that the large majority of young people left school without a proper preparation for the world of work. The remedy was not only to emphasize vocational and technical education, but also to make sure that it became easier to move from school into work and back into school. Education became a priority of policy-makers in the early 1970s. They progressively implemented ambitious programs with financial sup-

Table 3.2. Gross Primary Enrollment Ratio and Illiteracy Rates, 1970–2000

		Gross Primary Enrollment Ratio (%)	Illiteracy Rate (%) (Population Age 15 Years and Older)
World total	1970	90	37
	1980	96	31
	1990	99	25
	1995	100	23
	2000	102[a]	21
Developed countries	1970	99	6
	1980	101	3
	1990	101	2
	1995	102	1
	2000	103[a]	1
Least developed countries	1970	48	73
	1980	66	66
	1990	66	58
	1995	70	54
	2000	71[a]	49
Developing countries	1970	81	52
	1980	95	42
	1990	99	33
	1995	100	29
	2000	102[a]	26

Source: UNESCO, Statistics Yearbook 2000 (Paris: UNESCO, 2000).
[a] 1997 data are the latest for gross enrollment ratio.

port from donors and the technical assistance from the UN system. Table 3.2 shows the substantial progress made during the 1970s regarding both primary education enrollment and the reduction of illiteracy.

The policy instrument that makes this passage easier is called recurrent education. The Ceylon (now Sri Lanka) employment report of 1971 and the Kenya employment report of 1972 illustrated how the ideas of recurrent education could be applied to a developing country.[11] Basically, the idea behind recurrent education is that after a certain number of years of education early in life (depending on the circumstances in a given country), the remainder could be taken whenever an individual is motivated. The prerequisite is that a person's return to the classroom is guaranteed. This starkly contrasts with the dominant model that makes it extremely difficult to return to the educational system once one has left it.

The fifth idea was the discovery of a virtuous circle between employment creation, income distribution, consumption patterns, and production structures. In the economic textbooks of the 1970s one could still read that a skewed income distribution was good for economic growth because the wealthy save while the poor do not. This was a variation on Kuznets's U-curve hypothesis. During the second phase, the rich save and investments were therefore supposed to be forthcoming to boost economic growth further. But it was not mentioned that the rich may put their savings not in their own country but in Miami, New York, Zurich, or Amsterdam. Moreover, the rich have consumption patterns that favor capital- and import-intensive goods.

Equally seriously, many failed to recognize that the poor do save, but for them the act of saving and of investing is one and the same. When they make tools, prepare land, build simple housing, build a feeder road, or restore a school, the poor are saving and investing at the same time. Hence, when productive employment is stimulated in the least productive sectors—by boosting the productivity of existing employment and thus the incomes there—not only does income distribution improve and poverty diminish, but a virtuous circle is set in motion. When the incomes of the poor are raised, they consume more labor-intensive and locally produced goods. This results in a shift in the production pattern toward more labor-intensive economic activities, creates more employment there, increases the incomes of the poor, and so on.[12]

The sixth discovery was obvious but had been overlooked. How many times have so-called pilot projects been launched at the micro level that never could be generalized to the regional or national level? Inconsistencies in policies at different levels of decision making are major problems. With one stroke of a macro pen on the twelfth floor of a steel and glass building in the capital city, a minister can wipe out years of hard work at the micro level. So consistency is essential between macro and micro decisions.

In brief, the WEP brought employment—and people and human needs—back to the center of development strategy. This was directly in line with the centrality of employment in the early days of the UN and of the IMF as well. But ILO work in the 1970s enriched and elaborated the earlier concept of employment and strategies to deal with it by relating both directly to the situations and needs of developing countries.

Box 3.1. Employment Policies in the Interwar Period

During the 1920s and 1930s Arthur Pigou maintained that the causes of unemployment were both excessive wages and trade union pressures in favor of increased minimum wages.[13] He stuck to this analysis by pointing to the role of strengthened trade unions in rounds of wage bargaining, the effects of unemployment insurance, and the growing attention to increases in the cost of living that made things more rigid than they used to be. This resulted in "wage stickiness," which largely explained the high percentage of unemployed that prevailed after the end of the First World War.[14]

Pigou pleaded in favor of letting the market do the necessary adjustments with as little outside interference as possible. Keynes's truly novel idea was that an economic equilibrium could be reached while unemployment was still high. There could be considerable levels of involuntary unemployment in the sense that many workers may be trapped in a state of unemployment even if they would be willing to work at existing or even lower levels of real wages. In such cases, there would be failure of market-clearing mechanisms. The economy would be stuck in a state of equilibrium at high levels of unemployment.[15]

Keynes's central argument differed sharply from those of the classical economists à la Pigou, who argued that in the absence of state interference the existence of any type of unemployment would have the effect of lowering wages. Keynes argued that having millions of unemployed showed that the classical economic mechanism was not working, especially when millions were willing to work for less than the current real wage and still could not find a job.

Keynes's revolutionary *General Theory* analyzed the forces that determine changes in the scale of output and employment as a whole. He attacked the classical model of the labor market that starts with the determination of the real wage and the level of employment. For him, the level of employment is determined by the level of effective demand—that is, as the sum of the expected consumption and the expected investment—and not by changes in real wages. An important implication of this reasoning is the ineffectiveness of wage cuts in order to increase employment, because "the volume of employment is uniquely correlated with the volume of effective demand measured in wage units."[16]

Keynes established the view that there could be no presumption that in a *laissez-faire* economy effective demand would be at a level consistent with the full employment of resources. He, therefore, recognized a necessary place for state intervention. The current economic and financial orthodoxy has reverted to the views prevalent before Keynes, which held sway in the 1920s and 1930s (see Box 3.2).

All of this led to major rethinking of the conventional development policies that for the previous decade had been mostly focused on achieving economic growth. By the middle of the 1970s, when the ILO was in the midst of preparing for the World Employment Conference—but with assistance from other UN organizations and the World Bank—the idea of a basic-needs development strategy was born.[17] The idea of "basic needs" originated in the psychology literature of the 1940s. The best-known publication in this connection was the article by Albert Maslow in the *American Psychological Review* of March 1942.[18] Later, in India during the 1950s, the concept of "minimum needs" had been used within the Indian Planning Commission, with the creative contributions by Pitawber Pant. But basic needs had never become a mainstream approach in development, even if the attractiveness of the concept was clear. Francis Blanchard spent a lifetime in the service of the ILO including fifteen years as its director-general. He noted that basic needs was an inherently attractive concept "because, in the final analysis, what is missing for the majority of our contemporaries and for those who will come later is a job, an income, a roof, adequate education, minimum health services, and access to culture."

In the 1970s, "suddenly" this economic application took place in three different places, practically simultaneously: in the Latin American Bariloche project; in the Dag Hammarskjöld Foundation publication *What Now?*; and in the WEP.[19] It became clear that employment creation was not an end in itself but serves to fulfill the basic needs of individual human beings—more or less equivalent to Maslow's first of five rungs. Many people were already on the second, third, fourth, and even fifth rungs, but an important proportion were not even in sight of the ladder. And so the idea arose of designing a development strategy that had as its main objective meeting basic needs, including those of the poorest 20 percent of the population.

Basic needs were defined in terms of food, housing, clothing, and public transport. Employment was both a means and an end, and participation in decision making was included. The first task was to quantify basic needs for a target year—for instance, twenty-five years in the future.[20] In other words, what must GDP be in $t+25$ if even the poorest 20 percent of the population would have enough to eat, decent housing, high-quality education? Without going into the details of all the numbers and calculations, this quantification was feasible. Having quantified GDP for the target year, one could calculate the annual rate of economic growth required between the base and the target years. This approach reversed conventional practice, which was to project a desirable annual rate of per capita economic growth into the future. The latter was a forward-rolling approach, while the basic-needs approach achieved more precision by setting specific production targets and deriving the desirable rate of growth implied.[21]

Not surprisingly, in most cases the required rate of economic growth to fully meet basic-needs targets was unrealistically high by historical standards—well over 8 percent per annum over twenty-five years. East Asia has subsequently achieved such rates, but in the mid-1970s the East Asian miracle lay ahead. And so the only alternative to achieve the targets of basic needs was to work at two levels: the rate of economic growth *and* income distribution. Indeed, if income distribution improves, the overall rate of economic growth need not be so high. It was shown that with "redistribution from growth"—that is, marginal redistribution of future increase of income rather than redistribution of existing wealth—basic-needs targets could be reached with an annual rate of economic growth of 6 percent.

When this package was presented at the 1976 ILO World Employment Conference, it was greeted with enthusiasm. The two exceptions were the American delegation and some of the employer representatives from other industrialized countries. Opposition may have reflected ideological suspicions rather than well-founded fears. And with the election of President Jimmy Carter a few months later, Washington's official views changed so much so that the U.S. Agency for International Development (USAID) started preaching aggressively the gospel "basic human needs." The president of the World Bank, Robert McNamara, adopted the basic-needs approach wholesale and tried hard to steer his operational departments in that direction.[22]

By the end of the 1970s it looked as though a more appropriate development strategy had been designed that effectively combined economic growth, productive employment, and basic needs. At the core of the strategy was the shift to a pattern of economic growth that is more employment-intensive, more equitable, and more effective in the battle against poverty.

International Cooperation

The design of new strategies brought controversy, inside and outside of the United Nations family. Within the UN it centered on the question of why this work was done by the ILO and not by the UN Department for Economic and Social Affairs (DESA). Indeed, comprehensive proposals for full employment and for development had been prepared under the auspices of that department in 1949 and 1951 (see Chapter 1). Basic needs should have been a prime responsibility of the UN proper. But in the absence of appropriate action, the ILO filled the vacuum and turned itself into a broader development agency without loosing its narrower preoccupation with labor matters.

The ILO referred to the 1944 Declaration of Philadelphia, which had become an integral part of the organization's constitution. Written and adopted toward the end of the war when the League of Nations was moribund and the UN not yet born, this declaration was hardly noticed in San Francisco. But it gave the ILO a broad mandate in the employment field as a part of general economic and social development. It took the ILO another twenty-five years—until 1969 to be exact, when the ILO won the Nobel Peace Prize—to move from its narrower labor pre-occupations to broader employment-creation strategies.

This step was taken because of the urgency of the problem, because orthodox development strategies had been found wanting, and because decisive action by the UN was absent. It was also important that the initiative emanated from David Morse, the then long-serving director-general of the ILO and former New Dealer. Part of the task was to overcome Washington's indifference to and negligible support of, not to say hostility toward, American trade unions.

Once the WEP was under way, it became clear that this idea's time had come. Resources were mobilized—financial, institutional, and substantive. Donors provided substantial extra-budgetary financial contributions because employment was seen as a crucial problem that had been largely ignored in development theory and practice. But it was further stimulated because after October 1970, when Washington stopped paying its obligatory financial contributions in response to what was dubbed a "broken promise" by C. Wilfred Jenks—Morse's successor as director-general—not to appoint an assistant director-general from the Soviet Union. The fatal appointment came after Jenks's election. George Meany, the influential leader of the American Federation of Labor and Congress of Industrial Organizations (AFL-CIO) who could dictate American policy toward the ILO during the Cold War, reacted predictably. Twenty-five percent of the ILO's budget disappeared. From this vantage point, writing at the turn of the century, the UN has grown all too accustomed to American arrogance. But this "first" and shocking experience can be seen in retrospect as a harbinger of what Edward Luck has called American "exceptionalism" in the multilateral arena.[23]

Box 3.2. ILO and Employment in the 1920s and 1930s

The International Labor Organization (ILO) was formed in 1919 as a direct response to the First World War at the signing of the Treaty of Versailles. The new institution was affiliated with the equally new League of Nations. Both had to confront almost immediately the mounting unemployment of the early 1920s, which was followed by the even more serious unemployment crisis of the following decade.

In 1924 the ILO was central to a conference held in London on unemployment at which various aspects of the problem were discussed by "speakers of special competence."[24] Those discussions, three-quarters of a century ago, focused on issues that are eerily still central to the contemporary public policy agenda: long-term unemployment; youth unemployment; the impact of imports on the displacement of workers; the level of unemployment benefits; and the downward pressure on wages of trade and global competition.

When the Great Depression hit in 1931, the ILO published a seminal document that combined the usual report of the director (the title "director-general" came later) to the fifteenth session of the International Labor Conference with substantive studies by scholars from Brussels, Oxford, Frankfurt, and Geneva.[25] The number of unemployed "throughout the world" in 1930 was estimated at ten million. That number had doubled by the end of February 1931, and unemployment stood at ten million in Germany and the United States alone. The report reviewed possible causes and identified "the general lack of confidence as a key one." It stated: "Europe . . . is held in an abyss of unemployment by a spirit of universal distrust."[26]

On the question of international trade and protectionism, the report took a clear and unambiguous stance. The Smoot-Hawley Tariff on U.S. imports, a highly protectionist measure, had come into force 17 June 1930. Far from stabilizing employment among U.S. workers, the tariff had become a new element of disturbance. American exports had in fact fallen, "partly as the result of reprisals and partly from a natural reaction. . . . At the end of 1930, 6 months after the erection of the new tariff wall by the United States, the number of unemployed was still on the increase."[27]

The ILO was an early advocate of public works schemes. The director's report emphasized that it was not enough to organize employment exchanges and to pay unemployment benefits. Public authorities should do everything to ensure that the unemployed get work, if necessary creating jobs for them. Instead of paying unfruitful benefits, surely it is preferable—even if the cost is greater for a time—to ensure to the community the advantage of work voluntarily organized."[28] The question of international public works also was raised but not fully developed.[29]

The length of the work week, wages, and unemployment were also important topics. In those days the demand was for either a forty-four-hour week, or a forty-hour week, or a five-day week. Already the reasoning was that the same amount of work could thus be distributed among a larger number of workers.

In the increasingly globalized and regionalized economy of the new millennium, the importance of a clear and rational international division of labor should be more obvious than it was when the "countries of Western civilization"—the focus of the ILO's attention—reigned supreme and the rest of the world was largely under colonial domination. Yet the discussion seventy years ago was in some respects more forward-looking and more conducive to a rational division of labor than what passes for debate today.

The dawn of the twenty-first century finds the "West" still often opposed to the "rest." Much protectionism remains in place. On the employment issue, there are few imaginative proposals on the horizon. The old prescriptions are repeated: more economic growth, more labor market flexibility, the inevitability of lowering salaries and social security benefits, and so on. The refrain is monotonous. Moreover, no one really believes in the effectiveness of these measures for reasons that are often intuitive and implicit rather than explicit. By controlling and even lowering the level of wages and salaries, particularly of unskilled labor, Europe would hinder the progress and rate of adoption of technology rather than stimulating them, as it did in the 1960s when successive waves of "guest workers" were invited.

On the employment front, the discussion today is remarkably akin to the pre-Keynesian mood of the 1920s and 1930s. In retrospect, the Keynesian consensus proved to be short-lived (mainly from the 1940s to the 1970s). Before and after, there have been less agreement, more discussion, less action, and more dissension. The Third World dimension was almost entirely absent during the colonial days of the 1930s. Today Third-World voices are heard, often vociferously, even if the impact of majority voting is limited.

In these circumstances, many governments came to the ILO's rescue and, more particularly, to the rescue of programs deemed priorities. The WEP benefited. But before saying more about bilateral reactions, a word is in order about the multi-lateral response.

As just mentioned, the WEP filled a vacuum left by the UN proper. But once it was launched, the reaction by the rest of the UN system was admirable. The first two policy activities implemented by the WEP were to send high-level employment missions to selected countries and to establish regional employment teams in Latin America, Asia, and Africa. The high-level missions broke new ground in development theory and practice as they explored the form and nature of employment problems in particular countries—and what could be done to deal with them. The regional teams provided concrete follow-up and assisted other countries within a particular region to design more employment-intensive development strategies. Both of these instruments were financed to an important extent by the UNDP. Moreover, many other organizations contributed in kind, particularly by seconding personnel to the missions and regional teams. In addition to the core UN itself, participation came from the FAO; United Nations Educational, Scientific, and Cultural Organization (UNESCO); United Nations Industrial Development Organization (UNIDO); UNICEF; United Nations Population Fund (UNFPA); and others.

The UNDP, together with the ILO, invested substantially in the WEP, as did the UNFPA, then under the leadership of Rafael Salas from the Philippines. For instance, when it became clear that a WEP research component would be essential to thrash out the ideas explored initially by the high-level missions as well as to explore other ideas, the UNFPA was the first to help overcome the miniscule ILO budget and gave more than $1 million to establish the research capacity. As Aristotle Onassis is reported to have said, "The first million is the most difficult; once you have achieved that the rest is easy."

And in a sense it was. Individual countries weighed in. Sweden matched the UNFPA contribution and repeated that gesture many times. The Netherlands, Denmark, Germany, and other countries contributed, often annually. During the 1970s the research component of the WEP became one of the best-financed efforts in the world of policy research.[30] Without the intellectual sparkle, however, money alone would not have sufficed.

Both multilaterally and bilaterally, therefore, the WEP became an impressive showcase of a UN systemwide effort to try to shift the development focus back to people and to respond to a widely felt problem. Cooperation with the academic community, both in the basic research and in the applied field missions, was an important explanation for success. The role of the Institute of Development Studies (IDS) at the University of Sussex was especially distinguished. Its director, Dudley Seers, led the first two missions, to Colombia and to Ceylon (now Sri Lanka) in 1970 and 1971.[31] Its director-to-be, Richard Jolly, and Hans Singer together led the third mission to Kenya, which launched the debate about the informal sector as well as about the redistribution-from-growth strategy.[32] The Colombia mission had defined the employment problem as set out earlier in this chapter and had pointed to the errors inherent in the "rich save and poor don't" thesis. The previously cited Ceylon report broke new ground because it drew attention to the importance of educational restructuring in addressing development and employment problems, and to the mismatch between the supply of educated people and the demand for them.[33]

Other individuals and institutions played important roles. Gustav Ranis of Yale University's Growth Center led the mission to the Philippines, and Just Faaland of the Chr. Michelsen Institute in Bergen, Norway, headed the mission to the Sudan. The Ceylon mission benefited from the skillful support of Lal Jayawardene (who later headed the World Institute for Development Economics Research, or WIDER) and the Kenya report from Philip Ndegwa, each distinguished economists occupying senior positions in their own governments at the time. Many other academics, from North and South, who had never been associated with the ILO joined in the effort that was directed by Louis Emmerij.

As always, the role of specific individuals in the UN was crucial. The ILO senior deputy director-general, Abbas Amar, firmly believed in a comprehensive effort by the UN family. He recruited and protected "his employment people" within the ILO secretariat, many of whom were not conventional international civil servants. He understood the importance of fundamental research within an international organization in attracting world-class researchers and gaining respect in the wider academic community. Because of this attitude, Nobel laureates such as Jan Tinbergen and Wassily Leontief, and future winners such as Amartya Sen, were involved in research.

The role of the leaders of the high level missions was critical, as was their independence. Without diminishing the importance of others, the role of Seers should be singled out. Here was a man with ideas and convictions, an outstanding leader, and an editor supreme. He also had the experience and standing to insist that each of the mission reports was issued under the responsibility of the team leader, thereby avoiding any risk that the clarity of the messages would be stifled by bureaucratic interests or caution. Without such strong and clearheaded individuals and a team effort, the WEP would have been far less prominent.

What Happened to the Ideas?

The idea of a more employment-intensive development strategy leading to a basic-needs strategy was on the whole very well received by both the academic and practitioner communities. This was also true for both developing and developed country governments. In Congress and in the USAID there was much positive interest that led, as already mentioned, to strong American support after 1977.

And so the bulk of bilateral development assistance of the industrial countries was turned to basic-needs fulfillment as a top priority, including Washington's "basic human needs." The Development Assistance Committee (DAC) of the OECD issued policy papers on the theme, as did the organization's Development Centre. The World Bank joined the ranks of the enthusiasts, in part because of the great interest taken by Hollis Chenery, who was then the chief economist and vice president. Mahbub ul Haq and Paul Streeten developed the basic-needs strategy further, and McNamara pushed his operational people to start making loans in this area. Chenery together with the IDS in Sussex produced a seminal book, *Redistribution with Growth*, which was published by Oxford University on behalf of the World Bank.[34] The UN family jumped on the bandwagon as well. For example, the WHO, FAO, and UNESCO produced policy papers on basic needs, showing how they were qualified to foster one or more of them.[35]

In short, during the second half of the 1970s the idea was embraced by the entire donor community as well as by the UN family, including the World Bank, with the IMF as a sympathetic onlooker. The sensitivity of McNamara regarding basic-needs policies resulted from the acknowledgement in the early 1970s of the lack of impact previous economic growth had had on the actual living conditions of the most vulnerable groups. At the Annual Meeting of the Governors in Nairobi in 1973, McNamara pointed out that "despite a decade of unprecedented increase of the gross national product of the developing countries, the poorest segments of their population have received relatively little benefit." He continued, "Policies aimed primarily at accelerating growth, in most developing countries, have not benefited 40 percent of the population and the allocation of public services and investment funds has tended to strengthen rather to offset this trend."[36]

This general enthusiasm, perhaps predictably, meant that the initial positive reaction of developing countries was tempered and became skeptical. The G-77 was still calling for the establishment of the NIEO, approved only in April 1974. One of its central objectives was a radical improvement in the *international* distribution of income. And now, all of a sudden, the donor phalanx—the industrial countries, the DAC, the World Bank, and the UN system—clamored for basic needs and a better *internal* income distribution. Instead of seeing these two objectives as complementary, there was an initial and not entirely unfounded fear that the industrial countries would push for a better income distribution in developing countries as a prerequisite for what turned out to be a largely hypothetical commitment to the other goals of the NIEO.

Thousands of articles, hundreds of books, and countless theses were written on possible and impossible aspects of a basic-needs development strategy. The concept was rapidly on its way to becoming a fad, with all of the accompanying dangers. One of them was that basic needs became all things to all men and women. The concept was defined and redefined in myriad ways, as were the policies to achieve it. In other words, the distortion of the concept began almost instantly. This is the moment to remind the reader that a basic-needs development strategy is a comprehensive economic and social policy that demands quite crucial changes in macro and micro measures in order to steer the economy in a more employment-intensive and equitable direction with emphasis on a less unequal income distribution. There were two different approaches to a basic needs–oriented development strategy:

• A "strong" approach that emphasized the need for major structural reforms (in particular, land reform) aiming at redistributing resources and power more equally in developing countries. According to this approach, development strategies should strengthen the capabilities of populations to determine their own development priorities and to become the promoters of improvements in their own living and working conditions and not only the simple beneficiaries of top-down strategies. Empowerment as a political, economical, and cultural objective was at the heart of this muscular approach.[37]

• A "weak" approach was advocated by the World Bank, which tended to focus on growth, limit redistribution, underplay participation, and pursue basic need strategies in a centralized technocratic framework. The structural causes of poverty were not addressed. Basic-needs strategies were reduced to the definition by international experts and national administrations of basic-needs objectives—in terms of calories per day, doctors or teachers per inhabitant, drinking water, and the like—and policies to achieve them. Such objectives were formulated from the top down, without participatory process including the poorest groups of the population.

Box 3.3. Disarmament and Development

Efforts at reducing arms and defense expenditures are not new. The Covenant of the League of Nations emphasized that armaments should be reduced to "the lowest point consistent with national safety." Part of the work of the league after World War I aimed at formulating plans for a reduction of national armaments. The league was at the heart of important but unsuccessful efforts to increase international security, such as the Geneva Disarmament Conference in 1932.[38]

After the Second World War the UN's mandate was less clear. Arms control was not as prominent in the UN Charter. The use of collective military force was envisaged, albeit as a measure of last resort, to maintain international peace and security. The UN aimed more at regulating the armament process than at disarmament per se.

Atomic weapons were different. After Hiroshima, General Assembly resolution 1 (10) in January 1946 established the UN Atomic Energy Commission, to propose, or explore, measures for "the elimination from national armament of atomic weapons and of all other major weapons adaptable to mass destruction." In spite of this, the number of nuclear powers has risen to include China, India, Pakistan, and others.

For the most part, the superpowers have not chosen to use the UN as a forum for disarmament negotiations, which have often been conducted elsewhere—for instance, the Nuclear Test Ban (NTB) negotiations in 1963 and the bilateral efforts between Moscow and Washington on Strategic Arms Limitation Talks (SALT) in 1969.

In the mid-1970s the General Assembly took back the initiative. The Disarmament Commission was revived, and an Ad Hoc Committee established under the chair of the Swedish minister Inga Thorsson, to review the of the role of the UN in the field of disarmament. The UN Center for Disarmament was established.

One of the UN's clear successes—and where it has been ahead of the curve—is in exploring the link between disarmament and development.[39] The documents on the First Development Decade in 1962 emphasized the desirability of a reallocation of resources from military uses to development. Resolution S-10/2 of the Tenth Special Session of the General Assembly (1978) stressed "the necessity to release real resources now being used for military purpose to economic and social development." The UN played a major role in documenting the economic costs of the arms race and its social consequences. With the new committee and supporting publications, it quantified the challenge and explored other issues, such as the problem of the conversion of the resources employed for military purposes toward the civil sector.[40]

The UN explored internationally the idea of a "disarmament dividend." The Thorsson Report published in 1982 was a major attempt by the system to conceptualize the connections between disarmament and development.[41] Already several studies published in the 1970s showed the economic and social costs of armaments. Some underlined the reduction in the rate of economic growth and the lower investment levels associated with increased military spending.[42] They concentrated more particularly on the desirable shift of resources from the domestic military sector to domestic sectors for social and economic development. The Thorsson Report argued that the need for such a reallocation was shared by all countries. Arms spending was seen as a dramatic waste of resources, damaging the process and potential of development and leading to a poor allocation of scarce resources. Using Leontief's calculations, the Thorsson Report showed that shifting resources from military to civilian uses could increase consumption, investment, economic growth, and employment.[43]

The end of the Cold War altered the prospects for arms control. Military spending worldwide was reduced to levels which today are about two-thirds those of their peak in 1988. A major accomplishment of the UN was the 1993 Chemical Weapons Convention.[44] Moreover, the Review Conference of the Parties to the Treaty on the Non-Proliferation of Nuclear Weapons was held in New York in April–May 2000. The General Assembly had called upon all states that were party to the treaty to intensify their efforts toward reaching an agreement on nuclear nonproliferation and disarmament, and to reaffirm the decisions and resolutions adopted by the 1995 Review and Extension Conference.

Notwithstanding, in most parts of the world large amounts of scarce resources continue to be spent on arms. In 1998 more than 100 countries spent more than 1 percent of their GDP on military; 36 percent spent more than 3 percent. Only twenty-eight countries spent 1 percent or less.[45] In Asia overall expenditures have increased. Few countries have followed Cost Rica's example in abolishing their armies. The final document of the Social Summit + 5 in 2000 called, once again, for reallocating resources from excessive military expenditures to social programs. The Conference on Disarmament held in June 2000 lamented the difficulties of making international progress.

Viewed from the distance of a quarter-century, the employment and basic-needs strategies were weak on gender, the environment, and to a lesser extent international dimensions. But a historical context is important, because they had only just started through the 1972 Stockholm conference and the 1975 Mexico City conference (see Chapter 4).

Employment, basic needs, and much else were pushed to the sidelines with the debt crisis and the new pressures for structural adjustment. The succeeding "lost decade" in terms of growth was enforced by mean and lean policies that made it a tragic loss for millions. This led to the neglect of the employment question in the 1980s and 1990s at the very moment that it became truly a world problem, with high and often rising rates of unemployment in both Western and Eastern Europe.

With the advent of the 1980s and the Reagan and Thatcher administrations, economic and financial orthodoxy once again emphasized financial balance and low inflation over employment creation and income redistribution. The belief was propagated that with adjustment and sound economic policy would come economic growth, from which everything else would flow. In a sense, of course, this was true. With a rate of growth of 8 percent a year for a sustained period, employment and basic-needs goals could be achieved, as has been demonstrated by the fastest-growing countries in East Asia. But what about less fortunate countries? They would have to wait several generations, an irresponsible and unjust approach if alternatives are available. But the new orthodoxy emanating from the Bretton Woods institutions (and applauded loudly in Washington, London, and Bonn) succeeded in downplaying and discrediting most of the ideas that were launched during the 1970s. They were lumped together with a warning label, "danger: socialist ideas."[46]

The return of *"laissez-faire"* in the early 1980s constituted a strong political and academic offensive against "the predatory state" and led to the delegitimization of all interventionist policies. According to the new political economy based on rent seeking and collective choice, market failures were less costly in terms of welfare than state failures were. As state intervention was bound to make matters worse, the priority was to reduce the scope of its activities, pure and simple. Development strategies, including basic-needs strategies, that implied an activist state had no more *raison d'être* because the magic of the market would bring back rational growth and prosperity.

The idea of basic needs lived on, but without the strategy. The teeth were taken out of the concept. What remained were specific items that could or should be attained. For example, governments and institutions aimed to achieve universal primary education by year X, or to eradicate a certain illness by year Y. These were not unimportant goals, of course, but this approach had little in common with the idea as originally conceived. Even the employment-creation objective was downplayed in the financial and economic orthodoxy of the 1980s and 1990s. Other policy objectives—inflation, budget equilibrium, external balance, and interest rates—were considered higher or prior priorities. Moreover, the Washington consensus even held that employment creation should be left entirely to the private sector.

It took some time for policy-makers to realize once again that they should not be concerned solely with inflation, balance of payments, and GDP, but also with employment, individual incomes, income distribution, nutrition, food balances, and human growth. The role of the World Bank and the IMF in shaping and enforcing the new orthodoxy—in the shape of structural adjustment policies—was essential. The World Bank, in particular, went from one extreme to the other—

from emphasizing such flesh-and-blood issues as basic needs, poverty, and employment to stressing rather more "abstract" indicators such as inflation and external balance. The rest of the UN family was silent or at least largely absent from the visible international policy stage. The exceptions were UNICEF and the Economic Commission for Africa (ECA), at first the only members of the UN family that stood up to the Bretton Wood institutions during the harsh 1980s. We shall come back to this contemporary David-versus-Goliath story (see Chapter 5), with details of economic orthodoxy and alternatives.

Before that, we continue the story of the creative 1970s. The stage shifted to a series of global, ad hoc conferences to address such critical human challenges as the environment and population. However, we conclude here by stating that in the middle of the 1970s many thought that an operational set of policies had been designed—within the UN family and accepted outside—that did away with many of the weaknesses of the orthodoxy of the 1950s and 1960s. The hope thus held out was crushed by the advent of a new conventional wisdom that accompanied changes in the international political economy. The consequences of the oil shocks, the incapacity of governments to curb inflation while maintaining full employment, and the sea change in politics in the West led to a revival of neoliberalism. The new ideas could not solve the outstanding social problems and, in fact, created new ones. But they were an important part of the arsenal used by new administrations in London and Washington. Such is the power of ideas.

4

UN World Conferences
and Global Challenges

- **From Stockholm to Rio, Environment and Sustainable Development**
- **From Bucharest to Mexico City to Cairo, Population and Reproductive Health**
- **Rome's World Food Conference**
- **Sixth Special Session of the General Assembly, the NIEO**
- **From Mexico City to Copenhagen to Nairobi to Beijing, Women in Development**
- **From Vancouver to Istanbul, the Human Habitat**
- **Vienna's World Conference on Human Rights**
- **Copenhagen's World Summit for Social Development**
- **Conclusions**

From the vantage point of the beginning of the twenty-first century, it may be difficult to believe that in the 1960s environmental degradation, population growth, urbanization, and women's rights were being discussed but were not squarely on the international agenda. This changed during the 1970s. The United Nations system launched a series of global conferences on each of these challenges. Public opinion was mobilized. Action was often weak, inadequate for the challenges identified. But the long-run dynamics had been fundamentally altered.

International conferences about economic development were, of course, nothing new. Since the Congress of Vienna after Napoleon's defeat at Waterloo, conference diplomacy has been a common device for states to use in addressing new challenges. The League of Nations had convened them during the interwar period (see Box 5.1). But the UN institutionalized the conference system as a transmission belt for ideas in order to respond to common, global concerns.[1] The UN pioneered what became a template: establishment of a temporary secretariat headed by a secretary-general, often from outside the UN system; a series of preparatory committees; participation of NGOs; standard outcomes (final declarations and programs of action); and, increasingly in the 1990s, follow-up and monitoring institutions. These conferences were called "ad hoc" in that they were unlike annual or periodic conferences.

The UN system mobilized the community of states and international civil society to address global challenges. Table 4.1 lists selected UN world conferences of the 1970s and 1980s and summits of the 1990s, the latter often as a follow-up on the same topics.

The major goals of these conferences were to raise awareness of common problems, to promote a change in the dominant attitudes toward them, and to stimulate the establishment of programs of action to confront the challenges. The 1972 Stockholm conference was the first of the series and, from this perspective, a resounding success. Its worldwide publicity largely contributed to the inclusion of environmental concerns in national and international policy discussions. Environmental problems have played a crucial role in the growing awareness of interdependence and problems that countries could not solve alone.[2] The Stockholm conference illustrated also the importance of naming a strong personality like Maurice Strong to head the effort and of choosing a sympathetic host like Sweden.

During the 1990s the UN system went back to this method and continued the series begun in the 1970s, but this time with the participation of heads of state and government rather than "mere" ministers. In a new environment marked by the end of the Cold War, the UN convened a series of world summits to promote agendas for the 1990s and beyond. The objective was to mobilize governments and international civil society and to build a consensus around alternative approaches to development, centered on human beings and the protection of the environment. Major global conferences helped shape a new agenda for changes that went against the orthodox grain.

Toward the end of his term, UN Secretary-General Boutros Boutros-Ghali noted:

> The conferences of the United Nations, and the action programmes and agendas produced by these conferences form, together, an agenda for development committed to by the world community. Through these conferences, development cooperation will be revitalized and reinvented. The United Nations, its Member States, and you, the delegates at the conferences, are deciding development patterns for future generations. You are deciding the form of development cooperation to be adopted by the United Nations; you are setting the standards by which the actions of States, Organizations and individuals will be judged. This is the importance of the international conferences of the United Nations.[3]

Table 4.1. Selected UN World Conferences, 1972–2000

Conference	Number of Governments	NGO Presence	Principal Themes	Key Documents	Follow-up Mechanisms
UN Conference on the Human Environment, Stockholm, 1972	113	In addition to NGOs with status of official observers, representatives from 255 NGOs attended the parallel NGO Environment Forum and Life Forum	Human environment and the interactions between environment and development issues	Stockholm Declaration and Action Plan	Establishment of the UNEP; prior to the Stockholm conference, few multilateral treaties on the environment existed, and today there are more than 900 legal instruments that specifically address environmental matters
World Food Conference, Rome, 1974	133	Representatives of 161 NGOs	World food shortages, storage, drought, finances	*Assessment of the World Food Situation: Present and Future; The World Food Problem: Proposals for National and International Action*	Establishment of the WFC and IFAD; FAO technical assistance expanded
World Conference on Population, Bucharest, 1974	136	NGOs with ECOSOC consultative status	Population policy and development	Final Declaration and World Population Plan of Action	National population policies and family planning programs
Sixth Special Session of the General Assembly, New York, 1974	107	NGOs with ECOSOC consultative status	NIEO	Resolution 3201 on the Establishment of the NIEO and Program of Action for the Reform of International Economic Relations	Establishment of an Ad Hoc Committee on the special program
World Conference on Women, Mexico, 1975	133	114 NGOs attended the conference, and more than 4,000 participated in the parallel NGO forum	Integration and full participation of women in development and elimination of gender discrimination	Final Declaration and World Plan of Action	Establishment of INSTRAW and UNIFEM; beginning of the Decade on Women; adoption by the General Assembly in December 1979 of the Convention on the Elimination of All Forms of Discrimination against Women

Conference	Number	NGOs	Objectives	Documents	Notes
World Conference on Human Settlement, Vancouver, 1976	132	NGOs with ECOSOC consultative status	Management and improvement of human settlements in a context of uncontrolled urbanization in developing countries	Declaration of Principles and Vancouver Action Plan for National Policies to Improve the Quality of Life in Human Settlements	Establishment of the UNCHS
Tripartite World Conference on Employment, Income Distribution, and Social Progress, and the International Division of Labor, Geneva, 1976	Tripartite conference including government, trade unions, and employer representatives	None	Basic-needs approach; creation of productive employment with appropriate remuneration; income and asset redistribution; regulation of multinational firm activities	Report of the Director-General (*Employment, Growth, and Basic Needs: A One-World Problem*); Declaration of Principles and Program of Action	Continuation of the WEP; development of a basic-needs approach at the World Bank
World Conference on Science and Technology for Development, Vienna, 1979	142	Large number of NGOs with ECOSOC consultative status	Strengthening the technological capacity of developing countries and ensuring that scientific and technological potential be directed to constructive ends	Vienna Program of Action on Science and Technology for Development	
Second World Conference on Women, Copenhagen, 1980	145	9,000 NGOs attended the NGOs forum	Review and appraisal of the 1975 World Plan of Action	Program of Action for the Second Half of the UN Decade for Women: Equality, Development, and Peace	In 1980 the General Assembly, in resolution 35/56, adopted the International Development Strategy for the Third UN Development Decade and reaffirmed the recommendations of the Copenhagen World Conference

(continued)

Table 4.1. (continued)

Conference	Number of Governments	NGO Presence	Principal Themes	Key Documents	Follow-up Mechanisms
UN Conference on the Least Developed Countries, Paris, 1981	142	72 NGO representatives	Gravity of the deteriorating economic and social situation of the least developed countries	Substantial New Program of Action for the 1980s for the Least Developed Countries	The secretariat of UNCTAD had fulfilled the role of global monitoring of the program and reported on a regular basis to the General Assembly; the UNDP expanded its round-table conferences and the World Bank increased the number of consultative groups
UN World Conference Concluding the Decade for Women, Nairobi, 1985	157	15,000 NGO representatives attended the NGO Forum	Advancement of women	Programme of Action Nairobi, Forward-looking Strategies to the Year 2000	Establishment of the UN Division for the Advancement of Women
Second UN Conference on the Least Developed Countries, Paris, 1990	149	71 NGOs with ECOSOC or UNCTAD consultative status	Global review and appraisal of the implementation of the Substantial New Program of Action for the 1980s for the Least Developed Countries	Paris Declaration and Programme of Action for the Least Developed Countries for the 1990s	Least Developed Countries Report, prepared by UNCTAD, and the report of the secretary-general on implementation of the Program of Action, which highlights the main developmental difficulties the least developed countries continue to face
World Summit for Children, UN, New York, 1990	159, including 71 heads of state or government	45 NGOs participated in the summit	Goals for the year 2000 for children's health, nutrition, education, and access to safe water and sanitation	World Declaration and Plan of Action on the Survival, Protection, and Development of Children	Mid-decade reviews, with secretary-general's progress report; UN interagency task force; national program of action for children within each national government

Conference	Participants	NGO participation	Theme	Outcome documents	Follow-up
UN Conference on Environment and Development (Earth Summit), Rio de Janeiro, 1992	172, including 108 heads of state or government	2,400 representatives of over 650 NGOs; 17,000 people taking part in NGO forum activities	Environment and sustainable development	Rio Declaration on Environment and Development; Agenda 21; Statement of Forest Principles; UN Framework Convention on Climate Control and UN Convention on Biological Diversity	Commission on Sustainable Development; Interagency Committee on Sustainable Development; High-Level Advisory Board on Sustainable Development
World Conference on Human Rights, Vienna, 1993	171	2,000 representatives from over 800 NGOs attended parallel activities and forum	Promotion and protection of human rights	Vienna Declaration and Programme of Action	High Commissioner for Human Rights; fusion of the Centre for Human Rights and the Human Rights Commission; Commission on the Status of Women; five-year review of the implementation of the Vienna Declaration
International Conference on Population and Development, Cairo, 1994	179	4,200 representatives of over 1,500 NGOs attended the NGO forum	Population, sustained economic growth, and sustainable development	Cairo Programme of Action	UN Commission on Population and Development
UN Global Conference on the Sustainable Development of Small Island Developing States, Bridgetown, 1994	111, including 14 heads of state or government	1,200 NGO representatives attended the NGO forum, and 87 NGOs attended the official meeting	Development strategies respectful of fragile ecosystems	Barbados Declaration and the Programme of Action for the Sustainable Development of Small Island Developing States	Review of the implementation of the program of action by the UN Commission on Sustainable Development; establishment of a unit in the UN secretariat to monitor and coordinate follow-up to the conference
World Summit for Social Development (Social Summit), Copenhagen, 1995	186, including 117 heads of state or government	More than 4,500 representatives from NGOs attended the NGO forum, while 2,315 representatives from over 811 NGOs participated in the Social Summit itself	Social development, with three core issues: eradication of poverty, expansion of productive employment and reduction of unemployment, and social integration	Copenhagen Declaration on Social Development, and Programme of Action	Commission for Social Development; Comprehensive report of the secretary-general on the implementation of the outcome of the World Summit for Social Development; UN conference Copenhagen + 5 (Geneva, June 2000)

(continued)

Table 4.1. (continued)

Conference	Number of Governments	NGO Presence	Principal Themes	Key Documents	Follow-up Mechanisms
Fourth World Conference on Women: Action for Equality, Development, and Peace, Beijing, 1995	189	More than 5,000 representatives from 2,100 NGOs attended the conference, and nearly 30,000 individuals attended the NGO forum activities	Advancement and empowerment of women	Beijing Declaration and Platform for Action	Review of each of the 12 critical areas of concern by the Commission on the Status of Women; Comprehensive Review and Appraisal of the Implementation of the Beijing Platform of Action by the secretary-general; Special Session of the General Assembly for Beijing + 5 called "Gender Equality, Development, and Peace for the Twenty-first Century" (New York, June 2000)
Second UN Conference on Human Settlements (Habitat II), Istanbul, 1996	171	NGOs participated as partners in Habitat II to an unprecedented degree; some 8,000 representatives from 2,400 NGOs attended the NGO forum	Sustainable human settlement development in an urbanizing world, and adequate shelter for all	Habitat Agenda and Istanbul Declaration on Human Settlements; Catalogue of Good Practices	World's largest multidonor technical assistance program for urban management in developing country cities is established; publicity and exchange of best practices
World Food Summit, Rome, 1996	186, including 82 heads of state or government	Parallel international forum and activities attended by NGOs, farmer's association, and the private sector	Food security	Rome Declaration on World Food Security and World Food Summit Plan of Action	Technical assistance and support to developing countries from the FAO to implement the summit plan of action

Special Session of the General Assembly, "Women 2000: Gender Equality, Development, and Peace for the Twenty-first Century," Beijing + 5 Review, New York, 2000	182	Invitations to over 4,000 NGOs were issued, and a very large number of NGO representatives attended	Gender equality, development, and peace	Political Declaration and Outcome Document on Future Actions and Initiatives	The outcome document strengthened the Beijing Declaration and the Platform for Action in some areas through making the actions more focused, and encompassing the additional new issues which emerged or gained importance in the past five years; agenda expanded to include the signing and ratifying of the Optional Protocol to the Convention on the Elimination of All Forms of Discrimination against Women, adopted in 1999
Special Session of the General Assembly on Five-Year Follow-up to Copenhagen Social Summit, Geneva, 2000	130, including 18 heads of state or government	More than 6,000 individuals attended the Special Session and the Geneva 2000 NGO Forum	Reducing poverty, promoting job growth, and ensuring the participation of all people in the decision-making process; social development, and the challenge of globalization	A Review and Assessment of Implementation of the Social Summit; a Political Declaration; and a final document titled *World Summit for Social Development and Beyond: Achieving Social Development for All in a Globalizing World*	The Special Session called, among other things, for halving the number of persons living in extreme poverty by 2015; for the achievement of free and universal primary education by 2015; for avoidance of "unilateral measures" affecting the health and well-being of women and children; and for greater steps to ease the debt burdens of developing countries
Millennium Summit, New York, 2000	189, including 150 heads of state or government	1,350 representatives of NGOs from 106 countries participated in an earlier parallel Millennium Forum (May 2000)	Role and function of the UN in the twenty-first century	*"We the Peoples": The Role of the United Nations in the Twenty-first Century* (Secretary-General's Millennium Report); The Millennium Declaration	Secretary-General Kofi Annan offered a twenty-first-century action plan calling on all member states to commit themselves to ending poverty and inequality, improving education and human rights, increasing security, reducing HIV/AIDS, and protecting the environment

Boutros-Ghali also confessed that a key problem was fatigue—by donor countries, public opinion, and member states—and one of the achievements of world conferences was to counteract indifference.[4] The continuum of conferences maintained momentum and permitted a mobilization of public opinion. By legitimating the role of NGOs in conference processes and enabling them to contribute to the debate on global problems, UN gatherings also helped define the concept of global governance (see Chapter 8).

Here we explore the extent to which the agenda proposed by the UN at world conferences was ahead of the curve—in terms of formulating and nurturing both ideas and political will. We cannot undertake an exhaustive analysis, but rather we can provide a broad vision of the UN's role in consciousness-raising, agenda-setting, and the establishment of new commitments and programs of action. The true significance of these meetings must admittedly be measured by the way in which their recommendations have been translated into action at both national and international levels.

That is, we should distinguish the "two UNs" that we outlined earlier: the arena where states make decisions and the international civil service. In evaluating the extent to which recommendations have changed policies and behavior, it is the first UN, or the decision-making arena, that is crucial. Success or failure of this UN depends upon political will or lack thereof. However, the second UN is critical in determining the trajectory of ideas. Semi-independent secretariats, including outside experts, whose job descriptions include research about and articulation of ideas, are not, as we have underlined, independent of governments. Nonetheless, in the intellectual and advocacy realms, there is room for maneuver and autonomy. And individuals and leadership matter immensely for this second UN.

The reader will undoubtedly ask, "But in what time frame?" Given the nature of entrenched interests and cultures, any fair and definitive evaluation of the implementation of recommendations by governments must necessarily await the next generation of scholars. The relative importance of these conferences on the first UN will also be a major theme in the books that are being commissioned by the UNIHP. But we will, as promised in the introduction, run the risk of making our evaluation *avant la lettre*, which is more feasible for intellectual and advocacy contributions by the second UN.

It would be impractical to deal with all conferences in the same manner. The World Employment Conference was already sketched (see Chapter 3), and others will be dealt with briefly in boxes. This chapter concentrates on the environment, population, food, gender, NIEO, the human habitat (or the question of cities), human rights, and social development. And then there were others!

The reader should keep in mind two sets of factors to which we return at the end of this chapter. First, the role of two of the four powerful ideas (see Chapter 1) looms large. World conferences continued to redefine the contents of development and human rights. As we mentioned, peace was placed on the back burner because of the Cold War, but decolonization was basically achieved by the 1970s. Second, conferences are one of the main devices—some would say "gimmicks"—that are used to spawn, nurture, and massage new ideas as well as to nudge governments, international secretariats, and international civil society to alter their conceptions and policies. In short, UN world conferences have been one means through which ideas are translated into action.

From Stockholm to Rio, Environment and Sustainable Development

In 1968 ECOSOC adopted a resolution requesting the UN to address the problem of the human environment and to convene a conference. Sweden had played a major role and was invited to host it. Maurice Strong, a Canadian, became secretary-general. The conference was less universal than subsequent UN gatherings because the Soviet bloc boycotted it to protest the exclusion of the German Democratic Republic.

The United Nations Conference on the Human Environment (UNCHE) pioneered a pattern for future conferences in that some NGOs were invited to participate as observers at the conference but many more attended simultaneous, parallel activities called the Environment Forum and the Life Forum. And the media were present in large numbers, so that the events had a considerable impact on world opinion.

Stockholm put environment firmly on the international agenda—a subject that has expanded to include development, sustainability, and global resources management, which is why it will be treated in a book commissioned by the UNIHP.[5] Expectations were high regarding the prospect of multilateral cooperation. The preamble to the Stockholm Declaration noted that man's environment was essential to "his well being and to the enjoyment of basic human rights, the right to life itself," and that "man has the fundamental right to freedom, equality, and adequate conditions of life, in an environment of a quality that permits a life of dignity and well-being."[6] Because no country is an island, governments in Stockholm proclaimed common principles and actions to preserve and enhance the human environment, in a period growing conscious of the risk of massive, even irreversible harm.

Divisions between North and South were very much present in Sweden. Developed countries were mainly preoccupied with the negative impacts of industrialization (for instance, air and water pollution, and depletion of nonrenewable resources). By the beginning of the 1960s Rachel Carson's *Silent Spring* revealed the effects of toxic chemicals in the world's food chain; Paul Ehrlich's

The Population Bomb raised the specter of developing countries' breeding themselves into irredeemable, Malthusian misery.[7]

Developing countries viewed askance the rich countries' environmentalism as a blatant threat to their development objectives. They stressed that most environmental problems resulted from past industrialization of the now-developed countries. Developing countries explicitly proclaimed that they had a right to economic and social development and that environmental concerns could not be used to limit this right.

Strong organized a meeting of what he called "gurus" at Founex, Switzerland, in 1971, to articulate the interconnectedness of environment and development from a Third-World perspective. This meeting — which brought together Jan Tinbergen, Hans Singer, Mahbub ul Haq, and Ignacy Sachs, among others — emphasized that environmental issues should become an integral part of development strategy.[8] Many of its conclusions as well as the overall framing of the problem were reiterated in Stockholm and in subsequent UN publications:

- environmental problems experienced in the developing world are fundamentally different from those in the developed one;
- developing countries could and should avoid the degradation that can accompany development;
- all countries have the sovereign right to determine their development strategies, and approaches must be tailored to country specificities;
- the concerns of the North should not have a negative impact on the economic development of the South; and
- the transfer of resources from the developed to developing worlds is crucial to addressing the environment and development nexus of problems.

The Stockholm conference itself addressed two main problems. The first was the pattern of growth, which emerged from the first report of the Club of Rome issued the same year. A main point of this report, *The Limits to Growth*, was the question of the sustainability of past patterns from an environmental perspective.[9] Its conclusion was that a continuation along the lines adopted by industrialized countries — and its reproduction by developing countries — would lead to shortages of resources, result in major damage to the biosphere, and threaten the interest of generations yet unborn. Victor Urquidi, the developmental economist and former president of the Colegio de México who became a passionate supporter of sustainable development, recalled the initial reactions: "The critique of the study was tremendous. The economists in the U.S. just laughed at it, and in England, too. . . . In the end, however, the report was right."

This report was widely reviewed in the North, although the issue had been around for some time.[10] But the philosophy of "zero quantifiable growth" de-

The Earth Summit was held in June 1992 in Rio de Janeiro, after several years of in-depth preparations. The conference broke existing records in terms of both its size and the scope of its concerns. NGO participation and contributions were far more extensive than they had been twenty years earlier in Stockholm. As will become more obvious by the end of this chapter, NGOs had built steadily upon the precedents set by the conferences of the 1970s, which became especially pronounced after the Cold War's end facilitated the burgeoning of civil society throughout the socialist bloc and many parts of the developing world. NGOs mobilized public opinion around the world. That NGOs were able to shape to a large extent Agenda 21 (the final product of Rio) demonstrated the evolution of their relationship with the UN and their effectiveness in establishing political commitments. The present UN under-secretary general for policy coordination and sustainable development, Nitin Desai, noted two decades after Stockholm the extent to which NGOs "have increasingly assumed the role of promoters of new ideas" within the UN.[17] In his final speech at Rio, Strong acknowledged the role of the NGOs and called for a pluralization of UN consultations and an expansion in the participatory process throughout the UN: "I believe we need to review entirely the system of arrangements within the United Nations for greater participation of these organizations."[18]

The Earth Summit's call to integrate development and environment had a direct impact on subsequent UN world conferences of the 1990s. From Vienna on human rights to Copenhagen on social development, the point of departure was environmentally sustainable development based on a package of economic, social, and political rights. The Rio Declaration in many ways consummated the five key ideas put on the table by the meeting of experts at Founex in 1971.

However, the negotiating climate was tense, marked by the continuing confrontation of very different approaches to environment and development. The pressure from industrialized countries for action on climate change and deforestation was perceived by developing countries as an attack on their sovereignty and an unfair attempt to transfer to them the costs of industrialization and of the profligate northern consumption model. As in Stockholm two decades earlier, developing countries wanted to avoid any connotation that environmental concerns should limit their development.

The implementation of the outcomes from Rio was undermined by the position of the U.S. government. The treaty on biodiversity represented a threat to the interests of the pharmaceutical industry. The Bush administration was averse to any convention that would harm American competitiveness on world markets, and it refused to sign. At the same time, several developing countries, led by Brazil and Malaysia, resisted any incursion into the principle of sovereignty over their natural resources. The debate on forest principles, for example, led to sharp tensions between the North and the South. And in the end, Malaysia blocked consideration of a treaty on forests.

The conference led to a declaration of principles as well as an ambitious program of action, known as Agenda 21, and two conventions. The Rio Declaration on Environment and Development succeeded in balancing developed and developing countries' priorities by emphasizing sustainable development. The final document underlined that "human beings are at the centre of concern for sustainable development. They are entitled to a healthy and productive life in harmony with nature." The major insight of the Earth Summit, as had been the case at Founex and at Stockholm, was the need to integrate environmental considerations into all aspects of economic decision making. Agenda 21 represents a comprehensive framework—some might say *too* comprehensive at more than 600 pages—based on the recognition of the interdependence between economic, social, and environmental issues.[19]

The Rio conference also addressed global warming, which many scientists argued was increasingly a major global challenge. The UNFCCC acknowledged the risks of climate change and the need to take action to reduce carbon dioxide emissions, but participants failed to set reduction targets. A Framework Convention on the Maintenance of Bio-diversity was also signed, over the objections of the American delegation. Both documents define general principles and obligations but do not contain any binding targets or timetables. After Rio, however, steps have been taken to move forward with both. As Table 4.1 notes, prior to Stockholm there were few multilateral treaties on the environment. But today there are more than 900 legal instruments with specific provisions on the environment, and the Rio Earth Summit provided a healthy boost.

One of the summit's institutional outcomes was the establishment of the Commission on Sustainable Development (CSD). An intergovernmental body of fifty-three states elected by ECOSOC for a three-year term, the CSD has as its main task to monitor and review the implementation of Agenda 21. The CSD was seen as a complement to UNEP and a means to increase coordination among existing UN organs. Again, an idea became embedded in the form of an institution in order to maintain momentum.

To conclude, UNCED's results were mixed. Agenda 21 was weakened by compromise. The concept of sustainable development was the main intellectual input for Rio, but there were numerous bumps along the road to sustainable development. This weakened the Earth Summit's outcomes and explained the failure to establish an effective program of action for sustainable development. Agenda 21 is a comprehensive set of guidelines for action, but it does not include compulsory mechanisms for enforcement.[20] Governments were unwilling to establish binding targets for reductions in carbon dioxide emissions or the protection of tropical rainforests. However, the conference has shown the road ahead, and a number of follow-up activities have taken place since 1992, including the acceleration of legal conventions (see Table 4.1).

The idea that had been so unusual at Founex and Stockholm has become common for decision making at all levels. The World Bank, for instance, has substantially altered its lending policies to reflect concerns with sustainability.[21] The glass is considerably less full than environmental activists would have liked, but it undoubtedly is fuller than it would have been without Stockholm and Rio.

From Bucharest to Mexico City to Cairo, Population and Reproductive Health

While many developing countries initially paid little attention, population growth became a Western preoccupation during the 1960s. One perspective was strategic — political instability resulting from uncontrolled population growth in developing countries — and another was ecological as captured by such apocalyptic expressions as "population bomb." Many industrialized nations, with Washington in the lead, were calling for targeted family planning initiatives. The UNFPA was set up and later renamed the UN Population Fund.

The World Population Conference in Bucharest in 1974 was convened to address this global challenge during a period of growing concern. The draft plan of action reflected the Western position in favor of active social and economic measures to affect fertility.[22] However, several divergent and incompatible points of view surfaced during the conference — and again North-South divisions dominated because there was no agreement about either the nature of the problem or solutions. Developing countries believed that industrialized countries placed too much emphasis on fertility control and ignored the impact on fertility levels of genuine economic development. With echoes of Founex and Stockholm audible, the South argued in Bucharest that the problem of population growth should be addressed as an integral part of a comprehensive development strategy. Unwanted population growth was a consequence and not a cause of underdevelopment. The failure of many family planning programs illustrated, according to this logic, that the solution of population growth resided in accelerated development. As the head of the Indian delegation said, "Development is the best contraceptive."[23] Consequently, the G-77 put pressure to include references to the NIEO adopted three months earlier at the special session of the UN General Assembly.

The debate at Bucharest reflected deep North-South frictions, and the conference produced a much-debated and substantially redrafted World Population Plan of Action.[24] The final version eliminated earlier references to fertility reduction targets and situated population growth squarely within the broader framework of social and economic development. The final document represented a victory of sorts for developing countries with its emphasis that:

- the formulation and implementation of population policies are the sovereign right of each nation;
- all couples and individuals have the right to decide freely and responsibly the number and spacing of their children and to have the information, education, and means to do so; and
- population and development are interrelated.

A follow-up conference was convened in Mexico City a decade later, by which time a dramatic shift had taken place in developing countries' thinking. In a context marked by the debt crisis and structural adjustment (see Chapter 5), developing countries acknowledged the negative impact of population pressures on development. This more flexible attitude toward family planning and fertility control had led to the implementation of new policies in a number of countries, including well-publicized ones in both India and China. Many African countries began to emphasize measures to slow down some of the world's fastest growth rates. At the same time, and under the pressure of anti-abortion and anti–family planning lobbies, the Reagan administration became much less supportive and withdrew its financing for the International Planned Parenthood Federation (IPPF) and UN organizations that offered abortion information or services.

The final declaration from Mexico City greatly strengthened the provisions adopted at Bucharest. It recognized the role of development in lowering fertility but also the effectiveness of family planning *per se.* It also pointed out the obvious link between women's social and economic status and fertility rates and emphasized the need for women's advancement, a theme that had been put forward in the same city at a world conference in 1975. The growing relationships among debates at world conferences become clearer as the decade proceeds.

Twenty years after Bucharest, developing countries had taken important steps in implementing new population policies. In 1974 only twenty-seven countries had explicit population policies. In 1994 more than 100 countries had such policies, and most of the world's governments provided support for family planning. Hence, the seeds of ideas sewn in the 1970s had taken root by the time of the Third Population Conference in Cairo, which was given a broad mandate. In 1974 the link to development had been controversial, but by 1994 everyone agreed on its linkage with accelerated development. The point was to build consensus on a strategy to stabilize the world population and achieve sustainable development.

This International Conference on Population *and* Development (the title is significant) was the third UN world conference on this topic, and its program of action emphasized women's empowerment; interactions among population, development, and environment; as well as services to meet reproductive health needs for women and adolescent girls, including but going beyond family planning. The shift in emphasis is shown in the goals proposed for consideration by the Cairo conference were in three mutually reinforcing areas: reduction of infant, child, and maternal mortality; universal completion of primary education, especially for girls; and universal access to family planning information and services.

Cairo's controversial debate centered on abortion and reproductive rights, which attracted worldwide attention—among other reasons, because the Vatican and fundamentalist Islamic states were strange bedfellows. Who is more qualified to make decisions about birth control and abortion—political authorities or individual women whose health, and thus the survival of other children, may be at stake? The conference aimed to adopt a universally acceptable yet specific program of action. Participants acknowledged that no strategies were equally valid for all countries. In the name of cultural, ethical, and religious values, representatives from the Holy See and fundamentalist Islamic countries tried to restrict women's access to family planning choices. The representative of Iran argued, for example, that "women's pivotal role in determining population trends should not be exploited for the recognition of immoral behavior or for undermining religious and ethical values."[25]

The conference's program of action emphasizes empowering women and guaranteeing their choice with regard to family planning. Furthermore, it stresses that advancing gender equality and ensuring women's ability to control their own fertility are cornerstones of population and development.[26] The language about reproductive health and rights represents a breakthrough by recognizing the basic right of couples and individuals to decide freely and responsibly the number, spacing, and timing of their children and to have access to information and the means to do so.[27]

The conference also marked the emergence of a consensus around a framework to integrate population, environment, and development. Explicit integration of a population dimension into economic and development strategies would not only accelerate the pace of sustainable development and poverty alleviation but also contribute to the achievement of population objectives and an improved quality of life. Empowerment of women and eradication of poverty would contribute to slowing population growth. The text calls for improving the socioeconomic conditions of poor women in developed as well as in developing countries. Eliminating social, cultural, political, and economic discrimination against women is a prerequisite for eradicating poverty. With respect to population and the environment, the conference recommended integrating demographic factors into environment impact assessments. Among measures aimed at the eradication of poverty, special attention was given to income-generation and employment strategies directed at the rural poor and those living in fragile ecosystems. Policies should address the ecological implications of increases in population and other demographic changes.

The Cairo conference led to a paradigmatic shift in the recognition that women's empowerment and access to reproductive health were central to demographic control and development—in short, gender became central to mainstream population debates. The twenty-year program of action adopted in Cairo was based on a vision of women as key agents of social transformation instead of targets of demographic control. The Norwegian minister of development declared that "Cairo should be remembered for what it will do for women."[28] The need to improve the status of women, particularly their education, is the best strategy to cut birth rates. And so, the twenty-year trajectory from Bucharest to Cairo could, to paraphrase the Indian delegate cited earlier, be summarized as follows: Development plus education plus empowerment of women are the best contraceptives.

Rome's World Food Conference

The 1974 conference in Rome put food shortages on the international agenda. Poor weather two years earlier had considerably reduced harvests and the global production of food. Calculations showed that the world's margin of security against starvation had dropped precipitously from ninety-six days in early 1972 to only twenty-six days by mid-1973. At the same time, the severe drought in the African Sahel countries provided dramatic photos of the obvious implications for the starvation and malnutrition of millions.

U.S. Secretary of State Henry Kissinger proposed that a conference under UN auspices be convened as rapidly as possible to examine food supplies, storage, and starvation.[29] The U.S. position was not exempt from geopolitical considerations, ranging from allaying the possible political consequences of hunger and malnutrition to countervailing the OPEC oil price hike of October 1973.

Unlike Stockholm controversies a few years earlier, there was a consensus about the nature of the food problem and the priorities for action, which contributed to the success of the Rome conference.[30] There was unanimity among delegates that the UN gathering should produce concrete proposals for national and international action. The FAO offered suggestions to ECOSOC, which became guidelines for the preparatory committee and the conference secretariat. The latter called upon outside expertise to supplement the FAO's work. The preparatory committee emphasized that the food problem was not only one of more production but also of better income distribution, because a basic cause of hunger and malnutrition was poverty. The agenda represented agreement on three items:

- measures for increasing food production and consumption in developing countries;
- strengthening world food security (stocks, emergency relief, and food aid); and
- international trade and agricultural adjustment.

The first of two key background documents was *Assessment of the World Food Situation: Present and Future,*[31] which highlighted available data on the extent of global malnutrition. The second document, *The World Food Problem: Proposals for National and International Action,*[32] contained eighty-five specific recommendations. Although such a comprehensive set of proposals satisfying so many interests meant that contradictions were inevitable, the document had a substantive impact on subsequent governmental policy making.

The World Food Conference contributed to creating widespread interest and concern with regard to the problem of hunger and malnutrition. It spotlighted the dimensions of the problem and the magnitude of the effort needed to tackle it. Agricultural development was reconfirmed as an essential component of development strategies.

In terms of concrete action, one of the tangible achievements of the conference was the decision to set up the IFAD. Although some might argue that this decision marked the failure to reform the FAO, the IFAD was an attempt to rope in such new donors as Saudi Arabia by offering them weighted voting akin to that enjoyed by major Western donors in the Bretton Woods institutions. And for a time, additional resources were available. Competition may also have served to stimulate the FAO to react more effectively.

In subsequent years many of the priorities recommended by the conference to increase food security—such as the production of fertilizers, the elimination of the tsetse fly in Africa, and irrigation—were implemented. Finally, the conference led to the establishment of a World Food Council (WFC) to coordinate the efforts to follow up from the conference and to ensure that hunger and malnutrition received high priority. The creation of new institutions—that is, an idea embedded in organizational form to assure that attention does not wane—was as impressive in Rome as in any of the conferences under review.

Some twenty years later, the World Food Council was wound up as part of UN reforms of the 1990s. It had issued a number of important reports and calls to action, but it had always struggled to maintain its place alongside FAO and the other food institutions. The importance of global action on food and nutrition was revisited by the 1992 International Conference on Food and Nutrition sponsored by WHO and FAO and by the 1996 World Food Summit organized in Rome by FAO. The latter summit set the goal of halving the number of people hungry and without adequate access to food, estimated at that time to be about 840 million. Although this number had been reduced to 790 million by the year 2000, the rate of reduction is still below that required to reach the target of halving by 2015.

The Sixth Special Session of the UN General Assembly, the NIEO

As detailed earlier (see Chapter 2), the first United Nations Conference on Trade and Development (UNCTAD) was held in Geneva in 1964. Developing countries formally constituted the G-77, but the South's collective resistance to the North's dominance of the world's trading system received a boost from the economic muscle of one commodity-producing group, OPEC, following its ability to increase oil prices after the Six Day War in 1973. Michael Zammit-Cutajar, at the time in the front office of UNCTAD, pointed to two apparent lessons of the early 1970s: "One is that a developing country can beat a superpower in armed conflict, or force it to withdrawal. Two is that a group of commodity producers can set the price if they cooperate."

Optimism among developing countries reached an apex in April 1974 at the Sixth Special Session of the General Assembly — in effect, another setting for a global, ad hoc conference because it was the first such special session on development issues. The call for a new international economic order provided a framework to consolidate the numerous demands about the system of trade (preferential access on a nonreciprocal basis and mechanisms to stabilize developing countries' export earnings); sovereignty (in particular over natural resources); aid targets; debt alleviation; control of transnational corporations (TNCs); and new rules and procedures for decision making within the Washington-based financial institutions.

With their demonstrated bargaining power in oil, developing countries were persuaded that changes in the structure and mechanisms of the international economic system could be secured through global negotiations. On 1 April 1974 the General Assembly adopted resolution 3201 on the establishment of a NIEO based on equity, equality, sovereign rights, interdependence, common interests, and co-operation among all states, regardless of their economic and social systems. This document and its accompanying program of action for the reform of international economic relations reflected the temporary strength of developing countries buoyed by OPEC's success.

The then U.S. ambassador to the UN and future senator, Daniel Patrick Moynihan, dubbed the coalition of developing countries "the automatic majority" in the UN, which was "a dangerous place."[33] Donald Mills, the Jamaican ambassador, who was president of the G-77 at the time, explained why many in the West saw the NIEO as abrasive and hostile: "When two people come from very different points of view—if you would like to put it very roughly, advantaged and dis-advantaged—anything you say could seem to be aggressive." Jan Pronk, then a young minister of development in the Netherlands, put it in another way: "The oil shock had to be analyzed not only in terms of the production policy of the OPEC countries, but also as a North-South issue. It was North-South confrontation, where the oil-producing countries now had a weapon in the, say, labor union struggle by the G77 and non-aligned countries vis-à-vis the richer Northern countries."

In any event, the NIEO became the core of developing countries' demands on the international scene in the 1970s.[34] The G-77 continued the battle cry to es-tablish the NIEO at subsequent special sessions of the General Assembly and at other world conferences, including the twenty-five-country Conference on In-ternational Economic Cooperation (CIEC) organized by France.

The debate emphasized the need to replace purely market-centered measures of trade and investment with the modified alternatives embodied in the NIEO. In the mid-1970s the prospects looked good,[35] but the optimism was to be short-lived. Ironically, the cohesion and strength of the South eroded for the same rea-son that it had grown in 1974: namely, continued oil-price increases that led to overwhelming debt servicing for non–oil exporters, or the "NOPEC" countries. One exception was UNCTAD, where the G-77 remained united despite the oil shocks. But developing countries never seriously considered using UNCTAD as the OECD of the South, and the developed market economies would not have felt bound by resolutions adopted by UNCTAD. In fact, even on trade matters de-veloping countries by the 1990s recognized the reality of using the GATT and thereafter the WTO as the forum for specific trade negotiations.

Industrialized countries resisted the NIEO demands and focused on traditional forms of North-South cooperation rather than on any international measures to redistribute income and wealth. With few exceptions, Western governments did not take the North-South dialogue about the NIEO seriously. However, one vis-ible effort to continue the North-South dialogue began near Bonn in December 1977, when former West German Chancellor Willy Brandt brought together a dis-tinguished group "to study the grave global issues arising from the economic and social disparities of the world community." The twenty-one-member Indepen-dent Commission on International Development Issues (known as the Brandt Commission) included three persons who were or would be senior UN officials: Pronk, Goran Ohlin, and Dragoslav Avramović, the latter two as co-leaders of the secretariat.

Whatever the conceptual advances in the Brandt Commission's prose—and many judge it to be the most solid of the blockbuster reports—the timing of its publication in 1980 was unpropitious.[36] It coincided with the elections of Margaret Thatcher in the United Kingdom and Ronald Reagan in the United States, which

greatly altered the willingness of Western governments to confront openly the
Group of 77. This North-South dialogue, according to a cynical Northern view,
was "just a bit of international theater."[37] Proposals for radical changes became a
dead letter after the so-called global negotiations failed to achieve any substantive
outcome at Cancún in 1981. The degree of influence gained temporarily by the
G-77 in the 1970s was translated into few concrete policy changes in the North.
The major industrialized powers resisted from the outset, even though elements
of the NIEO were more popular in such Western countries as Sweden, Norway,
and The Netherlands. Except for a brief moment when OPEC was dominant, developing countries lacked the economic power to force Western governments to
commit themselves to the NIEO agenda.

The world economic recession and the manner of Third-World responses to
the debt crisis of the early 1980s drove the final nail into the NIEO's coffin for most
industrialized countries (see Chapter 5). Developing countries without petroleum
to export were obliged to set aside changes in the international economic system
and give priority to implementing structural adjustment programs (see Box 4.1).
The South failed to find an effective way of combining OPEC oil power with the
"NOPEC" majority into an alliance robust enough to achieve long-run change in
the South's economic position. In retrospect, the UN was too far ahead of the
advocacy curve. In addition to being a set of demands and negotiations, the NIEO
was also "a debate about the real and desirable basic structure of world economic relations."[38] In a sense, this was the first debate about global economic
governance (see Chapter 8) and about income distribution in the face of glaring
inequalities (see Chapter 7). The debate came too early and in too adversarial of
terms to succeed.[39]

Box 4.1. World Conferences on the Least Developed Countries, in Paris

Solidarity among developing countries was one of the key variables in the formulating and nurturing of new ideas about economic and social development from the 1960s
onward. One of the underlying assumptions of the Group of 77 was that all developing
countries were in the same boat, which would rise or fall with the tide of collective measures for the South. Over time it became clear that certain countries in the South were particularly poor and faced even greater Sisyphean tasks than others did.

At the same time, there was unease in the South about the creation of new categories—was this a new tactic of the North "to divide and conquer"? But the plight of dis-
advantaged countries became impossible to ignore.

The CDP in 1970 established a working group to define the hard-core poorest countries. Although statistics were disputed, low per capita income (less than $100 in 1968),
low contribution of manufacturing to GDP (less than 10 percent), and low adult literacy

(less than 20 percent) were used originally to identify twenty-four "least developed countries." Since that time, and although the criteria have been modified, the list has grown to
almost fifty. The UNCTAD secretariat assumed responsibilities for policy research on all
disadvantaged countries—least developed, landlocked, and small islands.

UN world conferences on the least developed countries were hosted by France in
UNESCO headquarters in 1981 and 1990. Both agreed on programs of action for these
countries, including special measures for aid disbursements and trade access. A third conference is to be held in Brussels, hosted by the European Union, in May 2001. Development has remained elusive for a significant number of least developed countries in the
1990s, particularly as globalization and liberalization have taken their toll (see Chapter 7).
About one-third of the group only achieved positive growth in the 1990s. Many were poorer
in terms of per capita income than they were many years before.

The final action programs for other global, ad hoc conferences of the 1990s also have
given attention to the particular needs of least developed countries. Thus has the controversial notion launched by the CDP become an accepted part of international public
policy.[40]

From Mexico City to Copenhagen to Nairobi to Beijing, Women in Development

Over the past quarter-century the UN has convened four world conferences on
women's issues. Each has marked a different stage of a process that has elevated
gender equality to the center of the global agenda. These conferences on women's
issues have also highlighted the contribution of NGOs in lobbying for a gender
perspective to be included in development policies and strategies.

In the two decades between Mexico City and Beijing, the process has changed
the way that women are perceived in the development struggle. With some regional
differences, women have been more and more viewed as full and equal partners
with equal rights to resources and opportunities. A similar transformation was taking place in development thinking, with the shift from an earlier belief that development served to advance women to a new consensus that development was not
possible without the full participation and empowerment of women. The 1995
Human Development Report argues that unless development is engendered, it is
endangered: "The new world order would thus put people—both women and
men—clearly at the centre of all development processes. Only then can human development become fully engendered."[41]Although some observers dismiss many international negotiations as the preoccupation of developmental elites, the four
conferences on women have generated remarkable cross-cutting coalitions from
all classes and socioeconomic groups from North and South,[42] with an indisputable
effect on changing awareness and programs for women in many countries.

The first world conference on the status of women was convened in Mexico City to coincide with the 1975 International Women's Year. Leticia Ramos Shahani was secretary-general of the third conference on women in 1985 but noted with some irony the situation in 1975: "Mexico was the host government, and the bias of the Mexican government and the foreign ministry was obvious—they couldn't allow a woman to chair the conference. Yes, Mexico was the host government of the first-ever World Conference on Women. But I guess that's how the world was then."

Nonetheless, the conference gave impetus to the dual recognition that discrimination against women persisted and that a gender perspective should be included in development strategies. In calling for the conference, the General Assembly identified three key objectives that would become the basis for future work:

• full gender equality and the elimination of gender discrimination;
• the integration and full participation of women in development; and
• an increased contribution by women in the strengthening of world peace.

The conference called upon governments to formulate national strategies and identify targets and priorities in their effort to promote equal participation of women. By the end of the United Nations Decade for Women in 1985, 127 member states had reported the creation of some form of national machinery dealing with the promotion of policy, research, and programs aimed at women's advancement and participation in development.

Within the UN system, the Mexico City conference led to the establishment of the International Research and Training Institute for the Advancement of Women (INSTRAW) and the United Nations Development Fund for Women (UNIFEM) to provide the institutional and financial framework for research, training, and operational activities. Moreover, the Branch (later the Division) for the Advancement of Women became stronger, and gender and development became increasingly embedded in the work of the UN system. States established a UN Voluntary Fund for Women and approved a World Plan of Action with minimum targets, to be met by 1980, that focused on securing equal access for women to resources such as education, employment opportunities, political participation, health services, housing, nutrition, and family planning.

The United Nations Decade for Women (1976–1985) was proclaimed by the General Assembly five months later. This launched a new era in global efforts to promote the advancement of women. Along with global, ad hoc conferences, the UN sometimes developed the idea of "special" decades as a device to maintain momentum in moving toward effective responses to global challenges. A major milestone was the adoption by the General Assembly of the Convention on the

Elimination of All Forms of Discrimination against Women in December 1979. This convention legally binds states and obligates them to report within one year of ratification, and subsequently every four years, on the steps taken to remove the obstacles they face in its implementation.

Momentum was also maintained by convening the Copenhagen conference in 1980, at the midpoint in the women's decade. This gathering pinpointed three areas in which specific and highly focused action was essential if the broad goals identified by the Mexico City conference were to be realized. These were equal access to education, employment opportunities, and adequate health care services.

The Third UN World Conference on Women held in Nairobi in 1985 marked the end of the Decade for Women, and its mandate was to review critically achievements and shortcomings. UN data revealed that improvements in the status of women and efforts to reduce discrimination had benefited only a small minority of women, mainly in the North. In short, the objectives of the second half of the UN decade on women's behalf had not been met. Shahani remembers the struggle to mainstream women: "Western feminists were saying all you need are daycare centers, family planning, equal pay for equal work. But the Third World women were saying, 'Oh, no; firewood is politics, water is politics, the North-South issues is politics. The conditionalities of the IMF are part of the lives of women.'"

The Nairobi conference's Forward-Looking Strategies to the Year 2000 broke new ground in declaring all issues to be women's issues. Gender should be included in every sphere of human activity from employment, health, education, and social services to industry, science, communications, and the environment. In addition, guidelines were proposed for national measures to increase women's participation in efforts to promote peace and to assist women in special situations of distress. Moreover, the UN Division for the Advancement of Women was established to monitor and implement this program of action.

At the heart of the final document were measures for achieving equality at the national level. Governments were to set their own priorities, based on their development policies and resource capabilities. Many referred to Nairobi as the "birth of global feminism." And indeed, the movement for gender equality had gained true global recognition across the world.

The Fourth World Conference on Women gathered in Beijing in 1995, and its Declaration and the Platform for Action aimed to accelerate the implementation of the Nairobi document and remove the obstacles to women's active participation in all spheres of public and private life.[43] The UN's comprehensive review and appraisal of the implementation of the preceding decade showed that little or no priority had been given to the advancement of women in many countries.

The Beijing Platform for Action identified twelve critical areas for action: women and poverty; education and the training of women; women and health;

violence against women; women and armed conflict; women and the economy; women in power and decision making; institutional mechanisms for the advancement of women; human rights of women; women and the media; women and the environment; and the girl child. The role and contribution of civil society, in particular non-governmental and women's organizations, in the implementation of the Beijing Declaration and the Platform for Action were recognized and encouraged. The document stressed the importance of targets and benchmarks and urged member states to translate them into national strategies with time-bound targets and benchmarks for monitoring.

The fundamental transformation in Beijing was the recognition of the need to shift the focus from women to the concept of gender, recognizing that the structure of society, and all relations between men and women, had to be reevaluated. Only through such a fundamental restructuring of society and its institutions could women be fully empowered to take their rightful place as equal partners. This change represented a strong reaffirmation that women's rights were human rights and that gender equality was an issue of universal concern.

The Beijing conference itself was the largest gathering of government and NGO representatives ever held, with 17,000 in attendance. The host Chinese government attempted to control the separate NGO gathering by locating it at some distance from the main conference, but to no avail. The NGO Forum also broke all attendance records, which brought the combined number of participants to more than 47,000. The presence and influence of NGOs, one of the most active forces in the drive for gender equality, had increased dramatically since Mexico City in 1975. In Beijing, NGOs directly influenced the content of the action platform and would eventually play an important role in holding their national leaders accountable for the commitments they had made to implement the platform.

In many ways Beijing benefited from other UN summits earlier in the decade, which had invariably referred to the need to involve women in decision making also. The international discussions of various aspects of development—the environment, human rights, population, and social development—had all stressed the importance of women's full participation in decision making.

In a rerun of earlier discussions in Cairo, many countries argued that the recommendations should be conditioned on respect for the right of national sovereignty and so-called local moral and religious values. The male delegation from the Holy See failed to appreciate the irony of their particularly active role in negotiations over women's right to control their sexuality and fertility, family planning services, contraception, and the question of abortion. Countries respecting the Islamic *Shariah* also put forward in their reservations about contravening the alleged customs and practices of Islam.[44]

Since Beijing, the Commission on the Status of Women has reviewed each of the twelve critical areas of concern contained in the Beijing Platform for Action. Progress has been achieved in some critical areas of concern, but, not surprisingly, many obstacles to gender equality persist, and some new ones have arisen. The UN comprehensive review shows that the goals and commitments made in the platform have not been fully implemented.[45] Despite the advances women have made in many societies, progress made toward achieving gender equality has been slow and erratic. Women still lag behind in virtually all aspects of life (education, health, literacy, access to income and labor market, and so on). Nonetheless, in most countries changes are occurring—and many female leaders believe that the UN conferences and the UN itself have been part of the process of change, especially through building international awareness and alliances.

The Special Session of the General Assembly on Beijing + 5 held in New York in June 2000 provided an opportunity to identify new ways to translate commitments by governments, the UN system, and other international organizations into effective actions. As a follow-up to the Beijing conference, this special session on "Gender Equality, Development, and Peace for the Twenty-first Century" focused on examples of good practices, positive actions, lessons learned, obstacles, and key challenges remaining. It has also considered further actions and initiatives for achieving gender equality at the outset of the new millennium. There is a division among observers about whether or not such frequently scheduled debates are useful or have become so routine as to be innocuous.

Box 4.2. The World Employment Conference

The World Employment Conference was convened in Geneva in 1976 (see Chapter 3). The ILO used conference diplomacy to advocate and publicize more widely its own cutting-edge economic and social development strategy.

This conference was different from others in three ways. First, it made use of ILO's tripartite model so that participants included representatives of workers and employers as well as of governments—hence there was no parallel NGO effort. Second, national as well as international aspects of basic needs were on the table because there was no substitute for appropriate domestic policies to satisfy such basic needs for the poorest citizens in developing countries. Third, the conference drew upon policy research from the field that examined the links among employment, poverty, and income distribution. Indeed, the meeting was called the Tripartite World Conference on Employment, Income Distribution, and Social Progress, and the International Division of Labor.

This attempt to create a more employment-intensive, basic needs–oriented development strategy was well received by the South, European governments, and trade union representatives. European employers' representatives and the American tripartite delegation were skeptical, but they went along with the consensus. An economic development pattern that combined high economic growth with a certain amount of redistribution of income and assets in order to satisfy the basic needs of populations (including of the poorest 20 percent) represented a discovery of the obvious, an egg of Columbus.

The approach was truly global, in scope and in substance. It was, and remains, ahead of the intellectual curve and addressed straightforwardly what remain huge challenges: namely, employment creation and poverty reduction. The ILO secretariat missed an opportunity to undertake follow-up activities at the country level in an active way, for which the conference had given it a mandate. When, four years later, the development paradigm shifted (see Chapter 5), employment and basic needs received much less attention. The idea did not die, the political will did.

This highlights the limits of world conferences and of the UN in general to transform ideas that are ahead of the curve into fresh national and international policies in the absence of political will at any point in time.

From Vancouver to Istanbul, the Human Habitat

The First World Conference on Human Settlements was convened in Vancouver in 1976 to respond to the growing concern over hyper-urbanization in developing countries. Migration to cities was the most common reaction to poverty and limited rural opportunities.

Urbanization *per se* was not the problem. Indeed, urbanization was associated with economic development, as had been foreshadowed in the 1951 *Measures for the Economic Development of Under-Developed Countries*. And some degree of urban poverty was inevitable in poor countries, just as it had been in the early stages of industrialization in Europe and North America. If he had been alive, Jacob Riis would have been able to photograph in barrios of Mexico City, the slums on the edge of Manila, or Cairo's garbage heaps scenes at least as appalling as those he captured in nineteenth and early twentieth century Manhattan.

Vancouver's focus was on the chaotic processes resulting in unplanned megalopolises throughout the developing world. The integration of planning, improving, and managing urban settlements went across the fields of housing, transportation, safe water, public health, waste management, and other essential community services. The challenge was to provide new housing, infrastructure, and services to cope with a population growing at historically unprecedented levels.[46]

In Vancouver states called for comprehensive development policies taking into account both the urban and rural environments.[47] Two years later and building upon the earlier establishment of UNEP, the United Nations Centre for Human

Settlements (UNCHS, or Habitat) was established, also located in Nairobi, and became the lead agency within the UN system for coordinating activities in the field of human settlements.

Since then the urban explosion has continued unabated, which has forced many governments to adopt and promote policies to improve human settlements. However, in many parts of the world, not only have the problems faced in the 1970s not disappeared, they have in fact worsened. For example, in 1996 it was estimated that at least one billion people lacked adequate shelter and were living in extreme poverty, at least the majority of whom lived in urban slums.

Two decades later the Second UN Conference on Human Settlements (Habitat II) in Istanbul addressed two main themes: "adequate shelter for all" and "sustainable human settlement development in an urbanizing world." Perhaps most importantly, Habitat II initiated new practices in the way that the UN prepares and conducts world conferences. Previously, fewer stakeholders had been involved. But in Istanbul in 1996, local authorities, businesspersons, NGOs, parliamentarians, women's groups, trade unions, scientists, engineers, religious groups, cultural societies, foundations, and other associations were involved from the outset. This conference established a formal mechanism through which a vast chorus of voices was mixed with those of government representatives.

Habitat II was the first UN world conference whose machinery included a platform for representatives of civil society. Unlike at previous UN world conferences, NGO representatives reported officially to the main conference rather than being relegated to the sidelines. As we have seen in other conferences, one of the main ways in which ideas matter is by facilitating new coalitions that view their interests as being served through working together to respond to a global challenge. In Istanbul the formation of such coalitions was consciously designed into the conference itself.

The final declaration in Istanbul recognized that the state system alone — neither governments nor intergovernmental agencies — could not solve or finance solutions to massive urbanization. The private sector, local authorities, grassroots organizations, and NGOs had to be drawn into the process of decision making to address the "urban question."

The global plan of action embodied a collective vision of human settlements for cities, towns, and villages that are viable, safe, prosperous, healthy, and equitable. Habitat II brought together different strands of development, moving beyond the issues of population movement and urbanization to employment generation, environmental infrastructure, living conditions, governance, finance, and sustainable use of resources. The conference emphasized that sustainable development is essential for human settlements. Hence, the Plan of Action for Sustainable Human Settlements Development in an Urbanizing World incorporated the main principles from the Rio and Copenhagen conferences along with provisions regarding gender equality from the series of conferences on women.

An important aspect of Habitat II was experience sharing. The UN launched the "Best Practices Initiative" to assist national committees in preparing their own national action plans before Istanbul. This initiative helped identify where concrete improvements have been made in human settlements around the world. Hundreds of communities and cities were thus able to learn and exchange problem-solving experiences. More than 100 national committees contributed more than 700 examples of "best practices." This was one concrete means by which the ideas originally placed on the table in Vancouver could in fact continue to be pursued even after the final gavel had sounded in Istanbul.

Vienna's World Conference on Human Rights

The 1993 Vienna conference should be assessed not as a single event but rather as part of an ongoing and long-standing (since 1948) struggle to strengthen UN mechanisms for human rights protection amid changing world politics. Controversy has surrounded international efforts since the original idea in the UN Charter was given more substance in the Universal Declaration of Human Rights.

The Vienna conference reaffirmed international commitments to human rights made in 1945 and strengthened mechanisms for monitoring and promoting them worldwide. However, the charter's original language contained clear tensions between sovereignty and human rights, and these tensions had not evaporated with the end of the Cold War. In many ways, the mantle of the restrictive interpretations against human rights passed from the members of the Soviet bloc to many countries in Asia and the Middle East.

The year 1993 was not 1948 or even 1968 (when a first review of the Universal Declaration took place in Teheran), but a substantial number of states still regarded human rights as purely domestic instead of a wider international concern. Ironically, the United States, which spearheaded the drafting of the Universal Declaration through the efforts of Eleanor Roosevelt, has a very restrictive interpretation of UN legitimacy. Turkey and the United States are the only OECD countries that have not ratified all of the six core conventions—in fact, the United States is in the bottom quarter of countries for having ratified only three of the six.[48]

Given the lack of initial agreement on the main agenda items, the output of the conference could be considered remarkable. The Vienna Declaration and Programme of Action focused on implementation and institutional reforms, of which the creation of the post of High Commissioner for Human Rights was the most important.[49] Five months later the General Assembly adopted a resolution creating the Office of High Commissioner for Human Rights (UNHCHR), whose responsibilities included "playing an active role in removing the current obstacles and in meeting the challenges to the full realization of all human rights and in preventing the continuation of human rights violations throughout the world."

As a concession to the many developing countries that sought to limit UN initiatives in this field, the first high commissioner was, ironically, a former military officer whose ministerial experience was with a Latin American regime that human rights watchdogs had lambasted. The present high commissioner is the former president of Ireland, Mary Robinson, whose own integrity and visibility have begun to transform her office and increase its budget so that it becomes a more powerful voice in defense of human rights.

During the Cold War the balance between first (civil and political) and second (economic and social) generation rights was the main flash point for human rights disputes between West, on the one hand, and the East and South, on the other (see Chapter 1). Mihaly Simai—at present a professor at the University of Budapest and former director of the Institute of World Economics of the Hungarian Academy of Science—was an ECE staff member in the 1950s and directed the UN University's WIDER in the 1980s. He commented on the two "flavors" of human rights during the Cold War: "One approach had been the approach of the socialist countries which considered economic and social rights as the fundamental rights of the people. The other was the Western approach, which considered human rights as an instrument of propaganda, the Western countries emphasizing the so-called political and civil rights." Economic and social rights were important, but members of the socialist bloc were hesitant—in spite of their desire to foster more civil and political rights—to speak against the Soviet position. Simai noted that it did not "make any sense to publicize the civil or political rights because this would serve only the interests of the Western countries which are using this as an instrument against the socialist countries."

In the words of the *Human Development Report 2000,* "The rights agenda and the development agenda followed parallel tracks." But by Vienna, the notion of a "package" of first- and second-generation rights had become widely accepted, and hence "human rights [are seen] as an intrinsic part of development—and development as a means to realizing human rights."[50] The Vienna conference went so far as to point out that extreme poverty and social exclusion are "violations of human dignity."

The main dispute in Vienna centered on whether human rights were actually universally applicable—as had been agreed in 1948—or were subject to local, religious, and cultural interpretations. Female genital mutilation in the Sudan, suppression of girls' education in Afghanistan, repression of dissidents in Singapore, or the use of the death penalty in the United States are illustrations. Stéphane Hessel, who worked on human rights at the UN in the 1940s, recalled in an interview that his compatriot René Cassin had insisted on the "U" in the Universal Declaration. Cassin would have been unnerved by the number of governments that used the conference to argue against universalism and for particularism.

In fact, however, the Vienna Declaration and Programme of Action re-affirmed the universality and indivisibility of human rights. Promoting and protecting human rights is the duty of all states whatever their levels of development, although a reference was worked in as part of a negotiating compromise, to the effect that "the significance of national and regional particularities and various historical, cultural and religious backgrounds must be borne in mind."

The Vienna conference made clear once again what had been obvious since 1948: namely, the crucial role played by human rights NGOs.[51] There were more than 2,000 NGO delegates in Vienna, who exerted pressure on governments to continue to expand UN rule making on human rights. For instance, Vienna was a critical opportunity to give full legitimacy to the claim that women's rights are human rights and to establish new mechanisms to enforce them. An "inalienable, integral, and indivisible part of universal human rights" was the language preferred by NGOs. They ensured that this language was included and that a special rapporteur on violence against women was appointed. Thus, women's organizations have developed an advocacy strategy for gender issues at UN world conferences not specifically focused on women.[52] Again we see the mutually reinforcing character of the ideas spawned and nurtured across global, ad hoc conferences.

Box 4.3. The Children's Summit

The World Summit for Children was held in New York in 1990. It was the first of the summits of the 1990s, the largest ever to have been held until that time and the first global meeting of heads of state to have had a human focus as opposed to a political or economic one. It launched the second phase of global conferences convened by the UN in the last decade of the twentieth century and, in several respects, provided the model for subsequent summits.

The Children's Summit was pioneering in other respects. It built on the "child survival and development revolution" (CSDR) of the 1980s, the UNICEF/UN-led efforts in more than a hundred countries, under which basic health actions such as immunization and oral rehydration had been enormously expanded. The result was greatly reduced numbers of child deaths from infectious diseases, diarrhea, and other common killers. In spite of increases in population, the total number of child deaths has fallen from fifteen million to twelve million each year. These achievements were all the more remarkable since many took place during the lost decade of the 1980s, during which income per capita had stagnated in Latin America and fallen by some 10 percent in sub-Saharan Africa.

The Children's Summit stimulated the final push toward these achievements and, at the same time, set new goals and laid the foundation for a further program of accelerated actions in the 1990s. The new goals were contained in the World Declaration on the Survival, Protection, and Development of Children and in a plan of action agreed to and signed at the summit. There were ten major goals and seventeen supporting targets, set for the year 2000, with "stepping-stone" goals for 1995. The major goals focused on further reductions of child mortality; increases in access to education and health care; and improvements in nutrition, water and sanitation, and family planning. Actions for the girl child were a particular focus, as early steps towards the empowerment of women and as necessary actions to end discrimination among future generations as well as the present. Accelerated ratification of the Convention on the Rights of the Child was a particular target—and the summit helped to raise awareness and commitment to this end.

In contrast to the 1970s, heads of state gathered—seventy-one of them, to be exact, with representatives of eighty-eight other countries present. This massive involvement of world leaders was a first. It proved effective in generating high-level commitments and publicizing the objectives of the conference. By the mid-1990s some 150 countries, including some developed countries, had prepared national plans for action.

In September 1996 the General Assembly examined a mid-decade review of the goals for the year 2000. About 100 developing countries, with about 90 percent of the children located in the developing world, were making substantial progress towards the targets for the turn of the century. The Convention on the Rights of the Child had broken all records in terms of the speed to transform itself into international law and the number of countries that had ratified it. As of this writing, it has been ratified by 191 countries, covering more than 96 percent of the world's children. Only the United States and Somalia have not ratified the convention.

The success of the summit owed much to the leadership of James Grant, UNICEF's energetic executive director from 1980 until his untimely death in 1995.[53] Initially there was great skepticism, with doubts about whether it was even appropriate for a summit to be held on a "soft" subject like the needs of children. Many doubted whether more than a few heads of state would come. And in fact the invitations for this first summit were sent from six heads of state—from Canada, Sweden, Egypt, Pakistan, Mali, and Mexico—because there were official doubts about whether the UN as such could sponsor a summit meeting. Grant staked his reputation on mobilizing the event, just as he had done in calling for a child survival revolution almost a decade before.

But once successful, innovation and initial struggle are quickly forgotten. The Children's Summit led on to the Earth Summit in Rio, the World Food Summit in Rome, the Social Summit in Copenhagen, and the Millennium Summit in New York. The Children's Summit Declaration and Plan of Action became models for future world gatherings. Time-bound, measurable goals for practical human action, which were pioneering approaches in 1990, rapidly became recipes for other programs. What is less clear is whether Grant's determined leadership of the Children's Summit can be reproduced for other global conferences.

Copenhagen's World Summit for Social Development

After decades of confrontation between the two ideological blocs, the end of the Cold War presented a historic opportunity to achieve a common vision of social development and poverty reduction. Although most of the commentary from pundits focused on the renaissance for international peace and security, the implications for development were also substantial. The beginning of the Copenhagen Declaration on Social Development points to the possibility of an emerging new economic and social agenda, which is the subject matter of the next chapter. The optimism of the moment is captured by the somewhat pompous words: "For the first time in history, at the invitation of the United Nations, we gather as Heads of State and Government to recognize the significance of social development and human well-being for all and to give to these goals the highest priority both now and into the twenty-first century." But as the largest gathering of heads of state ever held until the September 2000 Millennium Summit (117 attended) — and for a gathering whose purpose was to agree on actions to eradicate poverty — perhaps some pompous words were more acceptable than for a meeting to celebrate victory on the vanquished.

The 1995 Copenhagen Social Summit emphasized that economic and social development along with environmental protection were mutually reinforcing components of sustainable development, the idea that had emerged in the late 1980s and was baptized a few years later at the Earth Summit. The increased attention to the social dimensions of economic policies — placing human beings at the center of development — was based on three core themes: the eradication of poverty; the achievement of full employment; and the promotion of just, stable, and secure societies. Globalization was a new challenge because it was leading to unprecedented prosperity for some but intensified poverty, unemployment, and social disintegration for others. Fifty years after the creation of the UN, whose core goals included the promotion of "the economic and social advancement of all peoples," there were still 1.3 billion people living in absolute poverty and 1.5 billion without access to primary health care.

The Copenhagen summit adopted, as was by then the custom, a declaration and program of action. The first commitment was "to create a political, social, cultural, and legal environment that will enable people to achieve social development." The other commitments were linked logically to the first one, and they focused on eradicating poverty; achieving equality and equity between women and men; promoting full employment, social integration, and universal and equitable access to high-quality education and primary health care; and achieving human dignity.

A key aspect of the Copenhagen Declaration was the creation of a global framework for action that reaffirmed and incorporated commitments recorded at past world conferences in New York (children), Rio (environment), Vienna (human rights), and Cairo (population) as well as in core ILO conventions. The final declaration provided a new snapshot of the status of the four big ideas set out in the UN Charter and how they had been updated over the years at a variety of UN-sponsored gatherings.

In organizing the World Summit for Social Development, the UN surfed on the wave of what may be an emerging post-Washington consensus (see Chapter 5), but it was not ahead of it. The summit emphasized the threats to human security associated with unregulated globalization, but it never addressed the structural causes of poverty, unemployment, social disintegration, and environmental degradation. During the preparatory phase NGOs had pushed for a critical evaluation of the impact on human well-being of the current economic and financial orthodoxy in vogue since the early 1980s.[54] However, these questions were rejected during this phase. The summit never fundamentally challenged structural adjustment. Implicitly, higher priority was given to economic transformation than to social issues. Poverty and employment policies looked like second-order objectives after economic priorities were determined. The global challenge was thus defined as establishing social safety nets sufficient to put a more human face on structural adjustment.

The UN's "new approach" to development promoted in Copenhagen was based on the mainstream idea that global integration was not merely a desirable but actually the only road to accelerated development. The new international trade order defined by the Marrakech Agreement and the role of the WTO in the new global architecture was endorsed. The challenge became not to curb the emerging global economy but to adopt social policies to mitigate the human costs of the economic transformation associated with globalization.[55] The program of action, therefore, addressed more the symptoms than the causes of what we call "the new social question." This "failure" of the summit was stressed in the alternative declaration produced by the NGOs that severely criticized the conventional wisdom of the final declaration.[56]

On the recommendation of the Copenhagen summit, the General Assembly decided in 1995 to convene a special session in 2000 in Geneva to review and appraise implementation. Events organized outside of the Palais des Nations permitted NGOs, journalists, academics, and UN staff to pursue ideas. Overall, some progress had taken place. There is greater awareness of the human and environmental impacts of economic policies by both governments and the Washington-based financial institutions. A global consensus has emerged that development is more than economic growth. Poverty and employment are now, once again, at the top of the international policy agenda. Many governments have designed national plans and strategies for poverty eradication and employment creation. The summit also had an impact on the organizations of the UN system that have refocused their activities and promoted collaboration among different bodies and the Bretton Woods institutions on social development. This motivated, in part, the reforms instituted by UN Secretary-General Kofi Annan in 1997.[57]

On the other hand, increasing inequalities between and within countries continue as blights on the international landscape since the Copenhagen summit. The world has become a place of growing extremes with regard to income, employment, basic social services, and participation in the main institutions of society (see Chapter 7). Globalization—sustained by market forces—has accelerated, providing new opportunities for prosperity, but also limiting the capacity of states to manage it for the benefit of all.[58]

Conclusions

In the 1970s and continuing apace in the 1990s, the UN has made increasing use of world conferences to address new global challenges by involving states and increasingly members of civil society as well. These international gatherings have altered development thinking toward a more comprehensive vision.

Obviously, world conferences and summits can be viewed by cynics as jamborees in exotic places—expensive and futile attempts to force-feed international cooperation down the throats of actors having very different interests, priorities, and objectives. Their impact, according to this logic, has been little more than rhetorical.

That would be a misguided judgment. To be sure, their "utility is very uneven," to quote Zammit-Cutajar, who attended many of those conferences discussed above. Yet these conferences have been vehicles for the circulation of new ideas and for fruitful—albeit sometimes acrimonious—North-South dialogue. Their usefulness should be assessed in a long-term perspective of political forces mobilized, effectiveness of commitments, and implementation of outcomes. Many of them have successfully brought out new common concerns and generated new standards and guidelines for national and international policies.

Examples have been given in the preceding pages, but let us recall some of the ways in which the "second UN," that of individuals and secretariats, has pushed out the envelope of acceptable ideas and concepts. On the environment, Stockholm was definitely ahead of the curve in 1972, and both Stockholm and Rio have had many follow-up activities. On population, more than 100 countries now have active population policies, and it is commonplace to assert that "development is the best contraceptive," a proposition that had seemed outlandish to many in Bucharest in 1974. Cairo shifted the focus from fertility control to empowerment, recognizing that women are "key agents for social transformation."

The four conferences devoted to women and gender issues have created a worldwide dialogue on gender and given rise to a global women's movement. They have reinforced women's rights as human rights and made it possible for the Vienna conference to underline this position. They have confirmed women as essential actors rather than as passive recipients. Habitat II succeeded in involving a host of actors who have come up with many concrete illustrations of how things in the city can be done and can be done better. The Children's Summit adopted quantitative and time-bound goals, some now achieved and many pursued with more support from UNICEF than many conference commitments receive from other UN agencies. And the list could go on. For younger generations many of these examples now appear obvious and totally commonplace. Only a few decades ago, they were almost unimaginable.

UN world conferences also have generated a wealth of data and perspectives on practically all aspects of human rights and development. Background documents and position papers produced in preparation for conferences and summits have changed the ways in which states and civil society perceive such issues as the world food situation and growing inequalities in the global economy. UN conferences have stimulated research and integrated existing knowledge in new analytical frameworks. Moreover, they have facilitated the exchange of information and encouraged a process of action-oriented reflection and research that feed and sustain international discussion in both academic and policy-making circles.[59] For instance, "sustainable development" as an overriding development concept has spread rapidly, largely because it was at the heart of the conferences that took place in the 1990s.

A major outcome of the series of world conferences over the past thirty years is that they have resulted in a global realization of the essential role of civil society, and more particularly that of NGOs. Global, ad hoc conferences have opened the door to a growing pluralization of international dialogue and institutionalized participation by NGOs, whereas previously it had been circumscribed. A force for change was unleashed with the experiment in Stockholm to such an extent that global inter-*governmental* conferences without *non-governmental* organizations would now be unthinkable, except for gatherings organized by the Bretton Woods institutions.

NGOs have often been effective in using access to influence the outcomes of global conferences. They have targeted friendly governments, and a synergism emerged that led to the appearance of NGOs' ideas in governmental negotiating texts.[60] The World Bank and the IMF still hold their annual meetings without

NGOs, but the Inspection Panel is a precedent-setting step toward hearing private voices in relationship to projects.[61] And the cycle of UN world conferences is marked by a progressive recognition that NGO participation is essential to the attainment of policy goals. Brian Urquhart summarizes the situation in the following way: "Thank God for the NGOs, who have been the sounding board and the missionaries from these conferences. They also shame the governments into taking part in them." As already observed, civil society institutions—including the private for-profit sector—have changed the concept of global governance.

Perhaps the main weakness of the conference system is also its strength: namely, the politics of national interests that are the basic organizing principle of the UN system. World conferences and summits are political events that are affected by bargaining among states—especially between South and North, and, until the fall of the Berlin Wall, between East and West—as well as among different interests (for example, unions and business) and groups (for example, competing NGOs). Behind the calls to convene these UN meetings were powerful ideas and global challenges. The need to reach an agreement about the precise implications of ideas and the implementation of measures to address challenges necessarily led to compromises among actors with different priorities. It also often resulted in vague language that masks differences.

There inevitably are large gaps between rhetoric and reality, between commitments in international declarations and efforts in capitals to alter national policies and actions. Governments are ready to cooperate with the process only if the final agreement is in their perceived interests and if they are able to persuade important domestic constituencies and bureaucracies of this fact. There is no coercive capacity, and compliance with UN declarations, resolutions, and plans of action is voluntary. To restate the obvious, the UN is not a world government; the "first UN" is an arena in which states pursue their national interests.

This means, however, that the business of conferences has to be by persuasion, mobilizing public awareness. The UN has clearly had some success in this respect, although this research project must make a point of more thoroughly documenting the exact influences that have been brought to bear. Whether the UN succeeds in the short or medium term to promote new goals and secures new measures to achieve them, the world organization has influenced the international public policy agenda about human rights and development through ideas debated and fought over during global, ad hoc conferences. The cumulative impact of almost three decades of discussions is substantial. Ideas have helped define and redefine state interests to include such considerations as the environment and gender; if it occurs, sustainability would certainly have arrived more slowly without global conferences. When clashes occur about priorities or sequencing—is greater equity more important than faster growth?—ideas help to guide decisions. Moreover, ideas are important because they make it possible for new coalitions—including those that cross North-South borders, or governmental, intergovernmental, and non-governmental ones, or public and private ones, as well—to come together. And ideas are important because they have led to the establishment of a host of new institutions to address challenges.

A significant illustration of this line of argument is that in June 2000 the World Bank Group, the IMF, and the OECD seemed to have "got UN religion." At the request of the Group of Seven (G-7) they joined forces in Paris with the UN to prepare a report entitled "A Better World for All."[62] It would have been inconceivable, even a few years earlier,[63] to have imagined that the Bretton Woods institutions and the "rich men's club" in Paris would have aligned themselves so clearly behind the ideas and goals articulated during the UN's world conferences of the 1970s and summits of the 1990s. Indeed, many NGOs and developing countries in Geneva expressed deep suspicions about the alliance and expressed fears that in the long run it might mean that the UN's distinctive voice would be submerged under Bretton Woods or developed country pressure.

As we go to press, 150 heads of state had just gathered in New York for what Singapore's permanent representative to the UN, Kishore Mahbubani, called the "mother of all summits." In their final statement, the world's leaders committed themselves to "broad and sustained efforts to create a shared future, based upon our common humanity in all its diversity." Hence, poverty eradication, education, gender equality, child rights, reproductive health, and the environment have penetrated rhetoric. Although policies had begun to embrace these lofty objectives by the turn of the millennium, few would be satisfied with the political will to implement the kinds of changes required to meet the purportedly universally agreed-upon standards.

One final word is in order. The series of UN-sponsored conferences has changed the lenses through which policy- and decision-makers view many dimensions of economic and social development. New mechanisms have been set up, new coalitions shaped, and, yes, many tensions created. But on the whole these have been creative tensions. Obviously, the more one is ahead of the intellectual or advocacy curve, the greater the tensions. This is illustrated by the debate on the NIEO and at the World Employment Conference. On the whole, however, the UN succeeded in jumping on the beginning of a wave to surf to bigger ones, falling into the water from time to time, but often reaching a new shoreline, fatigued but still alive.

5

Current Orthodoxy, the New
Social Question, and Policy Alternatives

- **The Rising Power of the Bretton Woods Institutions**
- **The Drawbacks of the Current Orthodoxy**
- Ideas from the United Nations
- Ideas and Concepts Spread

In spite of the avalanche of ideas proposed by the UN in the 1970s, the re-action that took place within the 1980s ignored or abandoned much of what had gone before. Development in the 1980s was built more on market ideology than on facts and figures of specific problems.

The neo-liberal revolution of the early 1980s grew from four factors: the crisis of inflation and of Keynesian policies in the North; the global recession, balance-of-payments problems, and debt crisis throwing into disarray development strate-gies in the South; the growing internal contradictions of socialist economies; and the political triumph of Thatcher-Reaganism in the United Kingdom and the United States. The widespread acceptance of financial and market-oriented or-thodoxy in the 1980s was based not on clear evidence of its effectiveness—much after all was just reemphasizing the core of earlier liberal doctrine (see Box 5.1). Rather, it came as a reaction against previous interventionist policies and their failures.[1] A cynical vision of the state as a mechanism for rent seeking and self-interest replaced the Keynesian and developmentalist visions in which the state was a legitimate and purposeful contributor to development objectives.[2]

The new worldview gave high priority to the fight against inflation, and real interest rates rose sharply. This, combined with the monetarist policy imple-mented by the U.S. Federal Reserve Bank, led to a considerable appreciation of the dollar. Concentration on budgetary and monetary discipline in the North and the accompanying recession resulted in a strong contraction of world demand and a further deterioration of the terms of trade for primary products. Indebted developing countries faced a deep financial crisis, the combined result of the strong dollar, high rates of interest, and the drop in their export prices and incomes. This situation sparked the international debt crisis—with Mexico's refusing to service its debt in August 1982—and the "lost decade," or more, in Latin America and Africa.

Box 5.1. Current Orthodoxies: Remembrances of Times Past

Each generation often confronts old problems as if they were surprises and discusses remedies as if they had never before been discussed. This box recalls that present orthodoxies have old roots.

The interwar period was plagued by high inflation at the beginning of the 1920s and by the economic depression, obstacles to free trade, and high unemployment of the 1930s. These were the global challenges of the day. How did the League of Nations and the ILO face up to them?

Between 1920 and 1933 the League of Nations organized three major conferences on economic and financial problems. Each contributed greatly to the debate on international economic issues during the interwar period. The first general conference was held in Brussels in 1920 and dealt mainly with financial questions; the second, in Geneva in 1927, concerned more general economic matters; and the third, in London in 1933, dealt with major problems as they were seen at the time.

The first focused on the challenge of economic reconstruction and stabilization after the killing, destruction, and chaos of the First World War. The second occurred in a new era of optimism and addressed the question of international cooperation and liberalization of international trade. The last reflected the disturbing consequences of the Great Depression on both international political and economic cooperation. Jacques Polak, a young official in the 1930s who later became the IMF's director of research, recalled the oft-forgotten importance of these efforts and also their quality: "In the late thirties when the League was in desperate shape, the economic secretariat was considered to be first-rate. . . . Everybody who was anybody in economics came through Geneva."

The Brussels Financial Conference, 1920

The Brussels Financial Conference took place when many European countries were in the grip of severe inflation. Its aim was "to study the financial crisis and the means of remedying and of mitigating the dangerous consequences arising from it."[3] This was the first international conference since World War I in which the former belligerents participated in order to address their common interests. Thirty-nine countries were represented, including the United States and Germany, which were not members of the league at this time. The conference was not "a gathering of statesmen working at the solution of political difficulties in the interest of their particular countries, but a gathering of experts from all nations working for the solution of the common problem of the whole world."[4] Three sets of resolutions were adopted:

- "Proposals on public finance" argued for balancing the budget and restoring macroeconomic equilibrium. Balancing of budgets required reduced expenditures and increased taxation, the elimination of artificial controls, the withholding of subsidies, and the floating of loans only for the reestablishment of economic activity. These principles were presented as the way to strengthen market principles for economic efficiency, but also to make possible far-reaching social reforms, for which there was a strong and general demand.
- "Proposals on currency and exchange" urged the need to end inflation by returning to the gold standard, freeing banks from political pressure, and freeing trade as soon as possible from control and restriction of all kinds.
- "Proposals on international trade" declared that real peace is only possible by "reestablishing at once full and friendly cooperation and to arrange for the unrestricted interchange of commodities between the States which had been created or enlarged as a result of the war, in order that the essential unity of European economic life might not been impaired by the erection of artificial economic barriers."

The proceedings and views of the Financial Conference were closely followed in banking circles. They were used as a model by several governments that reformed public finance in their own countries until the Great Depression of the early 1930s.

The Geneva Economic Conference, 1927

With currencies stabilized and budgets balanced, wider economic problems connected with tariffs and trade attracted increasing attention in the latter half of the 1920s. At that time Europe's production was only about 5 percent greater than it had been in 1913, while its international trade had fallen to 89 percent of its prewar volume. (This was a far slower recovery than after the Second World War. The Marshall Plan and the Korean War made a big difference.)

The League of Nations in 1925 emphasized that economic peace would largely contribute to security among nations and make it necessary to investigate "the economic difficulties which stand in the way of the revival of general prosperity and of ascertaining the best means of overcoming these difficulties and of preventing disputes."[5]

The vast majority of the experts attending the 1927 conference recognized that the general level of prosperity and trade was far below the world's actual productive capacity. The final report surveyed the world's economic situation and formulated a series of policy suggestions. It was adopted unanimously and can be considered—like the report of the Financial Conference of Brussels—as an authoritative statement of orthodox economic doctrine at the time. According to a prominent economist of the time, Per Jacobsson, the conference reached a synthesis of two main economic ideas of the previous century: the Manchester School's belief in the advantages of free competition and the Manifold Movements' commitment to improvement in social conditions.[6]

This final report was acclaimed by government, leaders in commerce and industry, and representatives of organized labor.[7] As a follow-up to the conference, twenty-nine countries announced their willingness to join in collective action for carrying out the recommendations. The economic work of the league in the following years was strongly oriented toward helping and encouraging in every way the translation into concrete policy of the conference's statements. To that purpose, the league's Economic Committee was enlarged and strengthened by the addition of an American member, and a new Economic Consultative Committee was set up that included not only governmental but also labor, industrial, and commercial representatives.

The London Monetary and Economic Conference, 1933

This conference took place midway through the Great Depression. By that time, more than half of the league's member states had officially abandoned the gold standard, and some thirty had imposed foreign exchange restrictions. Some thirty million workers were unemployed by the end of 1932, according to the ILO, which meant that more than seventy million persons had been deprived of a means of livelihood (including dependents).[8] The effects of unemployment on public health were so considerable that the league undertook a special investigation.

The political situation was deteriorating dramatically. In January 1933 Adolf Hitler became chancellor of Germany, and soon after the Nazi Party won the elections of March. The disastrous effects of the economic crisis were exacerbated by the threat of war resulting from the stated platform of Nazi Germany to reverse the onerous provisions of the Treaty of Versailles. Moreover, Japan announced in March 1933 its withdrawal from the League of Nations two years after having attacked and occupied Manchuria in September 1931.

The London Monetary and Economic Conference convened in June 1933. Sixty-seven governments had been invited, and sixty-one participated, which collectively accounted for approximately 90 percent of world trade. The London conference was attended mainly by government representatives, whereas participants at the Brussels and Geneva conferences were experts nominated by their respective governments. Neville Chamberlain headed the British delegation; the French one was led by Prime Minister Edouard Daladier; the German one by Minister for Foreign Affairs Constantin von Neurath; and the U.S. one by Secretary of State Cordell Hull.

The general program of the London conference emphasized the gravity of three years of worldwide crisis generating so many tensions in the field of trade and international monetary and currency relations. "In essence," it pointed out, "the necessary programme is one of economic disarmament. Failure in this critical undertaking threatens a worldwide adoption of ideals of national self-sufficiency which cut unmistakably athwart the lines of economic development."[9]

The purpose of the conference was to address the urgent necessity for "a concerted and determined effort to rescue the world from the constantly deepening crisis against which it has been vainly struggling for some years." It recognized that "action must be on a world front covering a wide range of subjects, for experience had shown the difficulty, owing to the interdependence of the various problems, of reaching agreement internationally on some isolated point."[10]

As with so many other international undertakings to the present day, the success of the conference depended to a large extent on U.S. participation. Despite the initial objectives of the conference, hope for agreement disappeared when Washington stated its unwillingness to collaborate in any international plan to restore a stable international monetary standard. (The United States had abandoned the gold standard in April 1933.) Timing was also unfortunate in other ways. President Franklin Roosevelt's unprecedented recovery program—the New Deal—had just been launched and prevented Washington's agreeing about matters related to currency, debts, or tariffs. Roosevelt declared later: "The sound internal economic system of a nation is a greater factor of well-being than the price of its currency in changing terms of the currencies of other nations."[11] France refused to discuss a reduction on tariffs and Britain to discuss financing international public works.[12] The disastrous lack of agreement was apparent to all participants, and the year 1933 can be seen as a turning point. Governments looked inward and concentrated on their own domestic economic and financial situations.

Keynes's ideas were completely absent from the agenda. The conference reflected orthodox economics even though the United States was starting to implement a set of policies largely in accord with Keynes's subsequent analysis. Indeed, President Roosevelt in his inaugural address of March 1933 had said, "Our greatest primary task is to put people to work."[13] The failure of the London Monetary and Economic Conference showed the difficulties of trying to create worldwide economic cooperation in the midst of depression and growing nationalism.

Today the challenge is both different and more complex. The global economy is now subject to more forces. Multinational corporations, the media, NGOs, and other groups all play a bigger role. There are the major international economic institutions like the World Bank, the IMF, and the WTO. Many countries are benefiting from globalization—most of the OECD countries but also China and India, as well as Korea, Malaysia, and Thailand. The United States is still enjoying the largest sustained economic boom in history. Notwithstanding, global poverty remains widespread, and inequality has risen to record levels. Still, some seventy countries are marginalized, and their links and terms of trade with the global leaders are weak. The challenge is to find ways to get the attention and commitment of policy-makers, and their governments, at the same time as many in the rich countries are enjoying sustained and unprecedented prosperity.

This crisis amounted to a major threat to international capital markets. With strong U.S. support, the IMF intervened massively to help reschedule Mexico's debt and that of other developing countries. But having recourse to funds from the lender of last resort came with severe conditionality.[14] To gain access to IMF funds, borrowing countries were required to implement stabilization programs or structural adjustment programs (SAPs), which became a major force for implementing economic liberalization in developing countries. The success of applying conventional economic wisdom in the West was undeniable—especially in the United States, which rides the crest of ten years of expansion. However, the recipe produced different results elsewhere and should be examined in light of the performance of the rest of the globe.

The Rising Power of the Bretton Woods Institutions

The 1980s were marked by the increasing influence of the Bretton Woods institutions. To the stabilization policies aimed at restoring macroeconomic equilibrium, they added meso- and microeconomic interventions to address perceived structural problems within the economy. The World Bank proposed structural adjustment lending in 1979 to "support a program of specific policy changes and institutional reforms designed to reduce the current account deficit to sustainable levels."[15] The debt crisis made the need for stabilization and external financial assistance clear,[16] but the emphasis on trade liberalization and other components owed something to the weight of experience and something to Bretton Woods ideology. The original objectives had support as stabilization tools, but the more ideological effort to shrink the state was more controversial.[17]

Then came structural adjustment to suppress the alleged bias introduced by state intervention against the market. The withdrawal of the state from economic activities was linked to privatization. It was argued that even minimal state intervention would distort market mechanisms. Freed finally from all the distortions of such intervention, the totally unregulated market would bring optimal solution in terms of growth and welfare. Prices were seen as the primary determinant of the incentive structure for a rational economy. Thus, one of the major concerns of structural adjustment was to get prices right.[18]

In sub-Saharan Africa the power of the Bretton Woods institutions reached a zenith. A controversial report written for the World Bank by a team led by University of Michigan professor Elliot Berg played a key role in defining the new approach to structural adjustment and development in Africa over the 1980s.[19] The state was viewed as the cause of perverse effects that were counterproductive not only from an economic but also from a social point of view. Similar approaches were tried elsewhere with equal vigor, but the World Bank had less power outside Africa.

The reaction symbolized by the Berg report resulted, as already mentioned, from a variety of disheartening factors. They included ever mounting government spending; nationalized enterprises and parastatals; government regulations hampering competition; protectionist measures in international trade; international capital controls; and "runaway" inflation.

The new orthodoxy was neatly summed up as the "Washington consensus" by John Williamson, a senior fellow at the Institute for International Economics and former World Bank staff member.[20] "Consensus" is a misnomer in light of how many developing countries are and have been actively opposed to the prescriptions emanating from the Bretton Woods institutions. The "consensus" represents the views of the most powerful financial countries, but even here Japan and to a lesser extent France have dissented at times. Williamson's ten prescriptions fell into two major areas of policy:

- The establishment of a healthy base for growth through macroeconomic stabilization and austerity programs. This was seen as an important step on the road to the return of growth and prosperity. It included fiscal discipline to put an end to budget deficits, tight controls on public expenditure, and reliance on unified exchange rates in place of import controls or export subsidies.
- The restructuring of the economy toward export- and market-oriented activities through liberalization, deregulation, and privatization. The objective was to strengthen the private sector as the main actor of growth and development through tax reform, liberalization of trade and finance, privatization, deregulation, and strengthening of property rights. Countries should also be opened to foreign direct investment.

During the first half of the 1980s developing countries started to adopt policies based on universal IMF prescriptions. Mainstream discourse saw no need to debate issues like development and growth. The Washington consensus swept all before it, emphasizing the belief that the road to growth and development was open to any country ready to embrace structural adjustment and move toward an open economy and more rational market resource allocations. The 1990s "have been different in one significant respect," wrote Moisés Naim, a former Venezuelan minister and the editor of *Foreign Policy.* "During this decade the world has been under the impression that there was a clear and robust consensus about what a poor country should do to become more prosperous."[21]

This was a recycled version of trickle-down economics, with growth given greater weight than income distribution and social objectives. The underlying hypothesis was that policy reforms designed to achieve efficiency and growth would also promote better living standards, especially for the poorest.[22] The social costs of structural adjustment were inconvenient but temporary; in any case, they were inevitable in order for countries to return to more rational and viable economic structures: TINA—There Is No Alternative!

Alternatives may have been difficult, but there were also weaknesses in the orthodox approaches. Cutting government expenditures often meant cutting back in key areas such goals as education and health, and often worsening poverty and income distribution. Although undoubtedly there were areas of waste and inefficiency, public expenditures in most developing countries, in relation to GNP, were only about half the level in industrialized countries. Thus, when in the early 1980s the IMF recommended policies that heavily cut public expenditures, both physical and human investment was also reduced. Economic growth often came to a grinding halt. For many countries in sub-Saharan Africa and Latin America this was a period of stabilization and "adjustment without growth."

This was also the period in which Latin America transferred some $100 billion (between 1982 and 1984) to Northern Hemisphere banks.[23] Often savings and adjustment did not actually result in additional investments to stimulate economic development. Instead, they went straight into the bottomless pit of debt servicing and sometimes to direct savings abroad. The burden of adjustment was borne by debtor governments, in contrast to the approach proposed by Keynes some forty years earlier. The poorest of the poor were often affected, as they had less margin of maneuver. For the very poorest people in each country, the burden became intolerable. The commercial banks and creditor governments responsible for the enormous jump in the real rate of interest largely escaped. Indeed, they often benefited financially from net capital inflows from developing countries. Meanwhile, per capita income in Africa fell to the level of the 1960s, while in Latin America, on average, it regressed to levels that had prevailed at the beginning of the decade (see Table 5.1).

In the mid-1980s a second phase was started with the intention of achieving "adjustment with growth." In one of the Mexican "deals," in December 1985, it was explicitly agreed that if economic growth fell below a certain level, more capital inflows should be forthcoming. But this was not how adjustment has been practiced.

Although the IMF took the lead role, adjustment policies were pushed by the other international financial institutions (IFIs)—the World Bank and the regional development banks—and with the active support of practically the entire bilateral donor community. The UN largely remained on the sidelines.

When the consequences began to be clear, unease grew. UNICEF took the international lead, along with the ECA and a few scattered initiatives from others. Few would have expected the counteroffensive to emanate from an organization charged with care for children and mothers. But children were precisely those

Table 5.1. Evolution of GDP per Capita in Selected Regions, 1950–2000

Region	Per Capita GDP (US$ 1980)					
	1950	1960	1970	1980	1990	2000[a]
World	1,253	1,649	2,247	2,701	3,035	3,259
Developed market economies	4,133	5,609	8,178	10,192	12,637	15,010
Economies in transition	957	1,528	2,556	3,907	4,609	3,108
Developing countries	303	413	564	755	881	1,166
Latin America	936	1,208	1,610	2,144	1,986	2,154
North Africa	452	590	1,284	1,452	1,378	1,514
Sub-Saharan Africa	419	500	584	567	476	452
West Asia	1,839	2,246	3,510	4,277	2,794	2,839
South and East Asia	191	232	297	433	643	842
Mediterranean	603	934	1,390	1,953	2,096	2,084
China	96	179	205	299	619	1,300

Source: Development Policy Analysis Division of the UN Secretariat, based on Statistics Division of the UN, National Accounts Statistics, and other national and international sources.
[a] Estimates.

hardest hit by the events and misguided policies of the 1980s. In its *Adjustment with a Human Face*,[24] UNICEF argued that adjustment policies should safeguard the vital needs of a country's population. This approach went far beyond traditional concepts of social welfare and security. It sought to expand the basic rationale of economic policy to put human concerns and people at the center of development. It went back to the concepts of human investment and basic needs in an important attempt to construct a bridge between the old and the new orthodoxies.

The UNICEF study showed that the economic shocks and inappropriate adjustment policies of the 1980s had resulted in declining investment in health, falling school enrollments, and often rising malnutrition. Adjustment was necessary, but a different sort of starting point was the human consequences. They should not be viewed as unfortunate but inevitable by-products of adjustment. Rather, protecting and advancing the human condition should be treated as the essential challenge. Improving levels of nutrition and other basic human needs should be made as much part of the objectives of adjustment as improving the balance of payments, reducing inflation, and increasing economic growth.

The UNICEF study pointed out the three essential components of a broader approach to adjustment. The first was an acknowledgement, in the goals of adjustment policies, of concern for basic human conditions, including a commitment to protect the minimum nutrition levels of children and other especially vulnerable groups in a country's population.

The second was a broader approach to the adjustment process itself, including at least four elements: maintaining a minimum floor for basic needs, related to what the country could sustain in the long run; restructuring the productive sectors—agriculture, services, and industry; relying more on small-scale, informal sector producers and ensuring their access to credit, markets, and other requirements to stimulate growth in their incomes; and restructuring within health, education, and other social sectors to ensure cost-effectiveness and maximum coverage from constrained and reduced resources. In part, the task amounted to doing more and better with less. More international support for social aspects of adjustment was also stressed, including the provision of more aid, flexibly provided and for longer-term commitments.

The third was a system for monitoring nutrition and other key indicators of the human situation during adjustment. As UNICEF put it, "We should be concerned not only with inflation, balance of payments and GNP growth, but also with nutrition, food balances and human growth. The proportion of a nation's households falling below some basic poverty line should be monitored and treated as one of the relevant statistics for assessing adjustment."[25] Jacques Polak, the former director of research at the IMF, recalled that his own managing director was much taken by *Adjustment with a Human Face:* "Camdessus was very much influenced by this. The Fund got pushed in that direction, initially, I think, by this UNICEF report and similar reports. And the managing director pulled this little card out of his pocket when he addressed the annual meeting this year, and read out those seven pledges on development."

Why were so many of the UN family absent in this debate? This is one of the key questions that will be probed in future volumes. After all, the common element of the UN itself and its specialized agencies is and was their human focus. This is not absent from the programs of the World Bank and the IMF, but it is certainly less marked there than within the stated mission of the UN system. Bringing together these various UN institutions in support of some form of coherent commitment to the human dimensions of adjustment would be a crucial means for strengthening long-term development. This would imply, however, that the UN family itself is united in agreement on such a strategy and, while working with the World Bank and the IMF, presents a united front in pressing the case for more human concerns and priorities. It is important to explore the conventional wisdom in Washington and the reactions by the UN system.

The Drawbacks of the Current Orthodoxy

The UNICEF counter-argument was eventually accepted, at least in principle. It is interesting in this connection to quote the World Bank's *World Development Report 1990*:

> Many countries experienced macroeconomic difficulties in the 1980's as the debt crisis and international recession brought structural weaknesses into the open. But when structural adjustment issues came to the fore, little attention was paid to the effects on the poor. Macroeconomic issues seemed more pressing, and many expected that there would be a rapid transition to new growth paths. As the decade continued, it became clear that the macroeconomic recovery and structural change were slow in coming. Evidence of declines in incomes and cutbacks in social services began to mount. Many observers called attention to the situation, but it was UNICEF that first brought the issue to the center of the debate on the design and effects of adjustment. By the end of the decade the issue had become important for all agencies, and it is now reviewed in all adjustment programs financed by the World Bank. As UNICEF advocated, attention is focused both on how adjustment policies affect the poor and on the specific measures that can be taken to cushion the short-term costs.[26]

However, the World Bank has not always applied the good intentions laid out in its prose. In the early 1990s, with the end of the Cold War, one could observe an evolution of the mainstream discourse from a narrow economic one into a somewhat more flexible one that encompassed globalization and, later, poverty reduction at least as a goal. The new discourse beginning in the early 1990s is based on the idea that integration into the global economy is the only rational way to sustainable growth and prosperity. Thus, the highest priority shifts to include competitiveness and flexibility. The IMF, for example, argued that "to put themselves on a path of convergence with the advanced economies, developing countries must align their policies with the forces of globalization."[27] Deviation from the objective of global integration in the world economy was viewed as a sign of conservatism or nonmodernity that could jeopardize the achievement of sustainable growth and improvement of living standard of the population as a whole.

However, the combination of the current orthodoxy and of globalization often seemed to result in a dual process of integration and exclusion. It tended to marginalize regions, countries, social groups, and individuals who were not positively integrated in the new global economy and found it difficult to exploit the opportunities created.[28] In the mid-1990s, in particular with the preparatory work for the World Summit for Social Development in Copenhagen, UN organizations became more and more cognizant of the processes of pauperization and exclusion. The ILO emphasized that "rather than eliminating or attenuating differences and inequalities, the integration of national economies into a global system has on the contrary made those differences and inequalities more apparent and, in many ways, more unacceptable."[29] The UN Research Institute for Social Development (UNRISD) also pointed out this contradictory process of simultaneous inclusion and marginalization, where the incorporation of a large number of people around the world in an affluent global society was linked with processes that profoundly restrict the life chances of many.[30]

Twenty years down the road, it is more and more recognized that orthodox policies have three basic traits. They are crisis-prone. They are deflationary. And they stimulate the spirit of speculation. The crisis-prone system is obvious from the "lost decade" of the 1980s that was followed by the Tequila crisis in Mexico and Argentina (1994–95), the Asian crisis of 1997–99, the Russian debacle in 1998, and the Brazilian crisis in early 1999. In between, we witnessed attacks on the British pound ("the billion of Soros"), the Italian lira, and countless other currencies. Joseph Stiglitz—until December 1999 chief economist of the World Bank and formerly chairman of the Council of Economic Advisers (CEA) under President Bill Clinton—came to the conclusion that financial and capital liberalization can be an important source of macro-instability and financial shocks.[31] Something must be done about the free flow of money, and in particular of "hot money," as part of the problem of short-term capital and the concentration of foreign direct investment in a few countries.[32]

Implementation of the current orthodoxy often is so deflationary and slow-growth for poorer and weaker countries as to become anti-growth. This may come as a surprise, but data on economic growth—worldwide, and by income group—demonstrate a systematic slowing down of rates in all groups (excluding China) between 1970 and 1998. Table 5.2 also demonstrates very heterogeneous growth performances measured in percentages among low- and middle-income countries in the 1980s and 1990s. Asian miracle countries experienced very high growth rates during this period. But they were the countries that did not follow orthodox prescriptions. Sub-Saharan Africa and Latin America implemented massive structural adjustment programs but experienced extremely low growth in the 1980s and are recovering slowly in the 1990s. Moreover, most of Eastern Europe and the countries of the Commonwealth of Independent States (CIS) faced sharp economic declines during their dramatic transitions toward a market economy in the 1990s (see Chapter 6).

Table 5.2. Average Annual Growth Rate of GDP, 1970–1998

	Growth in GDP (%)		
	1970–80	1980–90	1990–98
World	3.6	3.2	2.5
High-income countries	3.2	3.1	2.3
Middle-income countries	5.5	2.6	2.2
Upper middle-income countries	5.9	2.8	3.9
Lower middle-income countries	5.1	2.3	-0.8
Low-income countries (except China and India)	4.4	4.1	3.7
Low- and middle-income countries	5.2	3.3	3.5
Sub-Saharan Africa	3.8	1.6	2.3
East Asia and Pacific	6.9	8.0	7.9
South Asia	3.5	5.8	6.1
Eastern Europe and Central Asia	5.4	2.4	-2.9
Middle East and North Africa	-	2.0	3.0
Latin America and Caribbean	5.2	1.7	3.6

Sources: World Bank, *World Development Indicators 2000* (Washington: World Bank, 2000), 184, Table 4.1; and *World Development Report 1995* (Washington: World Bank, 1995), 164, Table 2.
Note: The world by income per capita: Low ($760 or less), lower middle ($761–$3,030), upper middle ($3,031–$9,360), high ($9,361 or more).

Growth was always promised as one of the results of structural adjustment, but it has often failed to materialize. After two decades of structural adjustment, more than seventy developing countries still had levels of GDP per capita in 1998 below the levels that they had achieved many years earlier. Using the latest World Bank data on GDP per capita (in 1995 U.S. dollars), peak levels were achieved by twenty-five developing countries in the 1970s, thirty-nine in the 1980s, and eight in 1990.[33]

Perhaps the most telling illustration of this argument comes from Latin America. The cumulative average reduction of real wages during the 1980s had been 50 percent. Between 1990 and 1995 the average drop was "modest," only a further 10 percent (see Figure 5.1).

This should not surprise the seasoned observer if it is remembered that the priority policy objectives within the mind-set of today's economic orthodoxy are the fight against inflation, the reduction of financial deficits restoring external balance, and liberalization. More employment-intensive economic growth and

Figure 5.1. Real Wages in Latin America, 1980–96
(Index 1987=100)

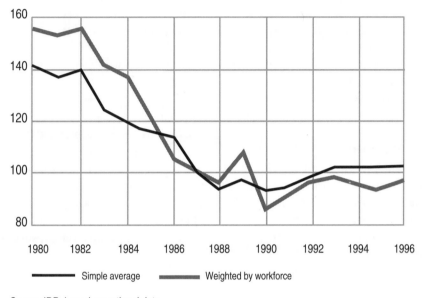

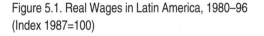

Source: IDB, based on national data.

poverty reduction are seen as automatic by-products. In spite of the lip service paid to them, they are not central.

Current policies (especially the liberalization of capital flows) stimulate speculation more than entrepreneurship. Incentives point to emphasizing the short-term, easy gains and to gambling, both of which in part are fostered by the uncertainties of a highly volatile marketplace. Many enterprises that produce manufactured goods have established financial services in order to participate in today's casino of global finance.

Why, then, it could be asked, was there such unalloyed optimism about this set of economic and financial policies as the best approach to the future of the world economy, at least until the Asian crisis in 1997? Even today, following the faster-than-expected recovery, optimism remains high among the governments of industrialized countries. The essential explanation results from the choice of indicators by which success and failure are measured. The prescriptions emanating from conventional neo-liberalism are successful if measured by such "abstract" indicators as inflation, external balances, debt ratios, and financial deficits. These Maastricht- or Washington-consensus criteria lead to a different view of success and failure than do those associated with the new social questions—a combination of traditional and contemporary social problems. Using criteria that capture such flesh-and-blood considerations as persistent poverty, unemployment, income distribution, and global crime would lead observers to different judgments.

The overall growth rates in the West also need to be dissected. For example, individual incomes in the United States for the great majority have decreased in real terms since 1973 and have only recently picked up.[34] Moreover, income distribution has worsened, as in most other countries.[35] For family income to remain at a decent level, more than one income earner is now the norm. The media trumpet fortunes made on the New York Stock Exchange, but almost 20 percent of Americans live in poverty. European Union countries have an average rate of open unemployment of 10 percent, and rates are higher yet in the large economies of Spain, Italy, France, and Germany.[36] This is the case despite the recent upsurge of economic growth in these countries. Real unemployment (including a lot of hidden unemployment) would be even higher. The recent decline in overall unemployment in Europe has not been accompanied by a change in long-term prospects for the chronically unemployed.

The situation in developing countries and those with economies in transition is more dramatic. To have some seventy countries with per capita incomes lower than they were eight or more years earlier can hardly be described as sustained economic growth. As for countries like Hungary or Poland—categorized as successful reformers—60 percent and 54 percent, respectively, of their populations thought that their living conditions were worse in 1997 than they were ten years earlier.[37] Until recently one could always point to East and Southeast Asia for stupendous economic and social results. But as observed earlier, it was rarely mentioned that these countries did not apply the current orthodoxy. They pursued their own way.

Moreover, there are the serious social consequences of current economic and financial policies, including globalization, that have given rise to what is called the "new social question." We illustrate its emergence by advancing eight propositions.

(1) Globalization is private sector–driven; regionalization is public sector–driven. The growing globalization of markets for finance and goods is being realized by private firms that function increasingly worldwide. It owes very little, if anything, to governments. On the contrary, when in March 1957 the Rome Treaty creating the European Common Market was signed, there were six heads of state or prime ministers sitting around the negotiating table with no private-sector rep-

resentatives in sight. The same can be said about the creation of the South American Common Market (MERCOSUR) and the North American Free Trade Agreement (NAFTA), although for latter business was more visible. In a sense these parallel activities demonstrate that the public sector at present is running several laps behind the private sector, in spite of a head start.

(2) Globalization is sharpening the intensity of competition and competitiveness. Competition is increasingly being seen as the only solution for survival, as well as the panacea for many social problems. Countries compete for capital, and companies compete for markets. And people are often affected by the intensity of both forms. If there are high levels of unemployment, the response is to become more competitive. If poverty is widespread, growth enabled by increased competition is once again the answer. However, extreme competition diminishes diversity in a society and contributes to social exclusion. Individuals, enterprises, cities, and nations that are not competitive are marginalized or excluded from the global economy. As systems lose their variety in this way, the more they lose the capacity to renew themselves. The Latin root of the verb "to compete" (*competere*) means "to seek together." This is a far cry from what competition is becoming in the global era.

(3) Technology, one of the engines of globalization, cuts as a two-edged sword. There was a time when futurologists explained the wonders that technology would have in store for individuals, enterprises, and countries alike. Francis Fukuyama, in a burst of technological evangelism, emphasized the path to "limitless accumulation of wealth" and "an increasing homogenization of all human societies."[38] People would be able to produce more with less labor and earn more by putting in fewer hours of work — Utopia, many thought at the time. But Utopia is here today. Societal restructuring has not kept pace with economic and technological restructuring. Labor markets, educational systems, and pension and tax regimes are largely as they were thirty years ago, whereas the economy and technology have changed dramatically.

(4) Orthodox, neo-liberal policies have not solved the old, outstanding social problems of unemployment, poverty, and income distribution. In fact, they have frequently intensified them. Life expectancy and school enrollment rates have improved in the world as a whole (although Eastern Europe has gone in the opposite direction), and East and Southeast Asia have done better than other countries (until recently). However, with respect to crucial indicators like unemployment, poverty, and income distribution, the situation has deteriorated in an unacceptably high number of countries.

(5) A new social question has arisen, which has two components. The first is the intensification of the "old" social problems. The second is the emergence of "new" elements — including international criminality, growing urban dualism,

new forms of international "migration" very often linked to civil wars and lack of economic opportunity, and drugs, which itself has become a global industry.

(6) The world has entered into a period of global wealth in the midst of increasing national and individual poverty. In spite of the hyperbole surrounding the increasing number of millionaires and even billionaires, almost half the world survives on the equivalent of less than $2 per day, and hundreds of millions of people are worse off today than they were ten or even twenty years ago. The absolute number of people living in poverty continues to increase in many parts of the world. Global enterprises are privately owned and in the business of profit making. They will, therefore, locate their multifarious activities in such a manner as to minimize costs (including paying taxes) and maximize profits. At the same time, the combination of neo-liberalism and globalization have given rise, as we have seen, to a growing social and economic vulnerability for a large part of the globe's population. It follows that while enormous global wealth is being created, the income of many governments is declining at the very moment that they require additional resources to pay for the increased financial outlays necessitated by the new social question. Globalization can be a very positive factor that contributes to the creation of wealth. Everyone is affected by it; many feel its negative aspects in their daily lives; and few really benefit. Globalization has given rise to a new distribution problem leading to social fragmentation and the loss of social cohesion.

(7) Mega-cities, particularly in the South, have become "Romes without Empires." Although rural exodus began long before globalization, the latter has exacerbated the problems of increased open unemployment and squattering. Mega-cities breed crime and waste resources, for instance, by travel to and from work. There has developed an urban question within the new social question, which has many dimensions — including poverty, housing, health, unemployment, slum areas, crime, drugs, street children, and quality of education. The urban question amounts to more than the sum total of the different problems just enumerated. It is difficult to calculate the "value added," but it certainly has a lot to do with the quality of life, or the lack of it, in urban settings. Common problems can be observed in urban conglomerates worldwide. The most important include growing inequalities, spatial and social fragmentation, and informalization leading to the phenomenon of "cities divided against themselves." The fundamentally social character of the urban problem is clear because poverty, social exclusion, and marginalization have become structural.

(8) There is no equivalent of social support at the regional and global levels. At the end of the nineteenth century capitalism had combined dynamic economic opportunity with persistent social problems at the national level. Extreme riches existed side-by-side with appalling poverty. It took strong and imaginative lead-

ership from German Chancellor Otto von Bismarck (hardly a progressive) to start building a national welfare state to balance the power of the market, to construct an income floor below which no one was allowed to fall, and hence to ensure a more equitable distribution of income. States were strong, and decision making mattered in a world economy that was largely organized along national lines. The private sector became somewhat less free, limited by social regulation.

Now, a century later, globalizing markets are giving private enterprise the freedom that their national counterparts had at the end of the nineteenth century. Thus, at the beginning of the twenty-first century a paradoxical situation has arisen, but this time at the global level. An economy propelled by energetic and dynamic global enterprises is booming, while many states grow poorer and have to shrink the welfare fabric that has been patiently constructed over the past decades, particularly since World War II. In many respects, a countervailing power is required for the planet. Overlooking for the moment the man's more bellicose aspects, what is now needed is a "new Bismarck," acting on a global scale to redefine the economic responsibility of states and the social responsibility of the business community and to develop a vision steering these two entities toward cooperation instead of cutthroat competition.

Ideas from the United Nations

The major development challenges to be distilled from the above analysis amount to a search for a new development paradigm that gives primary place to individual human beings. Such a paradigm should have concrete answers to the new social question and especially responses to the problems of poverty, gender, economic growth, employment, urban sprawl, and income distribution. How can all countries and all peoples take better advantage of the opportunities created by the technological revolution? How can negative externalities be minimized? How can societal restructuring catch up with economic and technological restructuring, given the lag between the two? How can the flourishing of local cultures be stimulated as well as their implications for variations in economic policy, for tolerance, and hence for human rights and peace? How can our environmental infrastructure be maintained? (See Box 5.2.) How can international action best be directed in support of national and regional efforts?

In the 1990s the UNDP led the charge for a more human-oriented development strategy based on poverty alleviation, social justice, participation, and employment creation. It took the lead, with others such as the UNRISD and UNCTAD also actively searching to adapt the economic and financial orthodoxy to the needs of the poorest citizens of the world (see Chapter 7).

Box 5.2. Culture and Development

For many decades culture has played a shadowy role in the development debate, but rarely with the emphasis that it deserved. More often than not, it was an afterthought thrown in once economic and social policies were already firmly established.

UNESCO—belatedly but still in sight of the curve—contributed to repairing this imbalance by setting up the World Commission on Culture and Development. Chaired by former UN Secretary-General Javier Pérez de Cuéllar, the group produced *Our Creative Diversity*, which was published in July 1996. The report defines culture as a way of life, which focuses on exploring culture and development as a means of living together in peace and tolerance but also enlarging human choices. Choice becomes the essence of development and builds on the series of *Human Development Reports*.

UNESCO produced its first two biannual *World Culture Reports* in 1998 and 2000. They combined quantitative and qualitative issues in the study of cultures and cultural processes. Culture gives people a sense of identity and helps to define an individual's place in the world. It fosters trust and cooperation and thereby facilitates working together, collective agreements, and fruitful exchanges of all kinds. But above all, culture can stimulate tolerance, an indispensable ingredient of development. Tolerance cuts across numerous issues, including attitudes toward immigrants and strangers, ethnicity, patience, and an understanding of "others." Most of the internal barriers to successful development are related to culture and education. The *World Culture Reports* cut across a broad spectrum of issues touched upon in UN world conferences, including the information and communication revolution; the link between human development and culture; the vexed questions of participation, empowerment, and rights; and the urban question.

They also touch upon—but do not elaborate sufficiently—the important problem of Western values and worldwide development. Western ethnocentrism has been the implicit culture of developmental theory. For a long time—and to this very day—equating development to modernization and modernization to Westernization has been very much the conventional wisdom. One of the paradoxes accompanying globalization is that local peculiarities are more in evidence than previously. Could it be that globalization stimulates localization? Cultural pluralism becomes more and more an all-pervasive characteristic of societies, and ethnic identification can often be a healthy response to pressures of globalization. The impression of growing global uniformity may, therefore, be deceptive as people turn to culture as a means of self-definition and mobilization.

We are discovering that globalization does not necessarily imply the spread of universal models or uniform sets of rules. In spite of French farmers' bombing a local McDonald's franchise, neither economic nor cultural homogeneity is likely. The Council of Europe has argued that a central priority is "to bring the millions of dispossessed and disadvantaged in from the margins of society and cultural policies in from the margins of governance."[39] If so, then adapting development models to the needs, institutions, history, and culture of different societies is essential.

The series of *Human Development Reports,* starting in 1990 and published an-nually, embodied precisely the critical evaluation of current orthodoxy called for in the preceding pages. These reports distinguished themselves in a number of ways.

First, they put people at the center of analyses and policy recommendations, building on the vision and creativity of Mahbub ul Haq as well as on the pioneer-ing work on entitlement and capabilities by Amartya Sen.[40] *Human development* was defined as the process of broadening choices for people and strengthening human capacities. Human development thus had a liberal-based philosophical foundation, but linked to the full range of human rights. Human development recognized the value of working with the grain of the market—while being nei-ther pure *laissez-faire* nor *dirigiste,* participation, empowerment, equity, and in-ternational justice were key concerns.

The *Human Development Report* also introduced new indicators for ranking countries in terms of their performance on human development, including the Human Development Index (HDI). Bernard Chidzero, in looking back at devel-opment over his forty years in the UN and the government of Zimbabwe, stated: "Thank God the UNDP and people like the late Mahbub ul Haq and Nobel lau-reate Amartya Sen are promoting the whole concept of human development. . . . Do we continue to define the development problem simply in materialistic terms? GDP, ten percent, fifteen percent? Even if it means there is poverty and people die early? Or do we not find new measurements of development?"

The HDI is a composite measure based on three indicators: longevity, as meas-ured by life expectancy at birth; educational attainment, as measured by a com-bination of adult literacy and the combined gross primary, secondary, and tertiary enrollment ratio; and access to resources for a decent standard of living, meas-ured by real GDP per capita (in purchasing power parities, or PPP$), with an ad-justment factor. The HDI is an alternative measure of development emphasizing the essential human aspects of life. It ranks countries from 1 to 174. In 2000 Canada was number one, the United States was in third place, and Sierra Leone came last.

In the *Human Development Report 1999* Sen recounted his initial skepticism about the merits of the HDI as an alternative indicator.[41] He agreed with the well-known shortcomings of GDP per capita as a way to measure meaningful devel-opment and with the necessity of broadening the view of development to include social and political as well as economic indicators. The problem for Sen is "to catch in one simple number a complex reality about human development and depri-vation." He quoted Mahbub ul Haq, the founder of the *Human Development Re-port*: "We need a measure of the same level of vulgarity as GNP—just one number—but a measure that is not as blind to social aspects of human lives as GNP is. Mahbub hoped that not only would the HDI be something of an im-provement on—or at least a helpful supplement to—GNP, but also that it would serve to broaden public interest in the other variables that are plentifully analyzed in the *Human Development Report.*" Sen added his view that "Mahbub got this exactly right." Sen notes, however, that the HDI is at least a fuller measure than GNP and that the *Human Development Reports* as a whole give richer and more complex information on development than simply the HDI. Indeed, they contain a broad variety of information and data on the multidimensional features of development, which provide a way to assess the evolution of human development.

Notwithstanding reservations about the HDI, it has taken its place as a widely quoted and influential indicator, which reoriented the debate on development toward human dimensions in the 1990s. It has given greater visibility to life expectancy, education, and well-being. Victor Urquidi, a young economist at the World Bank in the late 1940s and later president of the Colegio de México, recalled: "The Bank did not consider development as development. They considered it as projects. Bankable projects—that's what they called it: money for electric power development; money for railroads; money for irrigation districts. But no overall concept of what they were doing in a country in which they were lending money." The HDI has provided a new yardstick against which the impact of government policies and measures could be measured. Paul Streeten notes that "there is considerable political appeal in a simple indicator that identifies important objectives and contrasts them with other indicators."[42]

Since 1990 the HDI has been continuously refined in the light of better data and technical improvements. Refining and updating the HDI has also been complemented by adding more specific sub-indicators. Thus, there now exists a GDI (Gender-related Development Index), a GEM (Gender Empowerment Measure), and an HPI (Human Poverty Index) for developing countries, with a separate index based on more stringent standards, HPI-2, for industrialized countries.

Each *Human Development Report* has a theme, but there is consistency and continuity by viewing each issue through the lens of human development. Thus, reports have dealt with such themes as human development and human security, human development and gender, human development and globalization, and human development and human rights. They have systematically and constructively criticized the purported success of implementing the prescriptions of the conventional wisdom. Concentrating on flesh-and-blood indicators and pointing toward policies that could produce more human-oriented results have provided decision-makers and the general public with a broader perspective on the global results of neo-liberalism.

The reports have presented a great array of information on social, economic, and political features to spread awareness of human conditions in a world of unprecedented wealth. That the assets of the three richest men of the world are more than the combined GNP of all the least developed countries with their population of 600 million people is one such startling example.[43]

On an absolute scale, the international income distribution between countries has become gargantuan and grotesque. The gap between the richest and poorest countries in the world was just over 3 to 1 in 1820, 11 to 1 in 1913, 35 to 1 in 1950, 40 to 1 in 1973, and 72 to 1 in 1992.[44] We come back to the challenge of these widening global income gaps (see Chapter 7). Without a change in policies, these differences will become larger still, among other things because of unequal access to new technologies—for example, the richest 20 percent of the world's population accounts for more than 93 percent of Internet users; the poorest 20 percent, only 0.2 percent.[45]

Globalization has created tremendous riches but has also exacerbated distribution problems between and within countries (see Chapter 7). Nay-saying the unprecedented growth in the West, and especially in the United States during the 1990s, is not our point. Indeed, economic growth must be part of the global solution to world poverty. However, nationally and globally, income redistribution is also part of the solution. The industrialized countries also have their own poverty problem, as indicated by the HPI of the *Human Development Report 1999*: 16.5 percent in the United States and 12 percent in France. And even in "good" countries like Sweden and the Netherlands, different aspects of human poverty still affect an average of some 8 percent of the population.[46] The greatest challenge of the twenty-first century will be the creation of a democratic architecture that will lead to a form of good global governance, or the search for the new Bismarck (see Chapter 8).

Ideas and Concepts Spread

The UN made three contributions to rethinking conventional economic wisdom in the 1990s. The first was the series of world conferences organized by the UN system during the last decade of the twentieth century (see Chapter 4). The second was the series of *Human Development Reports,* just discussed. And the third was warning against the financial volatility and series of financial crises witnessed throughout the 1990s, ranging from the Tequila crisis in Mexico to the Russian and Brazilian crises, as argued earlier in this chapter. Indeed, in 1997—ahead of the actual downward curve of the Asian crisis—UNCTAD had predicted in its *Trade and Development Report 1997* that open and uncontrolled capital accounts would give rise to a crisis brought about by the extreme volatility in financial flows.[47] This was clearly ahead of the reactions in the Washington-based financial institutions, which were still preaching the virtues of open capital accounts.

Only in 1998 did the IMF and its member states agree that "something" had to be done about the volatility of financial flows. The turnaround in the World Bank was led by its president, James Wolfensohn, and by Stiglitz, its senior vice-president and chief economist. In January 1999 Stiglitz gave the first lecture in Helsinki sponsored by WIDER, and a few months later delivered UNCTAD's ninth Raúl Prebisch lecture. Significantly, he spoke in two forums for UN ideas—since 1985 WIDER has functioned as part of the UN University (UNU), established in 1973, and since 1964 UNCTAD has been part of the UN secretariat. Stiglitz acknowledged in no uncertain terms the failure of the Washington consensus. It had focused too narrowly on economics and resource allocation while ignoring such factors as quality of life, health standards, and education.[48] It also had failed to involve the countries and people concerned.

Although that may be a harsh judgment about the approach and results of the neo-liberal policies, it was welcomed by many UN member states as a fair evaluation of the actual impact of orthodoxy on a number of countries and certainly on vulnerable populations. Stiglitz explicitly pleaded in favor of a new development paradigm that would have a "focus on the whole" and move toward an overall "transformation of society."[49] The new development strategy should be more comprehensive. With a broader focus on overall development, such issues as health and living standards, literacy, and education should be given equal footing with capital allocation and increases in per capita income.

An environment that fosters organizational and social capital is key to development success. The *Human Development Reports* have made this point over and over again, picking up the theme from the 1960s and applying it within the perspectives of human development. Investments in human and physical capital are of the essence, and appropriate sustained development will improve the quality of life. Stiglitz stressed a point also made many times in UN debates: namely, that development must come from within. "The failure of the current orthodoxy," he said, "has proven that abstract prescriptions imposed by outside institutions cannot succeed."[50] The process for reform should evolve locally, at all levels of society. Development policies should be tailored to take into account both the public and private sectors, community, family, and the individual.

Moreover, Stiglitz also attacked the "single-minded focus on liberalization through reduction of trade barriers in developing countries." He pleaded in favor of "fair and open" trade policies on the part of the industrial countries. Without such a sense of fairness, the developing world will retreat from its reforms of recent decades. Worse still, the perception of hypocrisy reinforces the sense of unfairness. Stiglitz argued that "even as the more developed countries preach the doctrines of openness, they engage in restrictive practices. Even as they preach that countries must undertake the painful measures of liberalization—which may entail losses of jobs and industries—developed countries use antidumping and safeguard measures to protect their own industries that are adversely affected." Many welcomed a strong voice from within the Bretton Woods institutions joining developing countries and many NGOs and others who had claimed for years that industrialized countries too rarely practice what they preach when it comes to international trade (see Chapters 7 and 8).

Wolfensohn and Stiglitz were trying to nudge the World Bank and other development agencies toward policy changes in directions long advocated by the UNDP, UNCTAD, the UN's regional commissions, and the UNRISD. The World Bank's "Strategic Compact" pleaded in favor of "creating new and strong partnerships with other organizations thus enabling the Bank to be more selective and specialize in those areas where it has a comparative advantage."[51] Subsequent to these events, Stiglitz resigned in December 1999. And shortly afterward, in June 2000, Ravi Kanbur, who was responsible for leading the World Bank's work on the *World Development Report 2000,* did the same. The early drafts of this report had signaled a much more positive approach to participation, empowerment of the poor, and greater pragmatism in economic policy. The final version was toned down,[52] but the evolution is clear and a reversion to an earlier version of the Washington consensus unlikely. However, these well-publicized resignations signaled that not everyone in Washington had become a convert to the new approaches.

At the beginning of the twenty-first century and after some two decades into the current orthodoxy, the ideas and concepts advocated by such organizations as UNCTAD, the various UN regional commissions, UNICEF, the UNRISD, and the UNDP appear to be having an impact. Although more research is required to assess the results, UN ideas have begun to penetrate the consciousness and consciences of donor and recipient countries. Significantly, they have also begun to spread into the deliberations of the Bretton Woods institutions.

The IMF, together with the World Bank, agreed at the September 1999 annual meeting to put poverty reduction at the heart of the programs supported by the two institutions in the seventy-five poorest member countries. In his address to UNCTAD X in Bangkok in February 2000, Michel Camdessus, then still managing director of the IMF, acknowledged that the "market can have major failures, that growth alone is not enough, or can even be destructive of the natural environment or precious social goods and cultural values" and underlined that "if the poor are left hopeless, poverty will undermine the fabric of our societies through confrontation, violence, and civil disorder. We cannot afford to ignore poverty."[53]

Within this new comprehensive strategy for poverty reduction, the World Bank—along with the regional development bank and UN agencies—will discuss with national authorities the design of policies aimed at poverty reduction. Meanwhile, the IMF will seek to ensure that "these social and sectoral programs aimed at poverty reduction can be accommodated and coherently financed within a supportive, growth enhancing, low inflation, macroeconomic and budgetary framework."[54]

The World Bank has been continuously rethinking its overall development approach in light of the slow and uneven progress in poverty reduction and the social tensions that have been associated with it. The new framework developed jointly by the World Bank and the IMF is based on the recognition of the convergence between a respect for fundamental ethical values and the search for efficiency required by the market. Wolfensohn defined this framework as "a holistic and integrated approach to development strategies and programs that highlights the interdependence of all aspects of development strategy: social, human, institutional, environmental, economic and financial."

The *World Development Report 2000* proposes an attack on poverty on three fronts: ensuring empowerment of the poor by increasing their voice and participation in decision making, and managing the growth of inequalities; providing security against shocks at the individual and national levels, and for those left behind by rapid change; and creating opportunity for the poor by putting in place the conditions for sustainable economic expansion, to provide the material basis for poverty reduction. At the beginning of the new millennium, perhaps a new development orthodoxy is emerging. There is evidence of a vision more closely shared by the UN and the Washington-based financial institutions. The newly shared vision is not without irony, as former ILO Director-General Francis Blanchard noted: "What is surprising, without being encouraging, is to observe today, 25 years after the World Employment Conference, the World Bank's and the IMF's taking up poverty themes and adopting the language that the ILO has used since 1976."

Globalization is in many respects inevitable and an important engine for creating global wealth. In principle, it can be positive for many countries, rich and poor. But globalization requires a human face to address new threats to human security and new social problems. The policy prescriptions emanating from the dominant neo-liberal orthodoxy, even as modified, are not inevitable, nor are they the only path toward globalization. The search is on for alternative routes that benefit all people.

In his background document for the September 2000 Millennium Summit, UN Secretary-General Kofi Annan argues that "the central challenge we face today is to ensure that globalization becomes a positive force for all the world's people, instead of leaving billions of them behind in squalor." It is difficult to disagree. At the same time, many still feel that the UN is missing an opportunity to reassert itself as a significant and independent player on the field of economic and social policies. By seeking consensus with the private sector and OECD and close working relations with the IFIs, the value added by the UN in developing an alternative paradigm may be threatened. As mentioned at the outset, the so-called Washington consensus reflects the ideas of the major Western financial powers and the Bretton Woods institutions. A new "consensus" to tackle the new social questions must embrace the views of all groups of countries and a wider range of stakeholders, including NGOs, multinational corporations, and trade unions.

6

The Socialist Bloc's Collapse

- **Strengths and Weaknesses of the Socialist Model**
- **Transition Time: One Leap or a Crawl?**
- **Ten Years into the Reforms**
- **Would the ECE Approach Have Helped?**

Although it was not long ago that we watched dramatic televised images of men and women destroying it with their bare hands, somehow the fall of the Berlin Wall in November 1989 seems like ancient history. Vehement discussions about the transition period that took place in the early 1990s have faded. It is even difficult to remember the main lines of the different strains of arguments that confronted one another in those days. Since we have already witnessed the end of the end-of-history debate,[1] perhaps a quick reminder is in order.

Advice given to Eastern Europe by such Western experts as Jeffrey Sachs, Olivier Blanchard, and David Lipton largely followed neoclassical economic lines that had come back into vogue during the 1980s: free prices, remove subsidies, open up economies to international trade, free convertible currencies, privatize state-owned companies, open invitations to foreign investment, close inefficient plants, and retire redundant workers. It was recognized that such policies would involve costs — higher prices, unemployment, lost income, and more foreign debt and servicing. But, so it was argued, these costs would be short term and more than offset by longer-term benefits accruing from freer markets.[2] These experts urged that their recommended reform packages be adopted quickly and completely — which went by various labels including "big bang," "one leap," or "shock therapy."[3]

At the same time, other analysts insisted that a market economy was not a panacea for all economic ills. There would be a tortuous route toward the adoption both of a pluralistic democracy as a system of government and of the free market as a system of economic management.[4] Although the transition from a centrally planned to a market economy appeared, on the surface, to be composed mainly of practical problems of management, many observers argued that this in fact was not the case. They believed that a complete and rapid transition was

impossible and also undesirable.[5] There were neither preexisting appropriate theoretical solutions nor models for the momentous changes under way. An institutional structure for the new approaches would need to be built, often as a first
step. Gradualists emphasized the need for an original path of transition based
on a country-specific sequencing of policy measures.

This lower-decibel school argued in favor of recognizing the essential characteristics and internal weaknesses of Eastern European economies; it also expressed
doubts about continued public support for a reform process that would involve
hardships of unknown magnitude and unpredictable duration. It warned Eastern European leaders to think twice about the wisdom of exposing their still fragile democracies to shock therapy that might amount to economic free fall. Rather
than building economic sand castles, the adherents of this school argued that it
would be preferable to examine different models. Those that had met with solid
elements of success were found more easily in East and Southeast Asia than in the
Western Europe and North America of the 1980s.

This minority school realized that Eastern Europe confronted unprecedented
problems of the economics of transition. A panoply of questions arose when moving from a centrally planned economy—in which the ownership of the means of
production and the land are concentrated essentially in the hands of the state—
to a market economy—in which the ownership of the means of production and
the land are in private hands. What is the best means to privatize an economy?
To whom does one sell the enterprises? With what money will people buy shares?
Where can the new managers of privately owned companies be found when none
has been trained for the type of activity and, even worse, no one has actually exercised such skills in the past fifty to seventy-five years? What about competition?
What is the most effective way to liberalize foreign trade? What types of management tools are available for a new market economy–oriented government?

This second school also suggested that similar questions could and should be
asked about agriculture. The problems of ownership in the primary sector—as
well as in the industrial, services, and real-estate areas—should be settled before
governments embarked on wholesale or even small-scale privatization. In the
Soviet Union in the 1930s and in most Eastern European countries in the late
1940s, industry, services, and agriculture were nationalized with no compensation
for former owners. In the framework of formulating a business code and reestablishing commercial law in these countries, therefore, the status of former owners
should be settled first.

Moreover, the socialist bloc's transition from one economic system to another
entailed very different problems from those faced by the bulk of developing countries. The world had neither sufficient practical experience nor theoretical insights
for these immensely complicated challenges.

The World Bank, the IMF, and the European Bank for Reconstruction and De-velopment (EBRD) were closer to the "one leap" or "big bang" school. The UN— and more particularly its ECE—was closer to the second school. The former, however, became policy. As problems with the great leap began to appear and transitions extended with little light at the ends of tunnels, the second approach received more attention. The UN with its more pragmatic, less dogmatic approach may once again have been ahead of the curve.

Before examining the political and economic consequences of transition in Eastern Europe, we first look at the strengths and weaknesses of the old model prevailing in the former Soviet bloc. We then provide a more detailed look at the proposals for transition to a market economy propagated by the UN. The chap-ter ends with a provisional evaluation of where we stand after the first decade of transition.

Strengths and Weakness of the Socialist Model

After a decade in the dustbin of history, one can easily overlook the achieve-ments of the Soviet Union and the socialist countries of Eastern Europe. They had achieved substantial economic growth of net material product well into the 1970s. In the early years of Soviet and centralized planning, authorities grappled with the serious problem of urban unemployment and extremely low-productivity em-ployment in rural areas. The strategy was to link employment policy to a program of rapid industrialization. That is, the attainment of full employment became a by-product of the priority accorded to industry. This was a distinctive feature of employment policy, not only in the USSR but in other socialist countries as well.[6]

According to the official statistics, in all socialist countries except Yugoslavia open unemployment was virtually eliminated by the 1950s. In subsequent years a combination of a shift of labor out of agriculture, increasing female partici-pation in the paid labor force, and the coming of age of children born in the post-war baby boom ensured that labor bottlenecks did not arise until the 1960s.[7] In other words, the economic development pattern pursued by these countries until then was extensive rather than intensive. Economic growth came about by at-tracting more and more people into the labor force at relatively low levels of pro-ductivity. In short, full employment, a core goal of communist regimes, had been purchased at the price of low productivity.

By the 1970s the development of socialist economies had reached a stage of ap-parent labor shortage. This meant a change toward labor-saving techniques, effi-cient allocations, work incentives, and the sectoral composition of output and investment. Economic reforms had to be implemented to respond to emerging new problems in employment linked to the achievement of full employment and

were used (and often misused) by major economic powers in developing countries. This "impatient" group included the IMF, the World Bank, many Western experts, and the new leadership in several countries of the region. A more deliberate approach, or "crawl," was appropriate because Eastern Europe's crisis went back farther than 1945. Successful modernization was not a quick fix but demanded setting up appropriate institutions, careful trade liberalization, substantial inward transfer of resources, free access to major markets on which export-oriented growth could be based, and a sensitive treatment of the complicated heritage of "social welfare." This more deliberate school was represented by the ECE and by a number of individual experts. Let us examine these two schools in more detail.

Shock Therapy

The main organizing principle for the rapid integration of postcommunist regimes into the global economy has been through the adoption of what goes by the labels of the "Washington consensus," particularly in Latin America, or the "Maastricht consensus" in Europe. Leading proponents included Harvard University's Jeffrey Sachs and Central European politicians such as Leszek Balcerowicz and Vaclav Klaus.[14] For instance, the Czechoslovak comprehensive reform program of 1990 reflected this approach.[15] For the IMF, the "countries with economy in transition," as they came to be called, should reverse the inward-looking legacy of central planning and seek to catch up with a world economy whose performance has demonstrated the benefits of open international economic relations.

The Bretton Woods institutions assumed that implementing orthodoxy would be necessary and sufficient for shifting from an inefficient planned to a more efficient market economy.[16] Two main arguments framed this approach. First, stabilization would create the conditions for sustainable growth that in turn would increase the welfare of populations through trickle-down. And second, privatization and liberalization should be undertaken instantly, even if the institutional framework was absent, to create irreversibility and incentives for market forces. In fact, the neglect of institutions and the mistaken belief that, for example, the existing banking system could function combined with an overestimation of the state of productive infrastructure. It was, therefore, assumed that the appropriate regulatory and competition framework would be progressively and automatically introduced as a byproduct of the market. Transition economies should concentrate on trade and capital flows, liberalization, private ownership, and the private sector as the engines of growth.[17]

For the first few years of transition, the shock-therapy school did not accord priority to social policies. The assumption was that social problems were temporary and would improve after the return to sustained economic growth. Macroeconomic stabilization was linked to reform of the socialist welfare state, which was considered "irrational" and "premature."[18] Several targeted social policies were promoted as safety nets for those in dire straits, but access to social-protection benefits became restricted, and subsidies for basic products and services abolished.

There were obvious political considerations behind this school. Its partisans argued that it was essential to make a clean break with the past and to take maximum advantage of the "window of opportunity" created by the euphoria following the Berlin Wall's collapse. Eastern European reformers, the Bretton Woods institutions, and individual international advisers argued that it was imperative to exploit an exceptional moment to reach a point of no return in the process of transition. Radical, systemic changes were possible during the time period when there was strong popular support for transformations. Indeed, the historical context was purportedly unique and marked by strong expectations of long-repressed populations for a better life. Hence, the deterioration in living conditions was accepted as temporary and linked to the necessary changes viewed as prerequisites for "healthy" growth.

At the beginning of transition, people strongly supported the shift to anti-egalitarian and pro-market policies because, so they thought, this would give them access to opportunities with higher economic rewards. The shock therapists were particularly worried that more gradual reforms would give time and opportunity to conservative forces to block or slow reform processes and to restore vested interests.

A More Cautious Approach

Instead of rushing to global integration, the ECE argued in favor of enlargement and convergence toward the European social model. In April 1990, less than six months after the fall of the Berlin Wall, most of the themes that have been developed since were placed before the commission's members in the *Economic Survey of Europe 1989–1990*. In particular, the Western ECE members experienced considerable consternation with the call for a Marshall Plan for Eastern Europe.[19]

The following year's report was more restrained. The *Economic Survey of Europe 1990–1991* emphasized the extreme complexity of the reforms to be implemented.[20] It pointed out that the transition from a centrally planned to a decentralized market economy would be longer and more tortuous than the partisans of the shock therapy had imagined. This early publication by the ECE, when the dust had hardly settled from the demolition of the Berlin Wall, was an explicit critique of the relevance and desirability of shock therapy. In light of subsequent events, it appears prescient.

The ECE argued that "political, ethical and emotional questions are inextricably intertwined with purely economic issues"[21] and stressed the need for a wide social backing for the reform program in order to maintain a social consensus in favor of the shift to the market. It understood and emphasized the lack of political consensus in countries such as Russia and Yugoslavia and the possible consequences for economic reforms. The ECE stressed the inevitable painful effects of transition on the population. It warned in no uncertain terms that without a greater consensus, the prospects for sustained change were slight. The ECE was not alone. In the early 1990s many academics pointed to the risk of undertaking simultaneous economic and political reform; economic recession was seen as a major threat to democratic stability.[22] They posited that the dramatic social cost of the shock therapy would produce disruptive social tensions.

The ECE framework for the transition in Eastern Europe focused on comprehensiveness (how much to change), speed (how to introduce change), and sequencing (what to change first). It stressed the importance of careful sequencing to take into account the degree of consensus and the technical and organizational capacities of the administrative structures to sustain reforms. The ECE underlined the contradictions between speed and comprehensiveness, which, in extreme form, could be mutually incompatible and erode the support of populations. It also suggested the need for a country-specific approach that differed greatly from the uniform transition mold applied by the Bretton Woods institutions.

The ECE survey presented a set of reforms to implement at the outset: property rights, macroeconomic stabilization, price liberalization, micro reforms at the enterprise level, the establishment of a commercial banking infrastructure, trade and foreign exchange liberalization, creation of social safety nets, and labor market changes. Afterward came reforms with a lower priority, including current account convertibility, the establishment of legal instruments and institutions, easier foreign investments, and a more competitive environment. Finally, the ECE proposed changes that simply could not be addressed in the short term, including large-scale privatization, the creation of an adequate regulatory environment and of capital markets, and reform of the pension system.

The ECE was explicitly cautious about shock therapy. In such cases as Poland, where stabilization and the legal framework for a market economy could be achieved rapidly, large-scale privatization, the creation of competitive markets, the enforcement of tough budget constraints, and efficient public service would take considerably longer. The ECE's focus on social consensus resulted largely from the analysis of the failure of the draconian reforms implemented in the former Yugoslavia. The federal reform package for the introduction of a fully fledged market economy in the medium term never found deep support from the republics and fell apart as a result of the centrifugal political forces and political manipulation.

Awareness of possible social and political unrest largely explains the ECE's gradualism. In contrast, shock therapy implied separating the economic sphere from the political, social, and cultural. As one reflects upon the role of ideas and missed opportunities, the ECE approach provides some grist for analytical mills in light of the subsequent implosion of the former Yugoslavia and the unraveling of the social fabric in the fifteen independent states created by the dissolution of the former Soviet Union (including armed conflicts in Azerbaijan, Armenia, Georgia, Moldova, Tajikistan, and Russia itself).

A clash in ideas was not unusual. However, what was unusual was the extent to which virtually all financial resources chased the one-leap approach and none the more tailored ECE approach. The ECE had no resources of its own and was unable to mobilize support for its ideas. Advice without financial leverage is rarely taken seriously. The question arises as to whether there was anything so peculiar in the UN's processes of discussion that led to a better informed but less feasible line of analysis. Was there something in the very structure of its multilateral functioning that made its analyses less extreme, but also less convincing?

To what extent did the "culture" and standard operating procedures of the ECE make their analyses more in tune with local conditions? From the outset, the UN commission had to adapt itself continually to ideological confrontations between East and West. Under the leadership of its first executive secretary, Nobel laureate Gunnar Myrdal, the ECE developed technical capacity and emphasized pragmatic responses to the needs of its member states. The aim was to make it possible for governments from very different politico-economic systems to work together at an expert level and to join forces. No matter what the philosophical differences, they could address such common problems as trade and scientific cooperation.

After refusing to participate in the Marshall Plan, the socialist countries actually boycotted the ECE for the first decade of its existence. But the secretariat's technical, or non-ideological, approach made it possible to include relevant information from the East. In 1955 membership increased from eighteen to thirty countries, and gradually better dialogue and better-informed research became possible. In particular, the regional commission promoted independent data gathering, notably through the publication of the *Economic Bulletin for Europe* and the *Economic Survey of Europe*. It was logical that analysts with firsthand exposure to problems and data were in a better position than ideologues were to provide comprehensive looks into the conditions and prospects of Europe as a whole. It is possible that the necessity to examine all sides made the ECE more able to resist becoming "born again" neo-liberals in the 1990s.

The legacy of Myrdal was independence, long-established contact with governments across ideological divides, sensitivity to different values, and staff expertise. As such, this regional commission developed an open and eclectic style that permitted some of the only East-West economic cooperation during the Cold War.[23] In short, it played an important bridging role. This story, as well as the distinctive cultures of other regional commissions, will be explored in a future volume from the UNIHP, to be edited by Yves Berthelot.[24]

Ten Years into the Reforms

Everyone agreed in the short term that stabilization and adjustment would lead to recession and social dislocations. The debate was about how long and how severe the recession and about how disruptive the social dislocations would be.[25] The proponents of shock therapy asserted that the duration would be short and the costs bearable.

Their forecasts turned out to be wrong. Both the economic recession and the social costs turned out to be deeper than anticipated. "The results have been dismal," summarizes Bill Maynes, former editor of *Foreign Policy* and former U.S. assistant secretary of state for international organization affairs. "Tens of millions of people are being pushed out of the Second World into the bottom of the Third."[26] Output and employment slumped to a degree unknown in Europe since the Great Depression. During the early 1990s output fell by about one-quarter on average, unemployment reached unprecedented proportions, and poverty increased massively throughout the region. In spite of differences in phasing—the Polish economy recovered more quickly—large degradations in living conditions occurred in these countries in transition.

Although estimates of poverty varied widely, there was general agreement about the magnitude of its increase during the first half of the 1990s. The total number of people living in poverty rose more than tenfold between 1988 and 1994 in transition economies of Eastern Europe and the former Soviet Union: from 14 million to more than 119 million, which raised the percentage of the population living below the poverty line ($4 a day in 1990 PPP$) from 4 percent to 32 percent.[27]

The rise of poverty was uneven by country. Between 1988 and 1995 the poverty headcount ratio rose from around 6 percent to 20 percent in Poland, 6 percent to 59 percent in Romania, 1 percent to 29 percent in the Baltic countries, 2 percent to 50 percent in Russia, and 2 percent to 63 percent in Ukraine. Increases were modest in Central Europe (the Czech Republic, Hungary, Slovakia, and Slovenia), where the poverty incidence rose from less than 1 percent to 2 percent.[28] However, even in these countries, populations with low incomes (defined as those earning 60 percent of the average wage of 1989) increased dramatically. By 1995 they had reached 27 percent in the Czech Republic, 31 percent in Slovakia, and 23 percent in Hungary.[29]

Poverty has struck mainly the unemployed, the working poor, and retirees. In all of the transition economies, the link between the evolution of the labor market and poverty is clear. The sharp increase of unemployment, and especially long-term unemployment, largely underlies the increase of poverty. At the same time, the fall of real wages and the development of low-wage jobs led to the emergence of a large group of working poor. Between 1989 and 1995 real wages declined by 55 percent in Russia, 63 percent in Ukraine, 40 percent in Bulgaria, and 25 percent in Poland.[30] Many of these figures were compiled at the Innocente Centre in Florence, a UNICEF initiative with some support from the World Bank.

Children under fifteen years old have been the first victims of the breakdown of the socialist welfare states and the return of economic insecurity. The rising cost of transportation had a negative impact on school attendance, especially in rural areas. The reduction in state expenditures also affected nutritional levels. When the price of hot school meals provided by the state increased, fewer children had access to subsidized meals. Moreover, extracurricular free artistic and sport activities vanished for a great many of the region's children.[31]

Further evidence that poverty is increasing is also provided by changes in indicators of "income inadequacy" and "inability to pay."[32] The number of recipients of social assistance has increased, often dramatically. Evidence of a growing inability to pay can be deduced from rising delays and accumulating arrears in the payment of rent, electricity, gas, and water charges as well as from the settlement of mortgage payments and from the number of evictions and house repossessions. In the Russian Federation, where the percentage of the population living below the poverty line had decreased somewhat during the 1995–1997 period, the financial collapse of 1998 led to a sharp increase of that percentage, which reached almost 40 percent by the beginning of 1999.[33]

Small wonder, therefore, that during the first years of transition the UNDP's Human Development Index deteriorated dramatically. For the region as a whole, it stood at 0.625 in the 1960s, 0.838 in the 1980s, and then dropped to 0.75 in 1997.[34] In selected cases, life expectancy itself fell dramatically.

There is now consensus that the recession has been much deeper and longer than expected by the one-leap school and that the transformation has not delivered the promised benefits. This dramatic divergence between expectations and reality has been at the heart of the turnaround in the political climate in many countries of the region. Indeed, and as the gradualists had cautioned, recycled communist parties have made electoral comebacks in Poland, Hungary, Bulgaria, and Romania (see Box 6.1).

Besides the breakdown in the socialist welfare guarantees, several other interrelated factors explain this large and largely unexpected deterioration in human welfare. There are, for instance, the poor conditions, policies, and performance

Box 6.1. Democracy and Dissatisfaction in Selected Countries

The ECE forecast about the risk of diminishing consensus related to the implementation of shock therapy was on target. Indeed, the electoral successes in Poland (in September 1993) and in Hungary (in May 1994) by ex-communist parties or by a party with a distinctive leftist orientation like the Czech Social Democratic Party (in May 1996) only a few years after the beginning of the transition can be attributed in great part to the loss of basic social rights established universally by the now defunct socialist systems. In a 1999 Czech sociological survey, 27 percent of the voters believed that the Czech Communist Party would be able to take proper care of the poor, as compared with only 10 percent for the Social Democrats and 3 percent for the Civic Democrats.[35]

A Polish study found that 87 percent of the population felt that they had no influence over public policy.[36] There is a growing feeling of helplessness and disenchantment among citizens.

According to the Central and Eastern Eurobarometer,[37] between 1990 and 1994 positive replies concerning satisfaction with the functioning of markets dropped from 47 percent to 20 percent in Hungary and from 47 percent to 26 percent in Poland. Similarly, satisfaction with democracy dropped in both Poland and Hungary during the same period. In Poland 52 percent judged that their economic situation in 1999 was bad. Only 10 percent thought that it was good, and 41 percent thought the situation would get worse. These results capture the profound economic insecurities of daily life. Indeed, 50 percent judged that their household financial situation had worsened after the reforms, while only 11 percent felt that it had improved.[38]

A central problem is that such a large part of the population judges that their economic situation is unlikely to improve. Despite the return to positive growth in most Eastern European countries (except Yugoslavia and Romania and to a lesser extent Croatia and the Czech Republic), the average rate of unemployment in Eastern Europe at the end of 1999 was at its highest level since the beginning of the transition (close to 15 percent, or some 7.6 million people). The emergence of massive unemployment has been one of the greatest shocks during the transition. According to a labor force survey in Poland, the share of very long-term unemployment in total unemployment increased (over two years) from 13 percent to 20 percent.[39]

Social fragmentation is weakening the social consensus about the reforms. For example, in a another 1999 public opinion poll, the support for the pursuit of European Union (EU) membership in Poland had fallen to 55 percent in 1999.[40] The IMF has become aware of the feeble social basis underlying global integration: "The challenge therefore is how to minimize the tensions between globalization and the pressures for socialization of risk. If such tensions go unaddressed, the danger is that the domestic consensus in favor of open markets will ultimately erode and trigger a generalized resurgence of protectionism."[41]

"inherited" from the socialist era. Part of the decline in consumption and the increase in poverty are due to the suppression of inflation and artificial job creation imposed earlier.

Moreover, the external environment in which transitions occur has been far from favorable. The dissolution of the Council on Mutual Economic Assistance (COMECON) and the rapid elimination of oil and raw material subsidies in 1990 and 1991 produced large negative terms of trade shocks for all of the countries in the region (with the exception of Russia and Romania), but particularly for Ukraine and Bulgaria.

Policy design problems, particularly severe in view of the fragile initial conditions, have aggravated already complex conditions. The rigorous but orderly macroeconomic adjustment introduced in a few countries was required and unavoidable, and it has been preferable to spontaneous and confused adjustments. But the same cannot be said for the policies of simultaneous price and trade liberalization, large currency devaluations, and instantaneous privatization. Contrary to the misleading image implicitly suggested by the metaphor of shock therapy (a short and sharp jolt leading to a rapid, if painful, solution to economic maladies), this approach does not, cannot, and did not bring quick fixes.

In addition to being controversial, the one-leap school lacks historical precedents and has been ineffective. It raises credibility problems for the whole reform process and carries a heavy risk of aggravating the severe economic problems inherited from the past. The large annual increases in poverty rates have been directly linked to a large and unexpected "price overshooting" linked with simultaneous price and trade liberalization and exchange rate depreciation.

At the opposite end of the spectrum, failure to adhere to and maintain a modicum of fiscal discipline and macroeconomic balance or to introduce, at a human pace, much-needed structural reform (provision of greater incentives, privatization, and social reforms) should also be included among serious policy-induced problems. The continuation of lax monetary and fiscal policy is no solution to structural change, as underlined by the failure of the 1992 and 1993 stabilization programs in Russia and Ukraine. It certainly does not represent an alternative to the approach criticized above. While "shock without therapy" and continuous postponement of needed structural reforms may keep a surge of unemployment at bay in the short run, this approach has inflicted huge welfare costs on many weaker social groups through crippling hyperinflation.

Furthermore, and this factor has been less emphasized in the literature, another cause of the drop in welfare—particularly during the first five years but also beyond—relates to institutional vacuums and administrative weaknesses following the demise of the socialist model in Eastern Europe. What is underscored here is not so much the lack of new national economic institutions necessary for the functioning of a capitalist economy, or the breakdown of the former international socialist institutions, especially COMECON. Rather, the most troubling aspect may well be a more diffuse, less visible, but highly pernicious weakening of the social, administrative, and regulatory institutions that is causing considerable human and social costs even beyond those caused by more explicit economic factors.

The general problem is the abolishment of old institutions and rules of the game without having adequate substitutes in place or even on the drawing boards. For instance, many cultural and leisure associations for youth have been weakened or disappeared, while only a modest number of new community-based, religious, or even business-oriented institutions have been created. Restrictions concerning the freedom of movement and the importation of alcohol were lifted, but no parallel effort was made to address the exacerbated problems of vagrancy, alcoholism, and crime.

The elimination of nursery facilities for children of working mothers along with the drop in preschool enrollment rates and participation in much-needed summer camps for children can be explained by economic factors. But they also partly reflect the abrupt dismantling of services previously funded and provided by state enterprises. Along with child care, health and educational services have collapsed. Fewer girls are finishing school now than ten years ago. The number of working women has fallen by 25–40 percent within the region. As an opening sentence in a *New York Times* feature about the follow-up to the Beijing women's conference put it: "If anybody has borne the brunt of the changes in Eastern Europe and the former Soviet Union since the fall of Communism, it has been women." The article concludes that "women have not benefited from any economic gains," and "they appear to have disproportionately shouldered the stress brought by a total change of life style."[42]

Finally, there is ethnicity and fragmentation. The problems beleaguering various parts of Central and Eastern Europe spill over into neighboring countries. Large numbers of political, ethnic, and economic refugees are moving across the region and into Western Europe, which inevitably means considerable costs, including possible outbreaks of contagious diseases. Refugees in the region are estimated to number some 1.3 million without counting those from Kosovo and Chechnya. And economic migrants have burgeoned in the 1990s, legal and illegal. The push of war and the pull of economic opportunity are concrete indicators that all has not gone well with the transition.

Would the ECE Approach Have Helped?

It is fruitful to compare the ECE's recommended approach with what actually was implemented that emanated from the Bretton Woods institutions. From the comparison, seven points are particularly salient.

First, the ECE emphasized the crucial role of robust institutions and capacity building in the transformation toward a market economy. It also advocated careful sequencing. In retrospect, the approach followed was overly focused on destroying socialist institutions and insufficiently concerned with taking the requisite time to introduce and nurture appropriate institutional replacements. Ironically, there is now an emerging consensus that liberalization and privatization should be accompanied by appropriate institution building. As Joseph Stiglitz has pointed out: "All too late, it was recognized that without the right institutional infrastructure, the profit motive—combined with full capital market liberalization—could fail to provide incentive for wealth creation and could instead spark a drive to strip assets and ship wealth abroad."[43]

Second, one of the important outcomes of the Russian crisis has been to dampen the unabashed enthusiasm for the primacy of macroeconomic stabilization over microeconomic and institutional reforms. The potential inflow of foreign investment was vastly overestimated. In fact, most former socialist bloc countries have seen virtually no inflow of private resources—about 90 percent of foreign direct investment has gone to three countries (Poland, Hungary, and the Czech Republic).

Third, the advocates of shock therapy have tended to blame national reformers and their lack of aggressiveness for the failure of reforms. The culprit was not the design of reform, they argued, but its weak implementation. But as shown above, the one-leap approach failed to grasp the core elements that are prerequisites for a healthy market economy: institutions, fair government, and measures against monopoly and corruption. The lack of attention to these factors contributed to the weakening of the state through the development of corruption and rent seeking, while strengthening a contemporary version of "robber barons" who have been the big winners in privatization, especially in Moscow. Privatization can technically be done quickly, but the Russian case showed its ineffectiveness without an adequate institutional and regulatory framework, and a legal system. When rapid privatization results in the reallocation of state assets to former communist *apparatchiks* and state enterprise managers, there is little likelihood of a successful transition to an efficient market economy. Spontaneous privatization—for example, in Hungary, where it has been especially strong—was conceived as a vehicle for specific social groups to retain their former privileges. Privatization provided, especially in Russia, an "additional instrument by which special interests could retain their power."[44]

Fourth, a basic error of shock therapy was an insufficient appreciation for the necessary role of the state in development. State intervention as previously practiced by socialist governments was quite correctly identified as a major constraint to development. But there was too little attempt to think about possible synergies between state and market, to identify necessary public infrastructure. Clearly, the state has an important role not just in providing public goods but also in establishing the rule of law and regulatory frameworks. At the heart of any transition process, a complex mix of constraint and consent is required, which even the World Bank began to argue beginning with its *World Development Report 1993*. The analysis in Washington came full circle by the 1997 report, whose subtitle was *The State in a Changing World*. But the damage from the original ideas had already been done.

The irony is that precisely at the time when a well-functioning state was needed most, the reformers had dismantled the existing apparatus, weakened its legitimacy, and pushed for a withdrawal of many of its responsibilities. The problem was not so much to reduce the role of the state, although this was essential, but to restructure it in order to promote crucial functions in a market economy. The presence of a corrupt public administration and its lack of transparency have led to a vicious circle, leading in turn to a crisis of legitimacy of the state, but without any of the social benefits that had formerly been in its province, and to a "Wild West" atmosphere of quasi-lawlessness.

Fifth, it was assumed that the countries with economies in transition would react in the same way as industrialized capitalist economies to measures recommended by the advocates of shock therapy. The stabilization package promoted by the IMF was based on the assumption that supply responses would be broadly similar to those in developed capitalist countries. This was contrary to the ECE approach, which, in line with the lessons of the reconstruction after World War II, emphasized the importance of sequencing and of creating adequate breathing space for governments to implement sustainable reforms. At the same time, the regional commission was aware that the challenge of transition in the former socialist bloc was very different from the one faced by Western Europe after the war. Getting the global strategy right was more important than the volume of financial resources was. More particularly, the ECE stressed the need for country-specific reforms rather than a universal model that fails to reflect adequately the peculiar social and political strengths and weaknesses of target countries.

Sixth, the ECE underestimated the capacity of populations in Eastern Europe to endure the painful social impact of transition as well as their long-suffering patience. With the exception of the former Yugoslavia, massive political breakdown or even instability was not the rule. Indeed, populations have remained patient and channeled social discontent largely through democratic instruments. As noted earlier, this has resulted on quite a few occasions in the return of former communists to power. Contrary to predictions,[45] however, their return has not reversed the reform process in Poland, Hungary, Bulgaria, and Romania. The new democracies have survived; and so far the dramatic costs of transition and the

brutal deterioration in living standards have taken place without major social instability. They have proved to be crisis resistant despite ominous predictions. But
the jury is still out.

Seventh and finally, the ECE and the shock therapists alike emphasized that
popular support was linked to a specific but relatively short-lived period of euphoria. The shock therapists argued that this meant quick action. The ECE asked
instead how consensus could be maintained once the costs of adjustment became
more evident and onerous. It saw shock therapy as provoking dramatic social consequences that would render problematic most attempts to reach political and social consensus about future reforms. In a brief retrospective of the first five years
of reform, the ECE concluded that "popular reservations about the market reforms also pose a serious challenge to the international community, which should
read them not simply as symptoms of impatience and naïveté on the part of East
European population but as the reflection of real social distress and often disori-
entation—conditions which call for more not less cooperation and solidarity with
the transition economies."[46] The ECE survey of 1991 had already emphasized the
two main constraints affecting the speed and extent of implementation: the need
to preserve or build a consensus and to introduce country-specific reforms. Effectiveness and sustainability seemed more important than speed for the success of
the transition process.

As the number of potential donor countries and international organizations
has multiplied, it is increasingly difficult to coordinate bilateral and multilateral
efforts. There is no basic community of interest or experience, as there was in the
Great Depression, the Second World War, or the subsequent economic and political instability in which the Marshall Plan was introduced.

Why did the ECE approach not prevail? Why was shock therapy more palat-
able? The answer does not lie in the quality of ECE's analyses. Arguments began
shortly after the fall of the Berlin Wall. And the 1991 survey, *The Hard Road to the
Market Economy,* was more thoughtful and on target than the conventional neo-
liberal arguments were. There was support among some academics and Eastern
European research institutes, but in general they were not the people employed
by the IFIs or the European Union.

At the official level, the lack of support had several causes. First, the ECE is a
small part of the UN system with no financial resources to back its ideas, which
were flying in the face of the new triumphalism of the West. Second, Western governments were more interested in getting their own houses in order, particularly
by reducing deficits, than in providing the financial support for the transition in
the East. Third, many officials in the new governments of the East were anxious
to distance themselves from the past, and those proposing shock therapy had re-

sources. Fourth, there was very little support from the UN itself in New York. Fifth, the European Community (EC) took particular offense at the ECE's insistence that EC assistance was inadequate, incoherent, and badly coordinated.[47]

New ideas do not win public and professional support on the basis of cultural sensitivity and analytical merits alone. Victor Urquidi, former president of the Colegio de México and a development analyst for the past fifty years, commented on the tendency to overlook the need to tailor development policies: "It is very much the idea that you hit upon a model, an experience, maybe you have an econometric study to show that it is a good thing, which is full of assumptions. Then, you go on to sell it to other countries, saying, 'This is the way it worked over there, it will work here.' And it doesn't. Development is much more complicated." In speaking of so-called experts, he recalled: "They always came to say, 'This is the way that we did it in Mauritania, and this is the way you can do it in Puebla.' Well, Mauritania is not Puebla."

At the beginning of the transition, or "honeymoon," there were strong expectations and enthusiastic Western support for ambitious projects foreseeing rapid and radical transformations and instant results. Resources were marshaled by the European Union, the United States, and the Washington-based financial institutions. At the outset, decision-makers in Eastern Europe itself, pursuing reform, underestimated the complexity, duration, and difficulties of the transition process as well as the consequences of market failures along the road to transition. They paid too little attention to the foundations for an efficient market economy and especially to corporate governance, social and organizational capital, and institutional and legal structures. There is now a consensus that liberalization and privatization should be linked closely to institution building. The initial optimism about a rapid transition has, however, all but evaporated.

The actual experience of ten years of transition is summed up in Table 6.1, which shows above all the extent of "free fall." The contrast of low-growth countries in the CIS and Southeast Europe with the better performers in Central Europe highlights the difficulty of attaching a specific value to any reform strategy. Analysis shows no discernable correlation between shock therapy and growth. Of the three countries now having the strongest and steadiest records of economic growth,[48] Poland was the first to implement shock therapy. But we also see Hungary, which until 1995 followed a more gradualist path to stabilization, and Slovenia, which was criticized some years ago for the slowness and incompleteness of its reforms. At the same time, the economic situation of the Czech Republic— which chose the shock-therapy route to macroeconomic stabilization in the early 1990s—deteriorated dramatically in 1998–1999 and is now in the midst of a recession.

Table 6.1. Ten Years of Transition in Eastern and Central Europe and the Former Soviet Union
(GDP, Industrial Output, Employment, and Unemployment), 1989–1999

	Real GDP (Indices, 1989 = 100)				Real Gross Industrial Output (Indices, 1989 = 100)				Total Employment (Indices, 1989 = 100)				Registered Unemployment (Percent of Labor Force)			
	1989	1993	1996	1999	1989	1993	1996	1999	1989	1993	1996	1998	1988	1993	1996	1999
Eastern Europe[a]	100	79.0	90.3	95.2	100	61.4	73.8	77.9	100	82.6	82.7	83.1	<1%	14	11.7	14.6
CETE–5 [b]	100	85.0	98.1	109.0	100	70.4	86.3	100.4	100	83.3	85.5	87.4		13.3	11.2	12.5
SETE–7 [c]	100	68.5	76.7	70.8	100	47.0	53.9	42.1	100	81.7	78.9	77.1		15.1	12.5	16.6
Baltic states	100	58.2	58.8	65.4	100	44.4	38.9	40.7	100	89.0	80.1	80.5	<1%	4.5	6.4	9.1
CIS	100	70.4	55.0	55.5	100	68.3	48.8	52.1	100	94.2	89.7	87.4	<1%	3.6	6.6	8.4
Ukraine	100	68.0	41.4	39.3	100	81.9	48.7	51.2	100	94.1	91.3	87.9		0.4	1.5	4.3
Russian Federation	100	71.9	58.2	57.6	100	64.7	47.5	49.7	100	93.7	87.2	84.2		5.5[d]	10.0[d]	12.3[d]

Source: ECE, *Economic Survey of Europe 2000* (Geneva: ECE, 2000), no. 1.

a (CETE - 5) + (SETE - 7).

b CETE - 5: Central European transition economies: Czech Republic, Hungary, Poland, Slovakia, and Slovenia

c SETE - 7: Southeast European transition economies: Albania, Bosnia and Herzegovina, Bulgaria, Croatia, Romania, the former Yugoslav Republic of Macedonia, and Yugoslavia.

d Based on Russian Federation Goskomstat's monthly estimates, according to ILO definition.

In summary, the performance of some of the advanced reformers results from a combination of initial conditions, geography, history, external conditions, and the choice of a specific reform strategy. Moreover, it is important to emphasize the extent to which the prospect of enlargement of the EU has provided an incentive for Eastern Europe to implement structural reforms, whereas countries from the CIS had no such carrots dangling in front of them. Indeed, the requirement of the "*acquis communautaire*" to join the EU has shaped both reform programs and their timetables.

Apparently the ECE was too far ahead of the curve. Both scholars and practitioners are fond of counterfactuals, and we are led to conclude with a double "what if?" If ECE recommendations had been taken seriously, would economic and social outcomes have been different? But would the West have been any more inclined to provide the estimated $45–$50 billion of financial support that the IMF and the World Bank had called for? We are tempted to answer the former with an affirmative but the latter with a negative response. Ironically, both the ECE and the Bretton Woods recommendations can be seen as economically rational and politically impossible, albeit for quite different reasons.

7

Widening Global Gaps

- • **The Facts**
- • **Action or Inaction and the United Nations**
- • **Conclusions**

Today's world is very different from the world of 1945, when the United Nations began. Developed countries have become consumer societies, enjoying a widespread level of prosperity beyond anything available or even imagined when the UN Charter was signed. Global consumption has risen sixfold since 1950. Living standards have soared, benefiting at least 1.5 billion people, especially in North America, Europe, and East Asia. An increasing number of people in developing countries now live at levels comparable to those in the industrialized world. This is in line with the bold recommendations of the first major UN report on development, *Measures for the Economic Development of Under-Developed Countries* (see Chapter 1). In fact, achievements have been far in advance of what was generally believed to be possible, within fifty years of this report's publication.

In cultural and in communications terms, the world has also changed beyond recognition. In 1945 most intercontinental mail still went by boat across the seas, and radio communications crackled with uncertainty. There were no jet airplane services, and the cost of travel and telegrams limited them to a few people or a few words. Television had yet to arrive as a mass medium, let alone a medium with global outreach.

Today, in contrast with 1945, some part of the population in all countries is integrated into the global economy and culture. Businesspeople, government officials, civil society activists, artists, musicians, and academics act out an important part of their lives on a global stage. International marketing firms advertise to "global teens" — 300 million or more fifteen- to eighteen-year-olds in countries across the globe who share pop culture and cyberspace, who soak up many of the same videos and music, and who provide a huge market for designer running shoes, T-shirts, and jeans. Global awareness and interconnectedness have become immediate realities for many in the world, especially for the younger generation.

There is scarcely a corner of the planet that today is out of reach by cellular phone or e-mail. Even those who are unconnected are increasingly aware of what they are missing.

What is true for culture and communications is true also for many other technological advances as well. In crops and pharmaceuticals, transport and construction, industry and services, the face of production has changed beyond recognition. Scientific discovery, new materials, and genetic engineering have created a global-knowledge economy, displacing workers and others mired in "old-fashioned" ways who cannot adjust to or keep up with the pace of change.

The global economy has created a modern phenomenon of shrinking space and time, and of disappearing borders. As the links grow closer and faster, the gaps between the connected and the unconnected also grow wider, nationally and internationally. For all of the opportunities and benefits of globalization—which have made possible much of the progress just described—the world has become ever more unequal in many respects. It has grown more unequal in terms of the gaps between the poorest and richest countries, and very often between the poorest and richest people within those countries. The irony and tragedy are that these inequalities have grown so much just as advances in communications are spreading global awareness of them.[1]

In areas other than culture, communication, and technology, change in the world also has been much faster than anticipated a half-century ago. This has been true for education (see Table 3.2), although quality has suffered frequently. Access to basic health care has also improved, leading to longer life expectancy, even if the absence of a focused AIDS policy creates a devastating threat to life expectancy in many countries (see Box 7.1). Change has also been faster in decolonization, economic growth during the 1950s and 1960s, and the fulfillment of human rights in the 1980s and 1990s.

Box 7.1. HIV/AIDS: The United Nations behind the Curve

Today, in sixteen countries, all in sub-Saharan Africa, more than one adult in ten is infected with HIV. In seven of those nations, one adult in five actually carries the deadly virus. In Botswana, 36 percent of adults are infected; in Zimbabwe, 25 percent; in South Africa, 20 percent.

The world is gradually becoming more conscious of the magnitude of the problem. "We are at the beginning of a pandemic, not the middle, not the end,"[2] the director of the White House Office of National AIDS Policy stated. Alas, it is too late for the thirty-five million people now living with HIV and AIDS, and for the many who will follow. Indeed, the number of new infections is estimated at 15,000 a day, and growing. Member states of the UN have set as a goal to cut new infections among under-25-year-olds by 25 percent by 2005, but even that difficult feat would not stop the toll from doubling and doubling again in the near future.

Early in 1986, many in the WHO and elsewhere still regarded AIDS as an ailment of the promiscuous few. It was Jonathan Mann who convinced Halfdan Mahler, then the WHO director-general, that AIDS was not merely another infectious disease. It flourishes in, and reinforces, conditions of poverty, oppression, urban migration, and social violence. Discrimination is not just an effect; it is the root cause of the epidemic.

Mann persuaded Mahler that a pandemic was in the making, and so Mann was put in charge of a special program on AIDS. The UN seemed on its way toward moving abreast or even ahead of the curve. However, after Mahler's retirement in 1988, the WHO's AIDS program was slashed, financially and otherwise, by the new director-general, Hiroshi Nakajima. Mann resigned in protest and pursued his crusade from Harvard University, until his tragic death in a plane accident in September 1998.[3]

By 1990 the sense of urgency about AIDS in industrial countries had begun to wane. New drugs and other preventive measures meant that AIDS was no longer seen as the same threat to the West as it had been earlier. At the same time, it is hard to overlook the incompetence of ministries of health in many developing countries. The WHO was laggard in building on its promising start, and it was not the only UN agency to be so. UNICEF's efforts, which had been dramatically scaled up from 1991 to 1993, were subsequently displaced when priorities shifted to other mid-decade goals. The UNDP successfully argued that the approach must go far beyond bio-medical needs, but it failed to mobilize resources for an alternative strategy. UNFPA remained largely reactive, and HIV/AIDS concerns in most other UN agencies remained marginal.

By the middle of the 1990s, donor governments began to push for the creation of a joint UN/AIDS program, which was initiated in January 1996. However, in the first years of the program, the resources and personnel devoted by the participating UN organization were not much increased, and in some cases were actually reduced. And many donors failed to be as active in supporting the program as they had been in pushing for its creation.

By 1999, deaths from HIV/AIDS in Africa had surpassed all other causes of deaths in Africa. With increased advocacy and media attention, the priorities in the UN shifted. At the end of 1999, the UN Secretary-General convened a high-level meeting with participants from the most affected countries, donor countries, major NGOs, industry, and the major UN agencies. He pressed for a specific plan—elaborated as the International Partnership on Aids in Africa, with specific goals and milestones. A month later, U.S. Vice-President Al Gore articulated Washington's position before the Security Council, in a meeting called to address Africa's desperate social problems threatening security. Gore said: "Today, in sight of all the world, we are putting the AIDS crisis at the top of the world's agenda. We must face the threat as we are facing it right here, in one of the great forums of the earth—openly, boldly, with urgency and compassion."[4]

Unfortunately, to date the story of AIDS is a different story from that of smallpox (see Box 2.1). Of course, the clarity of understanding regarding the virology and epidemiology of smallpox was a precondition for its eradication. Nonetheless, the HIV-AIDS story is one of waking up after the disaster has struck.

However, there have been many other domains where progress has been disappointing at best. Many of the weakness are captured and symbolized by widening income gaps—globally, regionally, and nationally. This chapter examines global income disparities—that is, income distribution among countries—that in fact are a microcosm of other gaps.

The Facts

In sub-Saharan Africa, a large part of the population still lacks access to the basics of education, health, reasonable diet, and shelter, in spite of costly structural adjustment policies undertaken by most countries to integrate the global economy. The number of people with estimated incomes below US$1 a day rose from about 240 million to more than 290 million between 1990 and 1998 (see Table 7.1). As a result of substantial progress in Asia, the number of people living on US$1 a day, worldwide, fell slightly from about 1.3 billion in 1990 to 1.2 billion in 1998. This is a disappointingly slow and uneven progress over the decade of growing globalization. The poverty rate fell a little more quickly, from 29 percent to 24 percent. At the same time, the absolute number of people living on less than US$2 a day actually rose from 2.7 billion to 2.8 billion.

The facts are startling but not always simple. The gaps between the richest and the poorest countries have widened enormously over the past two centuries.[5] As a result, the United States is building a wall along its southern border. The Straits of Gibraltar are becoming the "boulevard" for Africans to sneak into the countries of the European Union, as is the Adriatic for East Europeans and Asians. In

Table 7.1. Population Living below US$1 per Day in Developing Countries, 1990 and 1998

	Number of People below US$1 per Day (Millions)		Poverty Rate (%)	
	1990	1998 (Estimate)	1990	1998 (Estimate)
East Asia	452.4	278.3	27.6	15.3
Excluding China	92.0	65.1	18.5	11.3
South Asia	495.1	522.0	44.0	40.0
Sub-Saharan Africa	242.3	290.9	47.7	46.3
Latin America	73.8	78.2	16.8	15.6
Middle East/North Africa	5.7	5.5	2.4	1.9
Europe and Central Asia	7.1	24.0	1.6	5.1
Total	1,276.4	1,198.9	29.0	24.0

Source: World Bank, *Global Economic Prospects and the Developing Countries 2000* (Washington: World Bank, 2000).

the spring of 2000, some fifty Chinese were found dead in a Dutch truck bound for Great Britain, losing their lives in a desperate effort to be smuggled across the English Channel.

Stefan Zweig's *The World of Yesterday* recounts how the author could travel to India without a passport at the beginning of the twentieth century.[6] Few were traveling over such distances then, and the deplorable living conditions in the colonies were a tale of mystery and indeed mystification. Now Westerners view televised images of hunger in faraway places, while those watching satellite TV in the shantytowns of the South and East see images of incredible riches in the West with the dollars, so it seems, growing on trees. They also see the wealthy denizens of gated ghettos in their own cities, but many believe that it is easier to move under the dollar-bearing trees than to undertake a revolution at home, at least for the time being.

Mainstream discourse on globalization in the 1990s emphasized the potential benefits from sustained growth and prosperity but neglected the sharp increase in inequalities within and among countries. Inequalities surged upward from levels that were already very high. In the new global economy, the poorest countries are not catching up with the richest, and both the absolute and the relative gaps between the two groups of countries are widening.

Table 7.2 presents the evolution of gross world product between 1950 and 2000, for the world as a whole and for selected regions. The changing gaps among regions present a mixed picture. Developed market economies have increased their already higher GDPs almost sixfold, and the sub-Saharan countries by more than fourfold, leading to the widening absolute and relative gaps referred to above. The GDP of economies in transition in the former Soviet bloc dropped by more than 40 percent in the 1990s, again leading to widening absolute and relative gaps. But there also have been important success stories since 1950: Japan, the newly industrializing countries of East and South East Asia, and more recently China have experienced sharp increases in per capita income. A small group of developing countries have sustained fast growth rates over a long period and are progressively catching up with developed countries, narrowing absolute as well as relative gaps. However, for the bulk of developing countries, per capita growth rates have lagged behind or been only marginally above those of developed countries. Absolute gaps have widened, although relative ones have not always done so. The growth differential in GDP per capita between the poorest and richest regions has widened since the 1980s (see Table 7.3). Although inequalities within countries often increased, it is this trend that explains most of growing total world inequality.

In a recent paper based on a sample of ninety-one countries, Branko Milanovic examined inequality in world income distribution (taking account of income distributions within countries and adjusting for differences in purchasing power parity among countries). Measured by the Gini coefficient,[7] it increased substantially

Table 7.2. Evolution of Gross World Product, 1950–2000

Gross World Product, Billions $US 1980

Region	1950	1960	1970	1980	1990	2000[a]
World	3,075	4,865	8,116	11,738	15,677	19,843
Developed market economies	2,326	3,562	5,791	7,858	10,352	12,919
Economies in transition	257	475	884	1,465	1,851	1,320
Developing countries	492	829	1,442	2,415	3,474	5,603
Latin America	146	250	438	744	858	1,124
North Africa	19	32	89	129	162	224
Sub-Saharan Africa	70	105	158	206	235	308
West Asia	60	98	212	364	344	477
South and East Asia	120	182	296	542	1,004	1,605
Mediterranean	23	44	79	132	169	193
China	53	118	170	298	703	1,672

Source: Development Policy Analysis Division of the UN Secretariat, based on Statistics Division of the UN, National Accounts Statistics, and other national and international sources.
[a] Estimates.

Table 7.3. Average Annual Rate of Growth in GDP per Capita (%), 1960–1998

	Growth in GDP (%)			
	1960–1970	1970–1980	1980–1990	1990–1998
World	3.2	1.9	1.3	1.0
Developed market economies	3.9	2.4	2.1	1.5
Eastern Europe and the CIS	6.2	4.2	2.3	-4.3
China	2.0	4.1	7.5	9.2
Developing countries (except China)	3.3	2.4	0.1	1.1
North Africa	8.2	1.2	-0.3	0.6
Sub-Saharan Africa	1.8	-0.4	-2.6	-0.4
Western Asia	4.1	1.0	-4.3	-0.1
South and East Asia	2.6	4.1	3.7	3.5
Latin America and the Caribbean	2.7	2.4	-1.1	1.7
Mediterranean	3.7	3.7	1.1	0.1
Least developed countries	1.1	-0.2	-0.3	0.5

Source: UN, *Global Outlook 2000: An Economic, Social, and Environmental Perspective* (New York: UN, 1990), 10; and Development Policy Analysis Division of the UN Secretariat.
Note: Gross world product is measured in US$ 1980.

in statistical terms from 0.63 to 0.66 during the period 1988–1993.[8] From a long-term human perspective, the most striking aspect of world income distribution is this large and rising disparity in incomes between the richest and poorest people in the world. Some of this results from rising inequality *within* countries—but almost three-quarters results from rising inequality *among* countries.

The long-term and widening income gap is well illustrated in Figure 7.1, which shows the income distribution between the five richest and five poorest countries over the past 180 years or so. In the first half of the nineteenth century, income distribution was only about three to one because both sets of countries had low levels of per capita income. But the richest countries took off economically, and the already remarkable acceleration really became impressive during the second half of the twentieth century. What is even more stunning is that the five poorest countries remain at essentially the same level of real income throughout the almost two centuries depicted in the graph. In other words, during the long nineteenth century (actually, until 1913) the gap between rich and poor countries stayed at a level that was "tolerable," but this gap has become a gaping abyss since 1950.

Figure 7.1. Widening Gaps between Rich and Poor, 1820s–1990s
from OECD, *Monitoring the World Economy 1820–1992* (Paris: ECD, 1995)

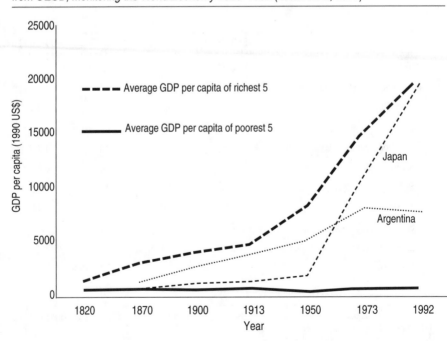

The graph also shows that there are exceptional winners and losers. Japan stayed at a level close to the poorest countries until practically the middle of the twentieth century. But during the second half of that century, it then enjoyed the most impressive economic growth sprint the world has ever seen and has now become—in spite of recent problems—one of the five richest countries in the world. Other East Asian countries have shown the same capacity for accelerated economic growth, largely because they had their own design for development policies that differed from the conventional mold (see Chapter 5). Argentina, by contrast, was one of the richest countries in the world during the first twenty years of the twentieth century and still in the top tier after the end of World War II but has lost its way since 1945. Since China—and more recently India—has been in this category of countries with accelerating growth, some two-thirds of people in developing countries have been in a position to benefit.

In addition to solid economic policies, the explanation has a lot to do with having a political commitment to development, a common enemy, and "a little help from your friends." This was the case in East Asia after losing the war (Japan) and in the divided countries (Taiwan, Korea, Hong Kong). Each of these countries was initially helped by impressive transfers of U.S. aid. We suppose that it also results from what we now call "good governance"—namely, having good policies and making good use of outside chances. But political will was essential.

This discussion has focused on growing inequalities among countries, but the same type of disturbing growth in gaps also has been occurring within countries. According to recent data compiled by the World Income Inequality Database (WIID), a joint undertaking of the UNU/WIDER and the UNDP, inequality has grown with increasing frequency since the 1980s. For the period 1947–1994 as a whole, inequality rose in 66 percent of the countries of the sample (seventy-seven, including OECD, transition, and developing countries), stopped declining in 3 percent, and declined in 29 percent (see Table 7.4).

In Western countries the media concentrate on the "new economy" and young "dot-com" millionaires, but they do not expose sufficiently the many countries and some three billion people left behind. In a global economy of some $30 trillion, this is the great failing. It is well known that important and costly measures are taken after a disaster. There are few exceptions to this rule, including the Marshall Plan.

Action or Inaction and the United Nations

The UN is by definition a global system. Thus, if there is one problem in the economic domain that it should have done its utmost to tackle, or at least publicize and mobilize behind, it is extreme and growing global inequalities. It should have done so because of the human rights and poverty eradication objectives in

Table 7.4. Growing Inequality within Selected Countries, 1947–1994

	WIDER Sample (77 Countries, Best-Fit Trends, 1947–1994)		
	% Countries	% Population	% GDP (PPP$)
Rising inequality	66	60	68
Continuously rising	33	40	29
U-shaped pattern	15	13	34
Stable–rising	17	7	5
Rising–stable	1	0	0
Slowdown in inequality decline	3	21	5
Falling inequality	29	19	27
No trend/stable inequality	2	0	0

Source: UNU/WIDER, World Income Inequality Database, 1999.

the UN Charter as well as the many other commitments taken during the series of world conferences and summits of the 1970s and 1990s (see Chapter 4).

Around 1980 the development paradigm shifted to pursue such objectives as lowering inflation and deficits in finance and balance of payments — in effect, coming full circle to an earlier paradigm (see Chapter 5). Erik Lundberg characterized the "establishment view" in the 1960s as follows:

> In the postwar period, the achievement of full employment and rapid economic growth has become a primary concern of national governments. Such policy targets certainly did not guide government activities during most of the inter-war period — instead, there were various policy aims that today would largely be considered as either intermediate, secondary, irrelevant, or irrational targets, such as the restoration or preservation of a specific exchange rate, the annual balancing of the government budget, and the stability of the price level at a prevailing or previously reached niveau.[9]

After 1980 conventional wisdom reverted to the old-fashioned religion. The pursuit of full employment and rapid economic growth was jettisoned, and older goals were embraced with a crusading zeal. We mention this leitmotif as a prelude to the discussion on action and inaction of the UN in the face of the tremendous difficulties that some hundred countries have experienced over the past two decades. The intellectual leadership in the international arena shifted from the

UN system to the Bretton Woods institutions (see Chapter 5). The UN too often reacted, standing on the sidelines and watching the match being played between the Bretton Woods' and developing and economy-in-transition countries' teams.

When it comes to the widening gap among countries, authoritative voices from the UN quantifying this gap and proposing alternative policies to attempt to remedy the situation were few and far between. This is in stark contrast to the situation in the 1940s and 1950s (see Chapter 1). There was at that time an intriguing exchange in 1952–53 in relation to the UN report *Measures for the Economic Development of Under-Developed Countries.* Herbert Frankel of Oxford University, among others, had strongly attacked the report, because it recommended the need for rapid economic development in developing countries. Arthur Lewis, one of the authors and later a Nobel laureate, replied:

> The relevance of a speed of 2 percent per annum (of per capita income) is this. We were informed that many member nations of the United Nations view with great uneasiness the increasing disparity of income between the developed and the underdeveloped world. . . . They would like to see the gap between income per capita in say, Western Europe, on the one hand, and say, India on the other hand, narrow instead of widen every day, as it does at present. This is why we asked what it would cost to bring about a rate of increase in the underdeveloped world comparable with that in Western Europe.[10]

This reaction is interesting for several reasons. First, it shows the importance UN member states attached, in those days, to closing the global income gap. Second, it reflects the belief that even a relatively modest growth rate, which was attained at least until 1973, could do the trick. Third, it indicates that reputable economics professors did not believe such rates to be feasible.

On the need to narrow global income gaps, Lewis never wavered. He was the leading economist on the Pearson Commission team that produced *Partners in Development.* The opening words of this book are reminiscent of the 1951 *Measures for the Economic Development of Under-Developed Countries*: "The widening gap between developed and developing countries is the central problem of our times."[11] In the past three decades, the gaps have widened. The *Human Development Report 1999* contains a host of statistics about the glaring and growing disparities resulting from globalization and states that "the opportunities and benefits of globalization need to be shared much more widely."[12]

Coming back to today's situation, three voices during the 1990s have spoken out most clearly against the widening global income gap: the UNDP, UNCTAD, and UNRISD.

The UNDP, through its *Human Development Report,* published annually since 1990, has quantified the gap at several occasions, perhaps most clearly in its 1998 report,[13] and proposed policies for developing and industrial countries alike in order to reduce this gap. UNCTAD has done the same, concentrating on international trade and investment measures in its annual *Trade and Development Report* and its *Least Developed Countries Report.* UNRISD, in its seminal report titled *States in Disarray,* concentrated on the social aspects of globalization resulting from relying upon measures dictated by current orthodoxy.[14] The UN Statistical Office has published data on gaps. Much of this has elicited controversy.

In successive *Human Development Reports* (which admittedly do not formally represent UNDP's opinion), the quality of governance in many developing countries has come under attack. Corruption, neglect of human development priorities, and excessive armaments expenditures had formerly been taboo but have become central in analyzing the problems and rankings of specific countries. In other words, the UNDP reports have made clear that national action is essential to capturing global opportunities in trade, capital flows, investments, and migration in order to speed up the rate of economic growth and development. But national action, however necessary, is insufficient. The widening global gaps in power and living standards and the feeble growth of the least developed countries are not only the result of national economic mismanagement and conflict. There is also the powerful impact of global tendencies toward marginalization in trade, aid, and investment as well as in management to address these issues.

But account should also be taken of the global economy in analyzing the causes of national decline and in identifying the actions needed to restore accelerated economic growth in the poorest countries. And so, issues should be considered in relation to a host of factors, including the terms of trade, the slowness of industrial countries to liberalize access to imports from developing countries, the slow pace and heavy conditionality of debt relief, declining levels of aid, and declining shares of foreign investment devoted to the poorest countries.

The importance of addressing the structural problem of declining terms of trade—which was among the first of many demands from developing countries (see Chapters 1 and 2)—can hardly be exaggerated. A World Bank report estimates that "for African countries that are not oil exporters and excluding South Africa, cumulative terms of trade losses in 1970–1997 represented almost 120 percent of GDP, a massive and persistent drain of purchasing power." It went on to explain that although grants and concessional loans had increased significantly since 1973, these amounted to "little more than the terms of trade losses." The bank added that "external factors, coupled with a failure to diversify exports and attract private capital in previous decades, lie behind the aid dependence of the 1990's." In addition, by 1997 these African countries had accumulated external debt equal to their GDP, raising their debt obligations.[15]

And so it is clear that national failures are not only to be found in developing countries. With respect to agricultural exports from the industrial countries, a

World Bank study points out that subsidies by OECD countries to their domestic agricultural sectors in 1996 were estimated at more than US$300 billion—about the same as Africa's total GDP! Removing these artificial supports would benefit Africa. Global trade in beverages, meat, and livestock products would grow greatly. Meat production in Africa could increase up to 20 percent. The World Bank estimates that if OECD countries reformed their agricultural policies, commodity prices would become more stable and real income in Africa and elsewhere would rise. The report adds that welfare in the OECD countries would also increase. This is an illustration of the challenge to global governance and global agreements. It also confirms the costs of industrialized countries' failing to practice what they preach (see Chapter 5).

The *Human Development Report 1999* reviewed the impact of debt, especially for the forty-one Highly Indebted Poor Countries (HIPCs), of which thirty-three are in Africa.[16] Only two of these countries have achieved economic growth rates of more than 2 percent per year since 1980, whereas nine did so between 1965 and 1980. Debt service payments exceed annual expenditure on health and education in nine countries, and they exceed spending on health in twenty-nine, including twenty-three in Africa. The report concludes that these countries need more support and more breathing space to restore growth and accelerate human development.

The sum required to fund the HIPC initiative has been officially estimated at US$7 billion—less than 5 percent of the US$170 billion mobilized for East Asia and Brazil in the aftermath of the 1997 and 1998 crises, respectively. The industrialized countries perceived their interests as being directly threatened by the economic turmoil in East Asia and Brazil. In contrast, the long-standing neglect of the poorest and least developed countries happens because rich countries do not perceive their interests to be at stake.

Globalization in the twenty-first century presents new opportunities as well as challenges. New approaches clearly are required to improve global governance so that all people in all countries can achieve their basic human rights. Although action must primarily rest with the people concerned in each country, improvements in global governance are also essential if the goal is to be achieved (see Chapter 8).

UNCTAD has also commented on the issue of widening income gaps. In the introduction to its 1999 overview of the situation of least developed countries, it underlines that at the end of the 1990s these countries (which have grown from twenty-five in 1971 to forty-eight today, with a combined population of more than 600 million people) have failed to derive appropriate benefits from the ongoing processes of liberalization and globalization. "Whilst the 1980's were dubbed the 'lost decade' for developing countries in general and the least developed countries in particular," the UNCTAD report argues, "the 1990's have become for the least developed countries the decade of increasing marginalization, inequality, poverty, and social exclusion. The violence and social tensions which afflict these countries are caused, in part at least, by increasing deprivation and inequality."[17] The report continues by arguing that the least developed countries are the big losers in the new global economic game. With more than 10 percent of the world's population, their share of world imports is only 0.6 percent and of world exports, 0.4 percent. Moreover, these minuscule shares represent declines of more than 40 percent since 1980, the year before the first world conference was organized in Paris to do something special to address their collective plight.[18] Table 7.5 shows the process of marginalization of sub-Saharan Africa within the global economy. Indeed, its share in world population increased from 6.8 percent in 1950 to 11.2 percent in 2000, whereas its share in gross world product decreased from 2.3 percent to 1.6 percent during the same period (see Table 7.5).

Net capital inflows into developing countries as a whole have risen more than twentyfold in nominal terms since 1970, reaching an estimated US$255 billion in 1998. Of this total, foreign direct investment (FDI) has expanded particularly rapidly. It accounted for 9 percent of capital inflows between 1975 and 1982, for 18 percent between 1983 and 1989, and for 34 percent between 1990 and 1998.[19] But inequalities in the distribution of FDI have also increased sharply. China, Brazil, and Mexico account for almost one-half of the total. Altogether, only twenty countries accounted for more than 90 percent of total net capital inflows to the South during the 1990s, whereas their shares were around 50 percent during the 1970s and 1980s.[20] In other words, more than 100 developing countries now share the remaining 10 percent. In this domain, Africa has been unable to take advantage of the new opportunities generated by the global economy. Sub-Saharan African countries' share of total FDI in developing countries fell from 11 percent in 1975–1982 to 4 percent during 1990–1998.[21]

UNCTAD has been a constructive critic of globalization and more particularly of neo-liberal orthodoxy as a panacea. The secretariat produced a comprehensive assessment in 1997.[22] It noted that average per capita income (in terms of purchasing power parity) in Africa fell from 14 percent of that of the industrial countries in 1965 to a mere 7 percent in 1995. In Latin America it fell from 36 percent in the late 1970s to around 25 percent in 1995. The report underlined the growing polarization among regions and countries leading to a transformation of the world economic landscape that is radically different from the Promised Land advocated by the proponents of deregulation and liberalization.

UNCTAD came back to this question in its 1999 annual report, and the question was a major theme at UNCTAD X in Bangkok in February 2000. This report observed that the conditions in the majority of developing countries had

should not be rationed to the lucky few, but be available to all. In this connection, the secretary-general expressed particular concern about Africa, which continues to be marginalized "despite real efforts made by African countries."[26]

During the Geneva special session, the UN system emphasized "the need for collective action to anticipate and offset the negative social and economic consequences of globalization and to maximize its benefits for all members of society, including those with special needs."[27] The dual nature of globalization was acknowledged, which has created "a world of 'winners' and 'losers' cutting across individuals, groups, nations, and even entire regions of the world."[28]

Conclusions

Here we summarize the main points made in this chapter and then review briefly suggestions made by the Bretton Woods institutions and by others. We summarize the main points in our argument as follows:

- Globalization is a positive force, but the current policies are not — and orthodoxy is changing. The search is for alternative roads to Rome.
- National policies are important and should, therefore, be adapted, in both industrialized and developing countries.
- To narrow the gaps in the global economy, improved global governance is of the essence not only to avoid instability but also to introduce social concerns and human rights, environmental sustainability, and human security.
- Urgent action is required because the gaps are rapidly becoming unsustainable; we should prevent economic and social disasters rather than take measures after they strike.

We discussed several reactions from the Washington-based financial institutions (see Chapter 5). There is a difference in views, of course. Jacques Polak, a staff member of the IMF for four decades (including as its director of research), was skeptical about the impact of the *Human Development Report:* "It's not put on the agenda of the Executive Board. I doubt many people in this building have even looked at it." In Hans Singer's judgment, however, "the World Bank and IMF have been taking over many of the original ideas developed in UNRISD and the UNDP and WIDER and UN University and in the research units of the WFP or FAO."

Our own view is closer to Singer's. The growing convergence with UN views was reflected, for example, by the joint report for the Geneva Special Session proposed by the UN, the World Bank Group, the IMF, and the OECD.[29] It is also illustrated by the speech of Michel Camdessus, his last as managing director of the IMF, at UNCTAD X in Bangkok.[30] James Wolfensohn, president of the World

Bank, has been crying in the wilderness for some time already that world poverty is taking on dramatic forms and that urgent measures should be taken. There has been a clear withdrawal by the IFIs of their earlier unqualified commitment to capital account liberalization.

There have also been a series of proposals to address the downsides of financial globalization by independent personalities.[31] We mention only a few:

- A proposal by George Soros to establish an International Credit Insurance Corporation, designed to reduce the likelihood of excessive credit expansion.
- A proposal by Henry Kaufman to establish a Board of Overseers of Major International Institutions and Markets with wide-ranging powers for setting standards and for the oversight and regulation of commercial banking, securities business, and insurance.
- A similar proposal for the creation of a World Financial Authority with responsibility for setting regulatory standards for all financial enterprises, off-shore as well as on-shore entities.
- The proposal to create an international bankruptcy court in order to apply an international version of Chapter 11 of the United States Bankruptcy Code for the orderly working out of debt.
- The proposal to manage the exchange rates of the G3 currencies through arrangements such as target zones, supported by Soros and by Paul Volcker.
- The Tobin tax to curb short-term volatility of capital movements and exchange rates.

There is thus a growing preoccupation about the social consequences and sky-rocketing inequalities resulting from contemporary globalization. The topic was on the agenda, for the first time, of the G-7 in Okinawa in July 2000. Virtually all sectors of society are aware of the problems—the private sector, academia, the public sector, civil society, and the UN, including the Bretton Woods institutions.

In many ways, however, we are all behind the curve, reacting to negative consequences rather than adopting a proactive mentality. What is, however, most striking is that so many practitioners of finance, development, and governance seem to be "out of line" and their considered recommendations to deal with the situation rejected out of hand by the powers of the land and the globe.

"What changes more often, the fashion designs coming from Paris and Milan," asks one commentator, "or the economic policy designs Washington and Wall Street prescribe for countries that are less developed or that are emerging from decades of communism?"[32] Nothing changes more rapidly than established orthodoxies. We hope that the change will come before the next disaster strikes.

8

Governance, Good Governance, and Global Governance

- • **Governance in the Early Years, 1945–1980**
- • **From Governance to Good Governance**
- • **Good Governance in the 1990s**
- • **From Good Governance to Global Governance**
- • **Conclusions**

The UN was directly concerned from its inception with four compelling ideas: peace and negotiation in place of war; national sovereignty in place of colonial status; accelerated economic and social development; and human rights (see Chapter 1). All had important implications for governance — for the objectives and operations of existing structures and for their transformation. The latter three ideas have formed the backbone of activities in the economic and social arena from the outset. Morever, since the 1990s peace has increasingly entered the economic and social arena as a condition for meaningful development.

Governance in the Early Years, 1945–1980

One of the earliest and most passionate preoccupations was decolonization. The logic behind self-determination was to move toward self-reliant structures so that people could control their own lives and countries through independent governments. In ending the exploitation of the colonized for the benefit of the colonial powers, the way was opened for government *of* the people and *by* the people. Bringing in concerns for accelerated development and human rights opened the way for government *for* the people. All of this introduced an important theme for the future work of the UN: Government *by* and *of* and *for* the benefit of each country's population was directly linked to what would later be labeled "good governance."

As countries became independent and the UN's membership burgeoned in the 1950s and 1960s, the policy and operational priorities of development rose to the top of the agenda.[1] Along with them arose the need for supporting administration in the new governments.

Many former colonies gained control of their own destinies in the 1950s and 1960s with only minimal preparations for governance. In an obvious and practical way, localization—replacing expatriates with nationals—became one of the world organization's highest priorities. Brian Urquhart looked back at the tumultuous period: "We roared into Africa the last years of the 19th Century, when nobody knew anything about it, for purely economic and imperial reasons. . . . And then, just when the Africans were making a huge effort to get used to it, we up and left within two generations. That wasn't, it seems to me, very responsible. Thus the Africans were stuck with the worst of both worlds. The original system, which in its own way had been quite effective, was gone, and they weren't used to the new political and judicial system."

Consequently, the UN was asked to provide accelerated training of nationals. Where their number with at least the basics of education and experience was insufficient, the UN provided expatriates to fill positions temporarily and also trained nationals in the country and on the job. This became the focus of the UN's early work on technical assistance, supported by the EPTA, which was created in 1949. This was more a pragmatic response than one that rested on deep analysis or great ideas. But by responding, the world organization proved to be ahead of the curve, in deeds as well as in words. Bernard Chidzero was the first black African to head a UNDP office in the mid-1960s. He later was appointed deputy secretary-general of UNCTAD before becoming the first minister of finance in Zimbabwe. According to him, one of the UN's main contributions was training and technical assistance; it played "a most constructive role . . . in promoting the independence or de-colonization process rather than simply talk, preach, make resolutions, and leave the process to take its own course."

One of the earliest expert groups organized by the UN examined in some depth what has come to be labeled "good governance." The distinguished authors of the 1951 report on *Measures for the Economic Development of Under-Developed Countries* (see Chapter 1) wrote that "the first thing that is demanded of governments is that they should be efficient and honest."[2] The experts, who included Arthur Lewis and Theodore Schultz, went on to stress that a "sufficient proportion" of budgets should be devoted to such social expenditures as education and health.

Several elements of the First Development Decade in the 1960s took further many of the specifics of "good governance." The broadening of the development agenda into such areas as land reform, urban low-cost housing, and new technologies expanded the areas where technical assistance and other support was necessary. The creation of UNCTAD reinforced the need for nationals to be well informed on issues of international trade and economic policy. Many specialized agencies developed new programs for training and technical assistance to deal with these. In 1966 EPTA and SUNFED were integrated to form the UNDP, intended to be the leader and coordinator of the UN's development efforts.[3]

From the 1960s, development became *the* work of the UN system, accounting for the lion's share of total staff and budgets. Then, as in the 1950s, the world organization was neither the only nor the main actor in the field. The United States and the Soviet Union had major programs of development assistance, and, relative to their resources, other industrial countries such as the Scandinavians were showing major interest and developing aid programs of their own. The former colonial powers—especially Britain, France, and The Netherlands—had many persons with experience and expertise to draw on. The best of the "colonial retreads" showed a ready willingness to adapt their attitudes and working styles to post-independence situations. In many cases, newly independent governments preferred to employ people who were accustomed to local procedures and administrative structures that had usually changed little from colonial times. By then the major colonial powers had accepted the need for independence and were providing financial support and were committed to working with the new leaders and their fledgling governments rather than against them.

What were first known as "underdeveloped" countries, in spite of their ancient civilizations, had priorities that were considerably more oriented toward development than were those of the former colonial powers. Decolonization altered priorities, national and international. Accelerated development moved to the top of the agenda. Resolutions at the outset of the development decades (in particular, the first two) established new vocabulary as well as new aspirations. Both were antecedents of thinking on governance.

Despite their macroeconomic core, many of the economic and social aspects of the development decades were harbingers of fundamental aspects of good governance. In the first decade, issues of rural and urban development carried major implications for improving national administrations. The Second Development Decade flagged such issues as gender.[4]

The context for the early decades was newly independent states. The focus was on economic development with the implicit assumption of a benign state, committed to improving the situation of the whole country's population. This, of course, was in line with the promises and expectations of independence. To the extent that political development entered the story, it was through decolonization, localization of staff, strengthening local institutions, and creating national plans. Nation building was a favorite theme of social scientists in the 1950s and 1960s,[5] a subject that would later be identified with good governance because the main goals and objectives were as much political as economic.

The 1970s marked the first round of the global conferences that identified both new issues and priority roles for the state in addressing pressing problems—the environment, population, food security, urban policy, women, employment, the informal sector, and basic needs (see Chapter 4). The UN was the midwife for many of these ideas, if not the parent. These ideas became guiding principles for governance and ultimately for good economic and social development. They often included "the new trappings of democracy," which were not always thought through well. The appearances of power and solidarity within the South were often stronger than the actual reality was.

National planning within what had by that time euphemistically become "developing" rather than "underdeveloped" countries often led to excesses and ultimately to reactions against the overly powerful, centralized, and rent-seeking states of the 1970s and 1980s. The need for *good* governance—essentially defined as the opposite of the state-dominated economic and social development models that had motivated a large number of developing and socialist bloc countries since 1950s—was the result.

In addition to ideas of national governance, however, the efforts of these decades also pointed to the importance of getting international-state relationships right. The most prominent negotiating effort of the 1970s was that of the NIEO, beginning in 1974 and ultimately coming to naught. Although it was a premature attempt to alter the distribution of benefits from growth and to ensure the provision of certain international public goods, it foreshadowed fundamental aspects of what is now known as global governance. The NIEO contributed to international discourse even if the abrasive rhetoric and confrontational tactics may well have been counterproductive to intergovernmental debates at that time.

From Governance to Good Governance

Since the early 1980s "governance" and increasingly "good governance" have become catchwords in development circles.[6] The idea now occupies a prominent place in the international public policy lexicon, especially in research agendas and other activities funded by public and private banks, bilateral donors, and private foundations. Scholars and eminent commissions extensively apply the concept to contemporary global problem solving.[7]

Governance may be as old as history, but at the country level, *good* governance is a more recent notion. It can be traced to increasing disgruntlement with the state-dominated models of economic and social development so prevalent throughout the socialist bloc and much of the Third World in the 1970s and 1980s. Only rarely do people remember the nineteenth-century experiences in Europe and the United States, when many of the modern forms of abuse of state power, corruption, and manipulation of the ballot box were invented. At the international level, *global* governance also is a more recent coinage that can be traced to a growing dissatisfaction with the shortcomings of both realist and liberal-institutionalist theories of international organization, so dominant in postwar analyses of international relations. In particular, they both failed to capture adequately the vast increase, in both numbers and influence, of nonstate actors and the implications of technology in an age of globalization.

The UN was built on unquestioned national sovereignty, although the alloy contained important references to human rights and "we, the peoples." Both sovereignty and noninterference in the internal affairs of states increasingly came under fire in the 1980s and 1990s. As then Secretary-General Boutros Boutros-Ghali wrote in *An Agenda for Peace*, "The time of absolute and exclusive sovereignty, however, has passed."[8] Governments, as well as NGOs, pushing forward the human rights agenda increasingly contested sovereignty's status within international organizations and forums.

Governance is a broader notion than government. It embraces the manner in which power is exercised. It involves both government and civil society. In the UN at least, it is national and international (see Box 8.1). In the words of Secretary-General Kofi Annan, "Good governance is ensuring respect for human rights and the rule of law."[9]

Box 8.1. Contemporary Views on Governance

Webster's Second New International Dictionary: "Governance is an act, manner, office, or power of governing; government; state of being governed; or method of government or regulation."

World Bank, 1994: "Governance is defined as the manner in which power is exercised in the management of a country's economic and social resources. The World Bank has identified three distinct aspects of governance: (i) the form of political regime; (ii) the process by which authority is exercised in the management of a country's economic and social resources for development; and (iii) the capacity of governments to design, formulate, and implement policies and discharge functions."[10]

OECD, 1995: "The concept of governance denotes the use of political authority and exercise of control in a society in relation to the management of its resources for social and economic development. This broad definition encompasses the role of public authorities in establishing the environment in which economic operators function and in determining the distribution of benefits as well as the nature of the relationship between the ruler and the ruled."[11]

Commission on Global Governance, 1995: "Governance is the sum of the many ways individuals and institutions, public and private, manage their common affairs. . . . At the global level, governance has been viewed primarily as intergovernmental relationships, but it must now be understood as also involving non-governmental organizations (NGOs), citizens' movements, multinational corporations, and the global capital market."[12]

> *International Institute of Administrative Sciences, 1996:* "Governance refers to the process whereby elements in society wield power and authority, and influence and enact policies and decisions concerning public life, and economic and social development. Governance is a broader notion than government. Governance involves interaction between these formal institutions and those of civil society."[13]
>
> *James N. Rosenau, 1996:* "Governance encompasses the activities of governments, but it also includes the many other channels through which 'commands' flow in the form of goals framed, directives issued, and policies pursued."[14]
>
> *UNDP, 1997:* "Governance is viewed as the exercise of economic, political and administrative authority to manage a country's affairs at all levels. It comprises mechanisms, processes and institutions through which citizens and groups articulate their interests, exercise their legal rights, meet their obligations and mediate their differences."[15]
>
> *Kofi Annan, 2000:* "Better governance means greater participation, coupled with accountability. Therefore, the international public domain—including the United Nations—must be opened up further to the participation of the many actors whose contributions are essential to managing the path of globalization."[16]

The UN system has a distinctive orientation and profile. The preponderance of developing countries in the membership, at least from the 1960s, often made UN deliberations drawn-out and messy, a reflection of the complexion and complexity of the planet after decolonization. Debates in New York and Geneva, in Rio and Cairo, were very different from those in Washington, where weighted voting privileges the voices of powerful donors within the Bretton Woods institutions.

The twin pillars of the postwar economic system, the World Bank and the IMF, traditionally have emphasized domestic policies.[17] Prior to the collapse of the Bretton Woods system in 1973, IMF pressure was not limited to developing countries but concerned all countries with balance-of-payments problems. Over the 1980s, with structural adjustment and conditionality, international pressure about the shape of national policies became obvious and direct, at least for the borrowing countries in the Third World.

The arrival of the Thatcher and Reagan administrations had a substantial impact on the UN system as well as on the Washington-based financial institutions. Robert Cox, who served a quarter of a century in the ILO before teaching at Columbia and York Universities, commented about the UN's "preaching the magic of the market" beginning in the 1980s. He remarked that this was "a big change from the emphasis in the 1960s and 1970s on the development of structures capable of managing and organizing the economy."

In Washington, international pressure to change domestic priorities assumed more weight and was increasingly pertinent after the controversial World Bank report on sub-Saharan Africa by Elliot Berg in 1981. In the UN the numerical preponderance of developing countries along with support from socialist bloc and like-minded countries made it possible at first to resist the policy "wisdom" from Washington. Later in the decade the World Bank developed a more holistic approach that emphasized political and institutional change as prerequisites for effective economic reform.[18] The promise of more aid and investment in exchange for economic liberalization eroded somewhat the reluctance to consider intrusion in domestic policies. But in philosophy and approach, it eroded "the global Keynesian social pact suggested by the Brandt Commission."[19] And the conditionality that accompanied the structural adjustment package meant some fairly direct arm-twisting over domestic policy.

In part in reaction to ideas from Washington, the UN in the 1990s began a broader and more serious debate about how state and society should be structured. This led to concern with how good a country's political and economic system of governance was. External economic factors such as declining commodity prices, rising debt, and rising interest rates were brought in as major and legitimate explanations for poverty and poor economic performance. Attributing all of the woes of developing countries to outside forces beyond their control was never the UN's official position, although some chose to caricature the approach from the world organization as just this. In any event, UN debates about international public policy began to occupy a newly plowed middle ground, emphasizing international as well as domestic changes in economic, social, and political approaches.

Several factors contributed to the changed intellectual climate. First, there was the glaring illegitimacy and corruption of regimes headed by such people as Uganda's Idi Amin, Kampuchea's Pol Pot, Haiti's Jean-Claude Duvalier, and the Central African Empire's Jean-Bédel Bokassa. The UN had been in the vanguard and successfully lobbied the international community to consider as genuinely "international" the domestic policies of white-majority governments in Rhodesia and South Africa. Concern for human rights in these formerly "domestic" situations meant that it was illogical to maintain that egregious violations in other situations were out of bounds.

Second, the end of the Cold War suddenly removed incentives for the West to support authoritarian rulers and cover up their failings. Without worldwide political competition, criticism of the weaknesses of corrupt and non-democratic regimes became more open.[20]

Third, both the Third World and the entire former Soviet bloc became engulfed by a tidal wave of political reforms, swelling further after the collapse of the Berlin Wall and the implosion of Moscow's empire. Samuel Huntington characterized this as the "third wave"[21] of democratic rule. Widespread democratization, including UN monitoring of elections in such former dictatorships as El Salvador and Haiti, brought squarely into focus the character and quality of local governance. Many regimes in the Third World and Eastern Europe adopted civilian rule, elections, and multiparty democracy. The form, if not always the spirit and content, of elections was often a prerequisite to legitimizing their rule and to attracting Western financing.

Fourth, the proliferation of nonstate actors changed the political landscape in most countries as well as the framing of issues within global debates. Our focus in this book has been largely upon the UN system and the international financial institutions that are *de facto* if not *de jure* part of that system. But such international NGOs as Human Rights Watch and CARE, such transnational corporations as Shell and Citibank, and such global media giants as the BBC and CNN increasingly contribute to global debate and policy and penetrate deeply what had formerly been something of a governmental *chasse gardée*.[22] They are exerting a growing influence on what once were almost exclusively matters of state policy.

What had once been more a phenomenon of the industrialized world has become more generalized. Within many developing and socialist bloc countries themselves, civil society burgeoned after decades of repression. Celso Furtado, the Brazilian development economist who in the 1940s and 1950s directed research in the ECLA and has written widely on development since, comments: "As civil society goes beyond states, they are in a somewhat different situation. States will have their own special roles, which are essential but differ from the past. This trend is spreading everywhere, and today states are recycling and modifying themselves, even in the Third World. . . . It is in such a world, I see the importance of women and, even more important, of civil society in its entirety." In short, economic and social policy is no longer the exclusive preserve of governments. Human rights advocates, gender activists, environmentalists, and groups of indigenous peoples have invaded the territory of states, literally and figuratively (see Box 8.2).

Box 8.2. NGOs in the 1990s: Bringing Civil Society in from the Cold

The growth of NGOs is a striking dimension of contemporary international relations, particularly evident in UN world conferences (see Chapter 4). The broader implications of this phenomenon for global governance and social policy in the UN system are only beginning to be understood and appreciated.[23] The term "NGO" refers to a nonprofit, voluntary, formal, nonviolent, nonpolitical organization whose objectives are the promotion of development and social change. Private organizations (or corporations) that seek to make profits are excluded, as are organized crime, insurgents, churches, mosques, and other institutions with strictly religious functions, as well as the media and political parties. Together with NGOs, these other nonstate actors constitute what is usually called "civil society," or the intermediary institutions between the individual and the apparatus of government.

The framers of the UN Charter had the foresight to include a far-reaching provision in Article 71 "to make suitable arrangements for consultation with non-governmental organizations." Although commentators tend to emphasize the last couple of decades, the NGO phenomenon actually has been gaining momentum for two centuries.[24] The UN system, especially ECOSOC, has been struggling to incorporate these voices, however cacophonous, in intergovernmental discussions. NGOs are becoming ever more numerous, vocal, visible, and operational, which has led to an increased supply of policy and scholarly publications about them.[25]

The sheer growth in NGO numbers has been nothing short of remarkable. The estimated number of international NGOs (those operating in more than three countries) hovers around 20,000, a figure that has doubled in the past decade and has exploded over the past half-century—there were an estimated 400 in 1920 and 700 in 1939.[26] National NGOs have grown faster still, if findings by more specialized development researchers are to be believed: 16,000 registered in Bangladesh; 21,000 in the Philippines; 100,000 Christian-based ones in Brazil; and 27,000 in Chile.[27] In Kenya about 250 are created each year. Throughout the Third World grassroots organizations are said to number in the millions.[28] The phenomenon certainly is not limited to the Third World. For example, in France in 1960 approximately 11,000 associations existed, but by 1987 the number had increased to 54,000. In the United Kingdom some 4,000 new charities were established each year during the 1980s and 1990s.[29] By one estimate there may be some two million in the United States alone. And in Russia, where there were virtually none a generation ago, there are now some 65,000.[30]

Charter Article 71 originally carved out some space for NGOs as observers of UN deliberations. But during the Cold War the socialist bloc and many autocratic developing countries resisted the intrusion of private and dissident voices. Nonetheless, ECOSOC in 1968 spelled out rules governing NGOs. Maurice Strong, secretary-general of the 1972 Stockholm Conference on the Human Environment, insisted on the presence of NGOs at the conference. Thereafter, NGO parallel meetings, usually called "forums," have become prominent in pressing for more forward-looking approaches during UN conferences. In the 1990s thousands of NGOs attended the Rio and Beijing conferences. Moreover, NGOs had become primary executors of UN projects by the time that ECOSOC agreed to more flexible accreditation standards in 1996. In short, the presence of alternative voices—one of the new characteristics of global governance—has become an integral part of the UN system's processes of deliberations.

Fifth, the 1990s witnessed a transformation of the widespread view that the "Charter is a Westphalian document *par excellence.*"[31] National sovereignty no longer rules without question. The UN's constitution, in Charter Article 2 (7), specifically does not permit the world organization "to intervene in matters which are essentially within the domestic jurisdiction of any state." Nonetheless, humanitarian interventions have encouraged the insertion of responsibility as a necessary additional component of national sovereignty, in addition to the three traditional characteristics of statehood (territory, people, and authority).

Leading the charge were none other than the last two UN secretaries-general, Boutros Boutros-Ghali (1992–1997) and Kofi Annan (1997–present), articulating the contingent character of sovereignty in spite of significant ire directed by some governments at their efforts. The acute suffering of people in such failed states as Somalia, the former Yugoslavia, and Rwanda opened the door to scrutinizing domestic policies that lead to mass displacement and even genocide. Given the need for the international system to respond and pick up the costly bill for such humanitarian tragedies, the prevention of future disasters lent additional weight—whether governments liked their presence or not—to the argument to examine governance patterns in weak and vulnerable states.[32]

By the end of the 1980s, probing domestic policies and priorities had become commonplace, in Washington if not always in New York. The efforts to come to grips operationally with governance, in UN debates and UN-executed projects, can be interpreted as part of an intellectual struggle to capture the energies and possibilities of the various units of governance that are not instruments of the state. At the national level, governance is embedded in and interwoven with state-civil society interactions, the part of the public realm that encompasses both. As Morten Bøås argues, "Governance is concerned with the regime which constitutes the set of fundamental rules for the organization of the public realm. Governance clearly embraces government institutions, but it also subsumes informal, non-governmental institutions operating within the public realm." He continues, "The World Bank operationalised 'bad governance' as personalization of power, lack of human rights, endemic corruption and un-elected and unaccountable governments." And so, "good governance must be the natural opposite."[33]

By conceptualizing governance in terms that transcend traditional notions of domestic politics, Bøås clarifies how national governance involves non-governmental actors exercising authority legitimately. The UN has similarly long made room for private voices and actors, despite the fact that it is an inter*government*al organization.

Good Governance in the 1990s

Since good governance has become an important component of the international agenda, discourse focuses on policies in those countries receiving development assistance or investments from international lending agencies. Good governance has become part of a new conditionality that is inseparable from levels of appropriate bilateral and multilateral financing for needy countries. International efforts in recent decades have supported political democratization (including elections, accountability, and human rights) and economic liberalization, somehow ignoring the social problems of markets and the traumas in societies with no history of Western-style democracy.

The UN system over the 1990s increasingly sought to broaden concepts of good governance. The argument introduced nuances into black-and-white notions about the pluses and minuses of undiluted market liberalization. The world organization also called into question the unabashed enthusiasm for political and economic conditionality, which were viewed by many recipient countries as unwelcome intrusions. The UN system put forward two sets of ideas, on the political and economic sides, that served to slow the momentum of the so-called Washington or Maastricht consensus.

The first was an emphasis on broader perspectives of political governance. Good governance is considerably more than multiparty elections, a judiciary, and a parliament—the traditional symbols of Western-style democracy. Other attributes were important. The list is formidable: universal protection of human rights; laws against discrimination; efficient, impartial, and rapid judicial processes; separation of powers; transparent public agencies; accountability for decisions by public officials; devolution of resources and decision making to local levels from the capital; and meaningful participation by citizens in debating public policies and choices. And it could be extended even further.

This thrust amounted to introducing more subtlety and playing down the infatuation with democracy and democratization as political surrogates for good governance. The reasoning that individual political and civil rights go hand in hand with good governance is not wrong. But the line of argument should be expanded to make sure that democracy is inclusive and ensures the fulfillment of all rights—economic, social, and cultural as well as political and civil.[34] In short, the "package" of rights—a UN theme for years—reemerged as a sensible middle ground. "We have moved beyond that confrontational discussion," writes UNDP Administrator Mark Malloch Brown, "to a wider recognition that both sets of rights are inextricably linked."[35]

The second contribution of the UN system was the commonsensical but, at the time, unusual emphasis on the need to strike a balance between the public and private sectors in the economic arena (see Chapter 5). The UN stressed elements of public welfare that had often been ignored in the undiluted version of the Washington consensus. The composite view of the UN system amounted to something of a *reprise* of Keynesianism by pointing to the ineluctable importance of many state decisions to determine the macromanagement of both supply and demand.[36] The UN system sought to leaven the heavy conservative doses in vogue since the beginning of the Reagan and Thatcher administrations—namely, that anything the government can do, the private sector can do better; and that more open markets, free trade, and capital flows are necessarily beneficial for all.

An unquestioned faith in the normative principles of neo-liberalism had become so widespread among Western and transnational elites that, for a time, seemingly the only acceptable prescriptions about restructuring political and economic life were those of the Washington consensus. The intellectual climate had changed so much that for a decade between the mid-1980s and mid-1990s it was almost heretical to argue that an efficient, thriving market economy and civil society require an effective and strong government. Antonio Gramsci would have found an apt illustration of his argument that ideologies have the "same energy as material force."[37]

The Washington consensus had created an artificial dichotomy between "state" and "market." The dissent by two of the UN's regional commissions—by the ECA regarding the overall impact of adjustment on Africa in the 1980s and by the ECE concerning the impact of applying the conventional wisdom about transition to Eastern Europe—were early signs of revolt (see Chapters 5 and 6). But the UN heresy was more widespread. In order to foster efficiency and effectiveness, adapting rather than "rolling back" the state became the main policy recommendation. For instance, a report from the UNDP's Regional Bureau for Europe and the CIS emphasized the prerequisites for equity, legitimacy, and efficiency: "A legitimately strong government can be described as one that commands sufficient confidence in its legitimacy to allow for a strong civil society, and for a network of non-governmental institutions and regulations that ensure the development of a well-functioning economic system, the strengthening of democratic procedures, and a widespread participation by people in public life."[38]

By 1997, in a departure from its previous orthodoxy, and as a sign that the pendulum was swinging in response to criticism and ideas from the UN and other sources, the World Bank's *World Development Report 1997* emphasized that the state is capable of, and indeed should perform the role of, producing welfare-enhancing outcomes. As the text argues: "There is a growing recognition that some needed public goods and services can only be secured through international cooperation. Thus, building state capacity will mean building more effective partnerships and institutions internationally as well as at home."[39] The report's subtitle, *The State in a Changing World,* was indicative of an internal policy challenge articulated by Joseph Stiglitz.[40]

It is fair to conclude that UN research and policy analyses contributed to a new balance between market and state and more widespread agnosticism about the potential for unfettered market forces—in short, what constitutes workable reforms and good governance. Rescuing the baby from the discarded bath water, today's mainstream debate about good governance has moved away from a visceral dismantling of the state. In contrast with narrower economic liberalization programs in vogue earlier, political liberalization programs of the late 1990s place a greater emphasis on leadership and management as well as democracy, human rights, rule of law, access to justice, and basic freedoms. They have weakened the force of arguments by the proponents of a "minimalist state."

Whereas the original debate about good governance was cast as the antithesis of state-dominated economic and social development of previous decades, today's debate is less about jettisoning state institutions than about improving and reforming the functioning of democratic institutions. "Deepening" democracy and exploring more active and creative roles for nonstate actors are now in the mainstream. Leaders are being held to higher standards of accountability even as they contend with the forces of globalization.

The World Bank's position is still distinct from the UN's, presupposing what is "good" and what is "not good" governance. The bank does not frame these issues as central to a conception of and strategy for governance that seek as a priority to maximize local participation in addressing the most pressing needs in a given community. In contrast, the UN system's multidisciplinary and evolving human development approach to governance exhibits relatively greater emphasis on empowerment — that is, providing space, freedom, and the tools of democracy that are necessary for the political and civic dimensions of governance. The World Bank may not be averse to these issues, and the *World Development Report 2000* spoke strongly in their favor (see Chapter 5). But it had in the past treated them as second-order concerns, "tag-ons," not so much valuable in and of themselves but rather desirable insofar as they contribute to efficiency and economic growth.

Debate has thus shifted toward common ground. Good governance does not necessarily mean less government but rather more appropriate government. In the 1960s and 1970s states often became overextended, but this does not remove the need for state actions in the public interest. Leaving everything to the private sector, particularly in countries with weak administrations, often leads to private exploitation of the public interest. There is need to balance the role of government and other political and economic institutions with efficient markets.

A great deal of ink has been spilled over the excesses of state authority, although much less on the excesses of the market and the social costs for vulnerable populations of forced-march transitions. It has long been recognized that some regulation is needed to ensure competition and some intervention is required to offset negative market externalities. The only candidate at the national level is the state, which the World Bank has recognized in its official position: "The central challenge is not to halt the expansion of the market but to establish proper rules and institutions so that the benefits of growth are more widely beneficial."[41]

In summary, debate over good governance shifted from an overly simplistic focus in the 1980s and early 1990s on reversing decades of state-dominated economic and social development to improving the political leadership in and for democracy. The debate rediscovered basic points made under different names in the 1950s, including in the path-breaking UN report, *Measures for the Economic Development of Under-Developed Countries.* Also involved in the approach is an openness to more active and creative roles for nonstate actors and the better integration of economic and social goals. Passive in the 1980s, the UN awakened to play a critical role, drawing heavily on perspectives from within its membership, in contrast to the more top-down perspectives of the Bretton Woods institutions.

The emphasis in UN circles in the 1990s also changed regarding human rights. Going beyond the Cold War clash between political and civil versus economic, social, and cultural rights, a package of comprehensive rights for all people increasingly was stressed. The present UN high commissioner for human rights, Mary Robinson, has continually stressed support for all rights as an essential for any well-governed society.[42] Better governance entails improving governmental institutions and development management. Mahbub ul Haq helped launch the idea of *humane* governance, in response to his own criticism that "the concept of good governance has so far failed to match the radicalism of the notion of human development."[43] Humane governance includes the notion of good political, economic, *and* civic governance.

The UNDP as the coordinating development agency within the UN system has taken this challenge as a new battle cry. Humane governance refers to civic structures and processes that support a participatory, responsive, and accountable polity (that is, good political governance) embedded in a competitive, nondiscriminatory, yet equitable, economy (that is, good economic governance). This requires that resources contributed by people be plowed back to serve their own basic human needs, which will in turn expand the opportunities open to them; people must be given the ability to self-organize (that is, good civic governance).

The definitions in Box 8.1 and the preceding discussion illustrate the importance of ideas. Governance and its prescriptive partner have elicited not only commentary by scholars and development practitioners but also policy changes by national governments and international funding agencies. The UN demonstrated a type of intellectual leadership by searching for common ground in a highly polarized atmosphere. The world organization probably would not have moved so quickly without the sea change in world politics after the end of the Cold War and without pressure from donors and simplifications from the Bretton Woods institutions against which to react.

From Good Governance to Global Governance

Global governance is distinct from either good or bad governance at the national level. At the national level, "good" governance is accountable, efficient, lawful, representative, and transparent. There is no such actor at the world level. "States need to develop a deeper awareness of their dual role in our global world," writes Secretary-General Kofi Annan. "In addition to the separate responsibilities each state bears towards its own society, states are, collectively, the custodians of our common life on this planet—a life the citizens of *all* countries share."[44] For all of the inadequacies, whatever order exists in today's international economic and political system results from international efforts, including those of the UN. Mark Zacher judged the world organization's efforts in this way: "In short, without these and other regimes and public goods generated by the UN system, it would truly be 'a jungle out there.'"[45]

At both the national and global levels, governance encompasses more than government. But for the world, governance exists without any government at all. "Global governance" is one contemporary formulation to express this reality. It perhaps is best seen as a heuristic device to capture the confusing and seemingly ever-accelerating transformation of the international system. The academic community is struggling with the notion. Since 1995 Lynne Rienner Publishers has, in cooperation with the Academic Council on the United Nations System (ACUNS) and the UNU, published an independent journal exploring the topic and titled *Global Governance*.

Even within a transformed international system, states are still central, although we have described above the extent to which their authority is receding in important ways. At the same time, intergovernmental organizations have not been strengthened and are no more powerful than they ever were. Multinational corporations have real power—but by choice and capacity mostly exercise it within a limited economic terrain. Local and international NGOs are proliferating and gaining authority and resources—but in an ad hoc manner. And technological developments are increasing the role and strength of some decidedly uncivil organizations—for example, the crime syndicates and the arms and drug smugglers. Within this context, the need for global public goods is ever more important—but their provision is even more of a challenge internationally than nationally.

On the one hand, a crucial contribution by the UN over the years has been ideas about global governance. For example, it would be sensible to review for a moment the four powerful ideas from 1945 (see Chapter 1). There have been numerous efforts at the pacific settlement of disputes, conflict management, and peacekeeping in the place of war. The process of decolonization and the training of nationals in place of outside exploitation was a crucial second set of principles and actions. Universal human rights is the most fundamental and humanizing principle of global governance. And, of course, there have been the host of international measures so that economic and social development is a reality rather than an aspiration, including international measures so that national efforts to maintain full employment in one country do not disrupt such measures in others; measures to avoid global recession and to achieve greater stability; actions to ensure that the benefits from free trade are more widely shared; efforts to iron out a global framework for development; and special attention to such key issues as sustainability, population growth, gender, and humane structures to provide basic needs. Surely all of these ideas were, and are, about the aims of global governance. And most of them came with proposals, right or wrong, about institutions and actions to achieve them.

On the other hand, while much of the UN's efforts have amounted to exploring elements of the *problématique,* in many key respects the world is no closer to achieving effective global governance than it was in 1945. In particular, there is at best only a feeble institutional capacity to come to grips with the regulation of market vagaries and inequalities. One could even go further, to state that "international institutions have weakened precisely at a time when global interdependence has increased."[46] The lacuna resulting from the lack of central guidance and countervailing power for the international system is clear. "Who plays the role of the development-oriented state in the global economy?" Canadian economist Gerry Helleiner asked the Second Committee of the General Assembly. "Today's global financial world . . . is utterly different from that facing the original architects of the Bretton Woods system in 1944."[47]

Even a relatively powerful institution like the IMF is a pale imitation of the global Central Bank for which Keynes was such a passionate advocate. Instead of reserves equal to half of world imports, as Keynes had urged, the IMF's present liquidity equals less than 3 percent of global imports.[48]

In the face of an anarchical system — that is, the absence of institutions resembling a global Bismarck to which we referred earlier (see Chapter 5) — some very big questions loom. What new or stronger mechanisms are needed for global economic and social governance? Is there a way to structure a reasonable measure of coordination and cooperation among governments, intergovernmental organizations, NGOs, and the private sector that would constitute meaningful or at least improved patterns of global governance? If global governance requires purposeful decisions and goal-oriented behavior, how can global governance exist in the absence of a clear consensus about goals? Can democratic global governance, in fact, exist without shared values?

A comprehensive and recent attempt to plumb the depths of global challenges and solutions came in 1995 with the Commission on Global Governance. This independent panel chaired by Sonny Ramphal and Ingvar Carlsson published its findings in *Our Global Neighbourhood* (see Box 8.3). The commission's chairmen were brought together by Willy Brandt shortly after the fall of the Berlin Wall. There was a sense that the world was "on the edge of a new time" which made possible "looking at the future of the world in a more integral way."[49] The effort made a conscious attempt to involve many of the participants from previous commissions and to pull together their recommendations. Like earlier eminent groups, this commission was a non-UN undertaking to ensure its autonomy but was nonetheless closely related. Its findings were presented to the secretary-general and to the heads of UN agencies and widely discussed within UN circles.

For instance, global governance was a major emphasis in the *Human Development Report 1999*.[50] Robert Cox, whose own writings emphasize the role of ideas and international organizations in sustaining the status quo, discounts the intellectual content of reports from eminent commissions and emphasizes their political impact. He compares such reports to the work of management consultants who are asked "to come in and give a sort of legitimacy to doing what you already decided to do. . . . They are a useful political device."

Interestingly, the commission was composed of twenty-eight women and men whose professional experiences were almost exclusively within governments and intergovernmental secretariats. It is noteworthy that "global governance" for the members of the commission did not imply a world government or even world federalism. Instead, "it is a broad, dynamic, complex process of interactive decision-making that is constantly evolving and responding to changing circumstances."[51] "Global governance" means making use of a wide and seemingly ever-growing number of public and private actors in every domain. Global economic and social affairs have traditionally been viewed as embracing primarily bilateral and intergovernmental relationships, but increasingly they must be framed in comprehensive enough terms to embrace local and international NGOs, grassroots and citizens' movements, multinational corporations, and the global capital market.

**Box 8.3. Some Recommendations from the
Commission on Global Governance**

The twenty-eight-person Commission on Global Governance set out numerous proposals in *Our Global Neighbourhood*.[52] They covered values, goals, and priorities as well as setting out several specifics for changing institutions and working methods of global governance. Their key recommendations included the following:

Governance, Change, and Values:

We call for a common commitment to core values that all humanity could uphold: respect for life, liberty, justice and equity, mutual respect, caring, and integrity. We further believe humanity as a whole will be best served by recognition of a set of common rights and responsibilities . . . to:

- a secure life,
- equitable treatment,
- an opportunity to earn a fair living and provide for their own welfare,
- the definition and preservation of their differences through peaceful means,
- participation in governance at all levels,
- free and fair petition for redress of gross injustices
- equal access to information, and
- equal access to the global commons.

At the same time, all people share a responsibility to:

- contribute to the common good;
- consider the impact of their actions on the security and welfare of others;
- promote equity, including gender equity;
- protect the interests of future generations by pursuing sustainable development and safeguarding the global commons;
- preserve humanity's cultural and intellectual heritage;
- be active participants in governance; and
- work to eliminate corruption.

Promoting Security

- All people, no less than all states, have a right to a secure existence, and all states have an obligation to protect those rights.
- The primary goals of global policy should be to prevent conflict and war and to maintain the integrity of the environment and life-support systems of the planet by eliminating the economic, social, environmental, political, and military conditions that generate threats to the security of people and the planet, and by anticipating and managing crisis before they escalate into armed conflicts.
- Military force is not a legitimate political instrument, except in self-defense or under UN auspices.
- The development of military capabilities beyond that required for national defense and support of UN action is a potential threat to the security of people.
- Weapons of mass destruction are not legitimate instruments of national defence and the international community should reaffirm its commitment to eliminate nuclear and other weapons of mass destruction progressively from all nations.
- The production and trade in arms should be controlled by the international community.

Work towards nuclear disarmament should involve action on four fronts:

- the earliest possible ratification and implementation of existing agreements on nuclear and other weapons of mass destruction;
- the indefinite extension of the Non-Proliferation Treaty;
- the conclusion of a treaty to end all nuclear testing; and
- the initiation of talks among all declared nuclear powers to establish a process to reduce and eventually eliminate all nuclear arsenals.

Managing Economic Inter-dependence

We propose the establishment of an Economic Security Council . . . to:

- continuously assess the overall state of the world economy and the interaction between major policy areas;
- provide long-term strategic policy framework in order to promote stable, balanced, and sustainable development;
- secure consistency between the policy goals of the major international organizations, particularly the Bretton Woods bodies, and the WTO; and
- give political leadership and promote consensus on international economic issues.

The decision-making structures of the Bretton Woods Institutions must be reformed and made more reflective of economic reality. . . . The role of the IMF should be enhanced by:

- enlarging its capacity for balance-of-payments support through low conditionality compensatory finance;
- having oversight of the international monetary system and a capacity to ensure that domestic economic policies in major countries are not mutually inconsistent or damaging to the rest of the international community;
- releasing a new issue of special drawing rights; and
- improving its capacity to support nominal exchange rates in the interests of exchange rate stability.

Reforming the United Nations

Much of the necessary reform of the United Nations system can be effected without amending the Charter, provided governments are willing. . . . UN reform must reflect the realities of change, including the new capacity of global civil society to contribute to global governance.

Strengthening the Rule of Law World-Wide

The global neighbourhood of the future must be characterized by law and the reality that all, including the weakest, are equal under the law and none, including the strongest, is above it.

Such overwhelming questions often lead to a common reaction, especially among representatives of governments. They fall back on familiar ways of thought by attempting to recapture the "good old days" of state-centric authority. One idea is to replace ECOSOC with an Economic and Social *Security* Council, modeled upon the Security Council, at present the most authoritative of the UN's six main organs.[53] This idea has received only modest support, although the Security Council itself has recently focused specifically on humanitarian and human rights problems. In January 2000 it also added Africa's problems of poverty and health to the "security" agenda.

Some seek to recapture the nostalgia and excitement of the period just after the end of World War II when intergovernmental organizations were charged with making the world safe from both war and economic recession. For instance, Lawrence Finkelstein—an intern in the U.S. delegation in San Francisco and now retired from university teaching of international organization—sees global governance as "doing internationally what governments do at home."[54] But his formulation leads one to ask: Which agents are supposed to accomplish globally the numerous tasks that governments, however inadequately, accomplish nationally? Who is at the helm?

The experiments with multilateralism in the past half-century have been useful, and the UN has certainly contributed many ideas about how to manage better the planet's affairs. However, neither our understanding nor our problem-solving efforts are any longer served, cautions James Rosenau, the scholar most associated with the analytical notion of global governance, "by clinging to the notion that states and national governments are the essential underpinnings of the world's organization."[55] With an increasing diffusion of authority and a corresponding loss of control, states and the intergovernmental organizations they create are no longer the only or even the most important actors on the world stage. Depending on the issue, member states retain many attributes of sovereignty, but they are past their prime and now share the spotlight with others.

Sovereignty is still alive and well, but it is hardly as sacrosanct as it once was. In attempting to protest too much, governmental representatives are highlighting daily in international forums the extent to which contemporary authority patterns are in flux and quite different from those of the past. The resistance to change among governments and intergovernmental secretariats contrasts markedly with the agility of most businesses and NGOs. There is no philosophical justification for assigning the highest form of authority to states, but representatives from national governments act as if there were.

It is in this arena that the UN is poised to play a crucial role on the world's stage. As Secretary-General Kofi Annan notes in his background document for the September 2000 Millennium Assembly, "The very notion of centralizing hierarchies is itself an anachronism in our fluid, highly dynamic and extensively networked world—an outmoded remnant of nineteenth century mindsets."[56] Both he and his predecessor sought to open the UN's door to civil society, especially to business and NGOs. More inclusive and participatory—hence, truly "democratic"—mechanisms for consultations and ultimately governance may and must be created at the UN. "Governance" is not "government." At the global level there can be no monolith, or even a single structure or set of structures.

The UN system at the beginning of the twenty-first century is a complex of small international bodies and institutions of modest capacity and very small budgets. With only some 50,000 UN staff worldwide, the UN system—even including the Bretton Woods institutions—has fewer employees than the local government in Stockholm has. The systemwide budget—excluding the Bretton Woods institutions—is less than the annual expenditure of the British government on public administration and policy. And the share of the UN proper is about the size of the budgets of the combined New York City fire and police departments.[57] Yet it is almost impossible to describe accurately all of the dimensions of international economic and social interactions—what Rosenau aptly calls "crazy-quilt patterns."[58]

The proverbial bottom line is this: There is no clear-cut global equivalent to the prescriptions of democratization and economic liberalization as the components of national governance. And there is no clear-cut institutional mechanism to ensure adequate supervision and monitoring of global economic and social affairs, let alone counteracting the excesses of globalization and markets.

Conclusions

In the light of its universality and scope, the UN has and will continue to have a special role, albeit hardly a monopoly, in exerting leadership for global governance. Indeed, virtually all of the world organization's work has been about aspects of global governance, although most of that work predates the term itself. The UN was in the *avant-garde* in the early years by helping spawn, nurture, and carry out the ideas for decolonization and localization. The development challenge and many solutions were articulated in early UN documents and conferences. Universal human rights have been a linchpin of national and international efforts. In terms of good governance, the world organization was at first in a reactive mode in the debate but later played a useful countervailing role even if originally it had been behind the curve.

In terms of the contemporary debate about what is now widely referred to as "global governance," the UN is ironically—since its mission is precisely this—groping and coping like everyone else in trying to find a conceptual handle for addressing contemporary global challenges. The UN system needs to match its best past performances in being ahead of the curve, rearticulate in the new context the four compelling ideas of its foundation, be responsive to reflecting the perspectives from all parts of the world, and be willing to swim against the powerful currents of orthodoxy whenever and wherever necessary. Amartya Sen, the 1998 Nobel laureate in economics, captures well the challenge: "The need for critical scrutiny of standard preconceptions and political-economic attitudes has never been stronger."[59]

To respond to globalization, intergovernmental organizations—both global and regional—undoubtedly should be strengthened. This is the most constant refrain throughout more than half a century of the UN's stewardship over economic and social ideas. There is, of course, more than a dollop of institutional self-interest behind this conviction. Notwithstanding, some countervailing power clearly is required to offset the excesses of the present system, where states pursue their national interests and the private sector pursues individual gains.

The need for a more cohesive and effective multilateral system is logical and evident. But no more than at the national level, we should not long for monolithic forms of global governance. The challenge is to find ways to pool the collective strengths and avoid the collective weaknesses of governments in managing intergovernmental organizations and global civil society. This is the paradox for proponents of global governance and the advocates of the UN.[60]

9

Conclusion: The United Nations and Ideas

- **The League of Nations and the Early UN Years**
- **The Creative 1970s**
- **The 1980s and Beyond**

What is the UN? Is it an assortment of governments that disagree on most issues? Does it reach beyond them to represent "we, the peoples"? Are there independent officials, or are staff enslaved to repetition of national party lines? Is it a family of organizations, some close siblings and others estranged cousins—like the World Bank and the IMF?

The answer is, "All of the above, and more." Concerning ideas and policies, the UN is a series of governments, secretariats, and individuals who produce them. But these same groups also can stimulate or bury these ideas, and launch others of their own.

In this volume we have not tried to probe original authorship. After all, ideas are virtually never the property of a single agent or single mind. They grow out of the interaction of many—international civil servants, academics, governments, journalists, and NGOs. This generalization is particularly true for the multilateral arena—indeed, consensus and wide ownership are signs of success.

The book opened with a brief introduction to the UNIHP. This effort is tracing ideas in the economic and social domain launched or nurtured by the UN system since its inception. The UNIHP will comprise some fifteen detailed volumes by the project's extended research family, and an oral history of some of the men and women who have played major roles in spawning or cultivating ideas on the UN's stage or in the wings of what unkind critics might label the "theater."

Ahead of the Curve? is the first book—an "appetizer" for later volumes. The question mark in the title indicates two things: the honesty with which we have tried to approach our task, and the early stages of our work. If we have achieved our culinary task, we should have instilled hunger pangs for the more substantive courses to follow. At the same time, we trust that this effort provides a satisfying introduction and also provides some guidelines to the authors of the books that we have commissioned.

We have had to be selective. The themes are necessarily based on choice. We have looked at UN ideas through the prism of a series of challenges that the world has faced over the past fifty years: unemployment, the search for development strategies, the importance of satisfying basic needs, the environment, gender, population, the battles around neoliberal orthodoxy, the collapse of Soviet-style socialism, growing global income gaps, and the challenge of improving national and global governance.

We began by setting out the four compelling ideas proclaimed at San Francisco and embodied in the UN Charter: peace, independence, human rights, and development. In each of these spheres we ask—and try to answer—the question: Were UN ideas ahead of the curve? In a surprising number of cases, the answer is "yes." In some, a resounding "no." There have been examples of intellectual and advocacy leadership as well as timidity and sheepishness. For the final section on global governance, the UN is at the epicenter of a world in flux. Ask again in another half-century.

The League of Nations and the Early UN Years

The reputation of the League of Nations is somber. Dramatic failures in Manchuria and Ethiopia usually jump to mind more quickly and often than achievements do. But in the economic and social arena it often succeeded—together with the surviving ILO—in doing useful work. It came up with policies that were successful in curbing inflation in Austria, Hungary, and elsewhere in the early 1920s. It proposed sensible economic policies based on open trade, and it discussed the mounting employment problem of the 1920s and 1930s in a clear and "modern" manner.

The problem with the league was not a lack of ideas, but the economic and political gales that it encountered. The Great Depression turned most countries inward and toward ferocious protective impulses, drowning the league's calls for open trade in the roars of protectionist reaction. The rise of fascist and Nazi regimes added a tragic political liability to the economic one. The world was swept in a downward spiral from which the league could not rescue it—a sad example of failing to take international measures. The political and economic situation was such, however, that common sense played, at best, a very modest role. Both the League of Nations and the ILO were at that time ahead of the curve in today's terms, but behind in Keynesian terms. In retrospect, the highly successful Keynesian policies lasted about twenty-five years *after* the Second World War—from the late 1940s to the early 1970s.

After the disaster, the San Francisco conference and the UN Charter came up with four powerful ideas. Peace became an endangered species when the Cold War started rapidly after the end of the Second World War. The arms race became the order of the day, not peace and disarmament. But no world war occurred during the second half of the twentieth century, and the UN's peacekeeping and conflict management efforts were a signal contribution recognized by the Nobel Peace Prize in 1988. We have not told this well-documented story here, but it should be kept in mind nonetheless.

Political independence, at the same time, turned out to be a triumph. Who would have expected in 1945 that in fewer than twenty-five years colonialism would largely be a thing of the past? But it was, and the UN played an essential role in ending it.

Human rights were the most radical and potentially subversive of the four ideas and also, with independence, the most penetrating. Human rights have acquired a status that is embraced worldwide. Well-publicized abuses attest, of course, that norms are often violated. Yet the idea has given the UN an opportunity to go beyond national sovereignty and explore a wider conception of governance. It has also made this opportunity available to others who may use military force more effectively but less legitimately than the UN.

Development became the battle cry of the world organization. This topic provides the bulk of the grist for our analytical mills in the preceding pages and will do so for the UNIHP more generally. Around 1950 the UN produced three pioneering reports covering employment, development, and international trade and investment. Contrary to the league and the prewar ILO, which had restricted their analyses essentially to "countries of Western civilization," each of these early UN reports took a global view. They were very much ahead of the curve in that sense. This continued and was given a boost by the creation of development decades, the first for the 1960s and others thereafter. Employment was high on the agenda, in both the industrialized and socialist countries. They and the reports saw the answer to full employment basically in industrialization. Both industrialized and socialist countries, each in their own and very different ways, succeeded in realizing full employment. Economic growth and industrialization were also vital to developing countries, but this was not enough to reach full employment in their case. And it was in that respect that the UN was found lacking during the 1950s and 1960s.

With decolonization mostly accomplished, newly and long independent countries of Africa, Asia, the Middle East, and Latin America joined forces in the political Non-Aligned Movement and the more economic Group of 77. Developing countries, or the Third World or the South as they came to be called, assumed a growing role in framing debates and in setting the UN's agenda. This was particularly the case after the institutionalization of North-South debates in 1964 with the establishment of UNCTAD.

At the end of the 1960s, after more than two decades of impressive economic growth, the world began to wake up to a host of challenges. The employment problem in developing countries had assumed horrifying proportions; environmental pressures were becoming urgent; population and urban explosions took their toll; and discrimination against women was rampant. The UN rose to the occasion by turning the 1970s into a remarkably creative decade.

The Creative 1970s

It became clear in the late 1960s that economic growth alone could not address unemployment and other social problems in the South. Unless the growth rate was "unrealistically" high, the answer had to be sought in the *pattern* of development—which had to become more labor- or employment-intensive. We have used "scare quotes" because later the Asian miracle meant that several of the so-called tigers of the region achieved exactly such "unrealistically" high rates of economic growth. However, full employment in these countries was not reached because of high growth, but rather because they fully used their factors of production, including labor. A country that has a quarter of its labor force idle and marginalized will never be able to attain growth rates of 8 percent.

In the 1970s the UN—and more particularly the ILO's WEP—elaborated an alternative development strategy that was more employment-intensive *and* directed to the basic needs of the entire population, including the poorest. This so-called basic needs–oriented development strategy was controversial at first. Yet within less than a year its converts included the entire UN system, the World Bank of Robert McNamara and Hollis Chenery, and practically the entire donor community—including the USAID, which labeled it basic *human* needs.

So overwhelming were the positive responses from industrialized countries that the attitude of the developing world—committed to negotiating the NIEO—switched abruptly from enthusiasm to skepticism. Indeed, their focus had been on international income redistribution, while basic-needs approaches concentrated on internal income redistribution. Obviously, the two go hand in hand, but that was too simple-minded for the Manichean world of North-South confrontation.

Notwithstanding, by the end of the 1970s economic and social policies had been widely embraced that addressed two of the most important challenges of developing countries: productive employment creation and poverty reduction. The 1980s changed all that, but first we should examine other creative outbursts during the 1970s.

Gradually, over a period of twenty years after World War II, the industrialized market countries began to realize that their economic approach put an ever-growing stress on the environment and drained nonrenewable resources. At the end of the 1960s the UN General Assembly voted to hold a world conference on environmental issues. The preparation of the Stockholm conference started out on the wrong foot, because developing countries saw the environment as a problem of the North. They were willing to consider a conference on the environment *and* development, just as a few years later they wished to link population *and* development. It took great skill to get developing countries on board after a highly successful preparatory meeting at Founex, which altered the agenda for Stockholm.

The 1972 gathering in the Swedish capital not only put the human environment on the agenda but also placed the notion of interdependence into the public policy lexicon. Afterwards, the Brundtland Commission and the Rio Earth Summit made sure that they remained so. That environmental issues, particularly among younger generations, are so central to domestic and international politics is due in no small measure to the Stockholm conference and its follow-up.

For developing countries, population issues also could not be isolated from development. Gradually, a balanced approach between population policy and development was achieved. The crowning achievement came at the Cairo population conference in 1994, where the conclusion was that women must be empowered so that they can decide on the number and spacing of their children. This also shows the interrelationship between the four conferences on gender, on the one hand, and issues such as population and environment, on the other. Over time these successive gatherings have built cumulatively one upon another. The controversial 1950s notion of a comprehensive development approach has become the standard bill of fare.

The long international march of women started in Mexico City in 1975, and the pace has accelerated almost continuously since. Women's rights are now accepted as human rights. Women are increasingly taking their place as recognized decision-makers in development, not just as targets for assistance and advice. The glass ceiling circumscribing women's advancement is not gone, but it is considerably higher than it once was. Discrimination has diminished. Opportunities have multiplied. This is an ongoing success story whose chapters have been written, published, or edited by the UN.

Employment, the environment, population, and gender meant that development strategies became more comprehensive and more realistic, leading to the notion of "sustainable human development" toward the end of the 1980s. Developing countries had, with the creation of UNCTAD, altered the dynamics of international negotiations. The Group of 77 became a formidable pressure group. Stimulated and strengthened by the action of OPEC in 1973 and later in 1979, the South launched a bid to create a NIEO that was formally adopted in 1974. This was a serious discussion of measures to foster fairer global governance but was often overshadowed by a long wish list, abrasive language, and confrontational negotiating tactics. As the influence of OPEC waned and the debt burdens of non-oil-exporting developing countries grew along with worldwide inflation, the industrialized market countries ignored more and more the demands emanating from the South. The NIEO was murdered, although it was reported to have died a natural death in the 1980s. It still may prove to be a Lazarus.

Other challenges in the 1970s — especially food and habitat — were addressed by the UN with varying degrees of success. We do not dwell on them in this brief summary, but they are central to the story told earlier.

In summary, the 1970s were a remarkable decade for the number of difficult global challenges that arose, and for the number and quality of normative and operational ideas that emerged from within and around the UN system in response. The decade was also a time when NGOs and civil society more generally came of age. Their participation in the series of UN world conferences was an essential element in formulating and advocating changes in ideas and approaches. Governance would never be the same.

The 1980s and Beyond

Drums and fireworks ushered in the 1980s. Margaret Thatcher and Ronald Reagan registered the loudest decibel levels. The worldwide economic recession and the international debt crisis sounded a death knell for many of the erratic propositions of the 1960s and 1970s. A paradigm shift took place, which was hailed as new but which, in fact, represented a return to policies of a previous age. Liberalization and privatization were dusted off and presented as new and insightful. The state was christened as the problem — a constraint on development and growth rather than a facilitator. Regulations were viewed as brakes on entrepreneurship rather than defenders. Liberalization and privatization became the new kids in town, and no one seemed to recognize them as the seductive and ambiguous saviors-cum-troublemakers of yesteryear. In short, liberalism (in the nineteenth-century European sense) made a comeback. The state was viewed as a parasite and source of evil, the market a source of salvation. Liberalizing trade and finance was good in any circumstance, and protectionism and controls bad.

Many of the ideas of the 1970s — particularly those related to development, trade, and income distribution — were relegated (temporarily, we would argue) to history's dustbin. Others such as population, employment, and habitat were put on hold. Still others — environment, children, human rights, and gender — continued to attract some attention and action.

The fulcrum of the development debate shifted from the UN to the Washington-based financial institutions. The NIEO debate seemed quaint. Attention came to be focused on *national* policies, and especially on structural adjustment to usher developing countries into the age of liberalization and privatization. What we call in this book the "current orthodoxy," also known in various circles as the Washington or Maastricht consensus, promised prosperity and stability after tough transitions. Economic growth was again viewed unequivocally as a panacea, and trickle-down its obedient servant.

Apparently each generation has to make some of the same mistakes that previous ones have made. During the 1980s many developing countries regressed to levels of economic development of ten to twenty-five years earlier. Income distribution and poverty worsened. The promise held out failed to be realized because — so it was said — more time was necessary. Now, at the beginning of the twenty-first century, after two decades, how much more time is required to conclude that the experiment has failed for the most vulnerable?

In the 1990s, after the collapse of the Berlin Wall and the implosion of the socialist bloc, the so-called countries with economy in transition were offered the same promises and the same medicine in spite of a remarkable analysis by the UN. In this case, the ECE called for a more balanced development path tailored to the particular circumstances of the region and of each country. The Bretton Woods institutions and others imposed shock therapy, which so far has not resulted in transformation but rather has exploded in the faces of the countries of Eastern Europe and of the former Soviet Union. The same remedies, the same medicine, and the same results.

The UN was sidelined economically during the 1980s. It largely accepted the role of observer rather than being an active participant on the intellectual economic playing field. It left the initiative to a very large extent to the Washington-based financial institutions. But there were exceptions. In the 1980s UNICEF's *Adjustment with a Human Face* attracted wide attention and had an impact. The ECA protested against orthodox belt-tightening measures, and the ILO made an effort. In the 1990s the exceptions became more numerous — the UNDP's *Human Development Reports,* UNCTAD's annual reports about trade and least developed countries, UNRISD's seminal *States in Disarray,* and various publications from regional commissions helped to make the current orthodoxy less current and less orthodox. The impact of these ideas can be found increasingly in the rhetoric, and occasionally in the policies, of the Bretton Woods institutions. By the late 1990s the heads of the World Bank and IMF along with the OECD were declaring poverty reduction to be their most important objective; insisting on the desirability of a more balanced view of the role of the state and of liberalization and privatization; and setting employment and other social indicators as crucial dimensions of success.

While the UN has on many occasions risen intellectually to face global challenges, it has also failed many — too many — times. We mention only a few recent examples. The world organization was very late in putting the relationship between culture and development on the map; however, under the leadership of UNESCO, it finally did so with a certain *panache* by the middle of the 1990s. The UN has also failed to live up to the challenge of global disparities of all stripes. Global income gaps, the most dramatic and easily quantifiable of indicators, are grotesque and in too many cases still increasing. As we have mentioned on more than one occasion, the ratio now stands at more than seventy to one between the per capita incomes of the richest countries and the incomes of the poorest. The gap between the incomes of the richest and poorest of the planet's citizens is even wider. A global body like the UN committed to justice should be especially sensitive to such global disparities. The world organization is aware but also has had too few ideas and proposals to attack vigorously this structural problem.

Finally, there is the question of good national and global governance. Governance is much more than government. The concept captures how different actors in a society (from churches to trade unions, from NGOs to corporations, from the media to the Mafia) participate in decision making. Good governance relates to the effective and transparent inclusion of numerous actors in national decision making and to their mobilization to provide public goods. Gradually over the past decade the world organization has moved into the forefront of debate about the character of good domestic governance. The same cannot be said about global governance, which is a concept tailor-made for the UN. The world organization, like the rest of the planet, is so far mumbling, fumbling, and stumbling its way forward, in part because of the difficulties of building consensus for new thinking and bolder action.

We return to the distinctions between the "two UNs" — the first of member states and the second of secretariats. Obviously, there are few if any governments, particularly among the more powerful, that will voluntarily abdicate power to universal multilateral organizations, although many have done so to a greater degree regionally. For instance, in the European Union national ministries of agriculture have delegated power to Brussels, and the same applies to international trade. But that is not the case, so far at least, globally. At this moment of more and more intense globalization when a global counter-force is required, the "first UN" has demonstrated its reluctance, if not to say ineptitude, to take many of the challenges of global governance seriously. The UN system is — indeed, all of us are — being let down by its more powerful member states, including its most powerful one. The September 2000 Millennium Summit was an impressive photo opportunity for some 150 government leaders of this first UN; if past is prelude, follow-up is hardly a foregone conclusion.

In terms of the "second UN," the persons who work on research and ideas, the preceding pages spell out a mixed record. There are important and substantial successes as well as unfortunate failures.

As this project proceeds, we hope to be able to make better and more definitive judgments about the nexus of states, secretariats, ideas and international public policy. Figure 9.1 is a first effort to diagram the kinds of evaluations that will be made. This matrix is an attempt not to quantify the unquantifiable, but rather to depict a qualitative balance sheet to guide our research and analytical efforts. On the vertical axis, we have placed the two UNs, the arena for states to make decisions and secretariats. On the horizontal axis, we have placed ideas and the separate judgments about whether the two UNs have been ahead of or behind the curve. International organizations use ideas as means to serve both conceptual ends (creating new ways of framing issues, incipient norms, and operational suggestions) and to advocate new policies and action. For both, any fair judgment about the relative effectiveness of the two UNs in putting ideas to use requires taking into account both the short- and the long-term impacts on concepts and advocacy/action.

Among the factors explaining success or failure are the quality of people and the quality of ideas. One of the essential dimensions of multilateralism, in our view, has been the vision and energy of individuals. In an age of cynicism, it is helpful to recall the role of dedicated internationalist pioneers: Ralph Bunche on decolonization; Maurice Strong on the environment; Jan Tinbergen, Arthur Lewis, and Raúl Prebisch on development; and Eleanor Roosevelt and Mary Robinson on human rights. Great human beings make a difference in the way that responses to global challenges are framed and in the actions taken by governments and civil society.

Figure 9.1. The United Nations and Ideas

	Ideas							
	Ahead of the Curve				Behind the Curve			
	Concepts		Advocacy/Action		Intellectual		Advocacy/Action	
UN as Arena: States	Short term	Long term	Short term	Long term	Short term	Long term	Short term	Long term
UN as Actor: Secretariats	Short term	Long term	Short term	Long term	Short term	Long term	Short term	Long term

Our examination of ideas themselves has not sought to justify the UN as a talk-shop, but rather to probe its capacity to create and nurture concepts that have not only permeated international discourse and changed the way that individuals think, but have also proved eminently implementable. UN ideas have helped redefine the nature and content of national interests and have generated new commitments. They have provided road maps for decision-makers when priorities have clashed or when sequencing has been necessary. They have made new coalitions of actors possible. They have also become embedded in local, national, and international institutions.

People matter.

Ideas matter.

Notes

Introduction

1. Edward Mason and Robert Asher, *The World Bank since Bretton Woods* (Washington, D.C.: Brookings Institution, 1973); and Devesh Kapur, John P. Lewis, and Richard Webb, *The World Bank: Its First Half Century,* vol. 1: *History* (Washington, D.C.: Brookings Institution, 1997), and vol. 2: *Perspectives,* especially Nicholas Stern with Francisco Ferreira, pp. 523–609.

2. See, for example, Margaret G. de Vries, *The International Monetary Fund, 1945–1965: The Twenty Years of International Monetary Cooperation* (Washington, D.C.: IMF, 1969); *The International Monetary Fund, 1966–1971: The System under Stress* (Washington, D.C.: IMF, 1976); and *The International Monetary Fund, 1972–1978: Cooperation on Trial* (Washington, D.C.: IMF, 1985). See also Norman K. Humphreys, ed., *Historical Dictionary of the IMF* (Washington, D.C.: IMF, 2000).

3. Ngaire Woods, "Economic Ideas and International Relations: Beyond Rational Neglect," *International Studies Quarterly* 39 (1995): 164.

4. See, for example, Benjamin Rivlin and Leon Gordenker, eds., *The Challenging Role of the UN Secretary-General: Making "The Most Impossible Job in the World" Possible* (Westport, Conn.: Praeger, 1993).

5. Kofi Annan, *"We the Peoples": The United Nations in the Twenty-first Century* (New York: UN, 2000).

6. For a longer treatment of this literature and the project's approach, see Thomas G. Weiss and Tatiana Carayannis, "The UN, Its Economic and Social Ideas, and Their Agents: Toward an Analytical Framework," *Global Social Policy* 1, no. 1 (April 2001): 25–47.

7. Judith Goldstein and Robert O. Keohane, eds., *Ideas and Foreign Policy* (Ithaca, N.Y.: Cornell University Press, 1993).

8. Kathryn Sikkink, *Ideas and Institutions: Developmentalism in Argentina and Brazil* (Ithaca, N.Y.: Cornell University Press, 1991).

9. Peter M. Haas, "Introduction: Epistemic Communities and International Policy Coordination," *International Organization* 46, no. 1 (Winter 1992): 1–36; and Peter M. Haas, Robert O. Keohane, and Marc A. Levy, eds., *Institutions for the Earth: Sources of Effective International Environmental Protection* (Cambridge, Mass.: MIT Press, 1992).

10. Peter A. Hall, ed., *The Political Power of Economic Ideas: Keynesianism across Nations* (Princeton: Princeton University Press, 1989).

11. Ernst B. Haas, *When Knowledge Is Power: Three Models of Change in International Organizations* (Los Angeles: University of California Press, 1994); and see Peter M. Haas and Ernst B. Haas, "Learning to Learn: Improving International Governance," *Global Governance* 1, no. 3 (September–December 1995): 255–284.

12. Kathryn Sikkink, *Activists beyond Borders: Advocacy Networks in International Politics* (Ithaca, N.Y.: Cornell University Press, 1998).

13. Alexander Wendt, *Social Theory of International Politics* (Cambridge: Cambridge University Press, 1999).

14. John G. Ruggie, *Constructing the World Polity* (New York: Routledge, 1998).

15. See, for example, Robert W. Cox, ed., *The New Realism: Perspectives on Multilateralism and World Order* (New York: St. Martin's, 1997); Robert W. Cox with Timothy J. Sinclair, *Approaches to World Order* (Cambridge: Cambridge University Press, 1996); and Quintin Hoare and Geoffrey N. Smith, eds. and trans., *Selections from the Prison Notebooks of Antonio Gramsci* (London: Lawrence and Wishart, 1971).

16. Thomas S. Kuhn, *The Structure of Scientific Revolutions*, 2d ed. (Chicago: University of Chicago Press, 1970).

17. Quentin E. Skinner, "Meaning and Understanding in the History of Ideas," *History and Theory* 8 (1969): 42.

18. Woods, "Economic Ideas and International Relations," 168.

19. Frederick Cooper and Randall Packard, eds., *International Development and the Social Sciences: Essays on the History and Politics of Knowledge* (Berkeley: University of California Press, 1997), 17.

20. See Ramesh Thakur, ed., *What Is Equitable Geographic Representation in the Twenty-first Century* (Tokyo: UN University, 1999).

21. Arthur O. Lovejoy, *The Great Chain of Being* (New York: Torchbook, 1960).

22. See Morten Bøås and Desmond McNeill, eds., *The Role of Ideas in Multilateral Institutions*, forthcoming.

23. Morten Bøås, "Ideas in the Multilateral System: Master or Servant? Thinking about Studying the Role of Ideas in the Multilateral System," Paper for the Forty-first Annual Convention of the International Studies Association, March 2000, 1.

24. See Albert Yee, "The Causal Effects of Ideas on Policies," *International Organization* 50 (1996): 69–108.

25. John Maynard Keynes, *The General Theory of Employment, Interest, and Money* (London: Macmillan, 1936), 383.

26. Quoted by Joseph Kahn, "Multinationals Sign U.N. Pact on Rights and Environment," *New York Times*, 27 July 2000, A3.

27. Ideas are both normative and causal. We conceive of normative ideas as broad, general beliefs about what the world should look like, collapsing the usual categories in the literature of "worldviews" and "principled ideas." Principled ideas refer, for example, to a more equitable allocation of world income as a normative idea. Causal ideas are more operational beliefs about what strategy will have a desired result or what tactics will achieve a particular strategy. For example, at the UN, causal ideas often take the operational form of such targets as the 0.7 percent of GNP to be contributed as overseas development assistance (ODA). Ideas are more than slogans, but they usually are less than

full-blown theories. Thus, they should have behind them some reputable research and analysis, even if they are often contested. At the same time that we disaggregate ideas, we will work to understand better the relationship between norms and causes; in other words, we hope to unravel the process through which causal ideas are derived from normative ones.

28. Robert W. Cox, "Social Forces, States, and World Orders," in Robert O. Keohane, ed., *Neo-Realism and Its Critics* (New York: Columbia University Press, 1986), 219.

1. Four Powerful Ideas and the Early Years

1. See Gaddis Smith, "Woodrow Wilson's Fourteen Points after Seventy-five Years," Twelfth Morgenthau Memorial Lecture on Ethics and Foreign Policy, Carnegie Council on Ethics and International Affairs, 1993.

2. Ruth Leger Sivard, *World Military and Social Expenditures, 1998* (Washington, D.C.: World Priorities, 1998).

3. Peter Baehr and Leon Gordenker, *The United Nations: Reality and Ideal* (New York: Praeger, 1999), 11, quoting memoirs by U.S. Secretary of State Cordell Hull.

4. In 1945 there were sixty-three states in the world, and fifty met in San Francisco from April to June 1945, signing the founding documents on June 26. Poland signed soon afterward, thus becoming a founding member. At the end of the nineteenth century there were some fifty states in the world, and only twenty-six participated in the 1899 Hague Peace Conference. At the Second Hague Peace Conference in 1907 forty-four participated. Following World War I some ten to twelve new states were created or old ones had their borders redefined. As the millennium dawned and we go to press, 189 states were members of the UN, and the number is likely to grow.

5. This sentiment echoed Keynes' own book, *The Economic Consequences of the Peace* (London: Macmillan, 1919), so unpopular with the establishment when first published.

6. See Craig Murphy, *International Organization and Industrial Change: Global Governance since 1850* (Cambridge: Polity Press, 1994).

7. Egon Ranshofen-Wertheimer, *The International Secretariat: A Great Experiment in International Administration* (Washington, D.C.: Carnegie Endowment for International Peace, 1945). For the best-known articulation of the principles, see Dag Hammarskjöld, "The International Civil Servant in Law and in Fact," lecture of 30 May 1961, published (Oxford: Clarendon Press, 1961).

8. See Ruth B. Russell, *A History of the United Nations Charter* (Washington: Brookings Institution, 1958); and Leland M. Goodrich and Edvard Hambro, *Charter of the United Nations* (Boston: World Peace Foundation, 1946).

9. Letter to the Secretary-General, February 1939, quoted by Francis P. Walters, *A History of the League of Nations* (London: Oxford University Press, 1952), 760.

10. This summary is from Brian Urquhart, *Ralph Bunche: An American Life* (New York: Norton, 1993), 21; the quote is from p. 272. See also Benjamin Rivlin, ed., *Ralph Bunche: The Man and His Times* (New York: Holmes and Meier, 1990).

11. Edwin Tetlow, *The United Nations: The First Twenty-five Years* (London: Peyter Owen, 1970), 26.

12. Roger Normand and Sarah Zaidi, *A Critical History of Human Rights at the United Nations* (Bloomington: Indiana University Press, forthcoming).

13. See David A. Kay, *The New Nations in the United Nations 1960–1967* (New York: Columbia University Press, 1970).

14. See Neta C. Crawford, *Argument and Change in World Politics* (Cambridge: Cambridge University Press, forthcoming), especially chap. 7, "Self-Determination."

15. See Robert Aldrich and John Connell, *The Last Colonies* (Cambridge: Cambridge University Press, 1998).

16. Julius Nyerere, "Foreword," in Chakravarti Raghavan, *Recolonization: GATT, the Uruguay Round, and the Third World* (London: Zed Books, 1990), 19.

17. Quoted by Stanley Meisler, *United Nations: The First Fifty Years* (New York: Atlantic Monthly Press, 1995), 24.

18. For a snapshot of the changes, see UNDP, *Human Development Report 2000* (New York: Oxford University Press, 2000). For examinations of the historical developments, see Jack Donnelly, *International Human Rights* (Boulder: Westview, 1993); Tim Dunne and Nicholas J. Wheeler, eds., *Human Rights in Global Politics* (Cambridge: Cambridge University Press, 1999); and David P. Forsythe, *The Internationalization of Human Rights* (Lexington, Massachusetts: D. C. Heath, 1991).

19. See, for example, Danish Institute of International Affairs, *Humanitarian Intervention: Legal and Political Aspects* (Copenhagen: Danish Institute of International Affairs, 1999); Jonathan Moore, ed., *Hard Choices: Moral Dilemmas in Humanitarian Intervention* (Lanham, Md.: Rowman and Littlefield, 1998); James Mayall, ed., *The New Interventionism* (Cambridge: Cambridge University Press, 1996); Oliver Ramsbotham and Tom Woodhouse, *Humanitarian Intervention in Contemporary Conflict* (Cambridge: Polity Press, 1996); John Harriss, ed., *The Politics of Humanitarian Intervention* (London: Pinter, 1995); Stanley Hoffmann, *The Ethics and Politics of Humanitarian Intervention* (South Bend, Ind.: University of Notre Dame Press, 1996); and Thomas G. Weiss, *Military-Civilian Interactions: Intervening in Humanitarian Crises* (Lanham, Md.: Rowman and Littlefield, 1999).

20. Francis M. Deng et al., *Sovereignty as Responsibility* (Washington, D.C.: Brookings, 1995); and Francis M. Deng, "Frontiers of Sovereignty," *Leiden Journal of International Law* 8, no. 2 (1995): 249–286.

21. Adam Smith, *An Inquiry into the Nature and Causes of the Wealth of Nations* (Oxford: Clarendon Press, 1869).

22. For a discussion, see Peter A. Hall, ed., *The Political Power of Economic Ideas: Keynesianism across Nations* (Princeton: Princeton University Press, 1989).

23. Paul Samuelson, *Economics* (New York: McGraw-Hill, 1970). This point was made by Devesh Kapur, John P. Lewis, and Richard Webb, *The World Bank: Its First Half Century*, vol. 1: *History* (Washington, D.C.: Brookings Institution, 1997), 67.

24. UN, *National and International Measures for Full Employment* (New York: UN, 1949); *Measures for the Economic Development of Under-Developed Countries* (New York: UN, 1951); and *Measures for International Economic Stability* (New York: UN, 1951).

25. Signed (May 1950) "Preface," *Economic Survey of Europe 1949* (Geneva: UN, 1950), prepared by the Economic Research Division of the ECE, iii and iv.

26. UN, *Measures for Full Employment*, 5.

27. Ibid., 9.

28. Ibid., 10.

29. Political independence was spread out over the next three or four decades, although most of the larger countries achieved independence by the 1960s, far ahead of the timetable then anticipated by the colonial powers. These came to independence after 1950 — about ten in the 1950s, almost forty in the 1960s, another twenty in the 1970s, and a final ten in the 1980s. The disintegration of the Soviet empire and the breakup of the socialist bloc added another twenty in the 1990s.

30. In the early 1950s the other pioneering document was also published by the UN: Raúl Prebisch, *The Economic Development of Latin America and Its Principal Problems* (New York: UN, 1950).

31. Arthur Lewis, *The Theory of Economic Growth* (London: Allen and Unwin, 1955).

32. Walt W. Rostow, *The Stages of Economic Growth: A Non-Communist Manifesto* (Cambridge: Cambridge University Press, 1961); and "The Take-Off into Self Sustained Growth," *Economic Journal* 66, no. 261 (1956): 25–48.

33. Peter Bauer and Basil Yamey, *The Economics of Under-Developed Countries* (Cambridge: Cambridge University Press, 1957).

34. Gunnar Myrdal, *Economic Theory and Under-Developed Regions* (London: G. Duckworth, 1957); see also Gunnar Myrdal, *Development and Under-Development; A Note on the Mechanism of National and International Economic Inequality,* National Bank of Egypt fiftieth anniversary commemoration lectures (Cairo: National Bank of Egypt, 1956).

35. Albert Hirschman, *The Strategy of Economic Development* (New Haven: Yale University Press, 1958); Ragnar Nurkse, *Lectures on Economic Development* (Istanbul: Istanbul University Press, 1958).

36. Eugene Staley, *World Economic Development* (Montreal: ILO, 1944).

37. Roy Harrod, "An Essay in Dynamic Theory," *Economic Journal* 49 (1939): 14–33; and *Towards a Dynamic Economics* (London: Macmillan, 1948).

38. UN, *Measures for Economic Development,* 9.

39. Ibid., 17.

40. Ibid., 29.

41. Ibid., 32.

42. UN, *Measures for International Economic Stability,* 3.

43. Ibid., 6.

44. Ibid., 25.

45. Ibid., 12.

46. Ibid., 13.

47. Independent Commission on International Development headed by Willy Brandt, *North-South: A Programme for Survival* (London: Pan Books, 1980). See also the follow-on report, *Common Crisis: North-South Cooperation for World Recovery* (Cambridge, Mass.: MIT Press, 1983).

48. Peter Bauer, 'The United Nations Report on the Economic Development of Under-Developed Countries," *Economic Journal* 63 (March 1953): 210–222.

49. Ibid., 213.

50. UN, *Measures for Economic Development,* 21.

51. World Bank, *Report on Cuba* (Baltimore: Johns Hopkins University Press, 1951), 425. As far as we know, Peter Bauer never commented on whether this was appropriate language for a World Bank report—but it certainly made reading more interesting, and perhaps more realistic!

52. Bauer, "The United Nations Report," 214–215.

53. UN, *Measures for Economic Development*, 73.

54. *Measures for International Economic Stability* had itself stated that "it would certainly be wrong to think that the supposedly unfavourable trend of the prices of primary products relative to manufactures in the half century ending in the 1930s leads to any presumption that the trend in the next half century will be in the same direction." (p. 15).

55. Data and analysis are taken from Alfred Maizels, T. Palaskas, and T. Crowe, "The Prebisch-Singer Hypothesis Revisited," in *Development Economics and Policy*, ed. Hans W. Singer, David Sapsford, and John-ren Chen (London: Macmillan Press, 1998), 65.

56. "Could It Happen Again," *Economist* (20 February 1999).

57. See, for example, Prebisch, *The Economic Development of Latin America and Its Principal Problems*; and Hans Singer, "The Distribution of Gains Between Investing and Borrowing Countries," *American Economic Review* 40, no. 2 (1950): 473–485.

58. Kapur, Lewis, and Webb, *The World Bank: Its First Half Century*, 92.

59. Herbert Frankel, "United Nations Primer for Development," *Quarterly Journal of Economics* 66, no. 3 (August 1952): 303.

60. Bauer, "The United Nations Report," 222.

61. Arthur Lewis, "United Nations Primer for Development: Comment," *Quarterly Journal of Economics* 67, no. 2 (May 1953): 275.

2. Development Hits Its Stride in the 1960s

1. For a discussion, see Peter Willets, *The Non-Aligned Movement: The Origins of the Third World Alliance* (London: Pinter, 1978); J. W. Burton, *Non-Alignment* (London: Deutsch, 1966); C. V. D. Crabb, *The Elephants and the Grass: A Study of Non-Alignment* (New York: Praeger, 1965); and L. W. Martin, ed., *Neutralism and Nonalignment: The New States in World Affairs* (New York: Praeger, 1962).

2. See Sidney Dell, "Economics in the United Nations," in *Economists in International Agencies*, ed. A. W. Coats (New York: Praeger, 1986), 44–45.

3. Devesh Kapur, John P. Lewis, and Richard Webb, *The World Bank: Its First Half Century*, vol. 1: *History* (Washington, D.C.: Brookings 1997), 154.

4. UN, *The United Nations Development Decade* (New York: UN, 1962), 6.

5. Ibid., 7. In fact, by 1995 it seemed that growth in the developing countries had been more like 4.5 percent per annum from 1955 to 1960, but that it had slowed to 4 percent from 1960 to 1963. See UN, *The United Nations Development Decade at Mid-point* (New York: UN, 1965), 6. For a discussion of the entire period, see Colin Legum, ed., *The First U.N. Development Decade and Its Lessons for the 1970's* (New York: Praeger, 1970).

6. UN, *The United Nations Development Decade*, vi.

7. The hoped-for centralization turned out to be less complete than many had hoped. For the most critical report at the time on this topic, see UNDP (Robert Jackson), *Capacity Study* (New York: UNDP, 1969).

8. UN, *The United Nations Development Decade,* 11.

9. See Richard Jolly, Louis Emmerij, Dharam Ghai, and Frédéric Lapeyre, *International Development Strategies: New Approaches in the 1960s and 1970s and New Orthodoxies in the 1980s and 1990s* (Bloomington: Indiana University Press, forthcoming).

10. Frank Fenner et al, *Smallpox and its Eradication,* History of International Public Health No. 6 (Geneva: WHO, 1988); and Maggie Black, *The Children and the Nations: The Story of UNICEF* (New York: UNICEF, 1986).

11. Hans Singer, *Men without Work* (Cambridge: Cambridge University Press, 1938).

12. See Peter T. Ellsworth, "The Terms of Trade between Primary Producing and Industrial Countries," *Inter-American Economic Affairs* 10 (Summer 1956): 47–65; Hans Singer, "The Terms of Trade Controversy and the Evolution of Soft Financing," and Bela Balassa, "Comment," in *Pioneers in Development,* ed. Gerald Meier and Dudley Seers (New York: Oxford University Press, 1984).

13. For a comprehensive study see, for example, Dimitris Diakosavvas and Pasquale L. Scandizzo, "Trends in the Terms of Trade of Primary Products, 1900–1982: The Controversy and Its Origin," *Economic Development and Cultural Change* 39, no. 2 (January 1991): 231–264; and Paul Bairoch, *The Economic Development of the Third World since 1900* (Berkeley: University of California Press, 1975).

14. See John Toye and Richard Toye, "The Origins of the Prebisch-Singer Thesis," Chapter 3 in John Toye and Richard Toye, *Trade, Finance, and Development* (Bloomington: Indiana University Press, forthcoming). The key document on which Singer worked is UN, *Relative Prices of Exports and Imports of Under-Developed Countries: A Study of Post-War Terms of Trade between Under-Developed and Industrialized Countries* (Lake Success, N.Y.: UN Department of Economic Affairs, 1949). Singer's first independently signed and published article was later, "The Distribution of Gains between Investing and Borrowing Countries," *American Economic Review* 40, no. 2 (1950): 473–485.

15. General Agreement on Tariffs and Trade, *Trends in International Trade, A Report by a Panel of Experts* (Geneva: GATT, 1958).

16. For details, see Michael Zammit-Cutajar, ed., *UNCTAD and the South-North Dialogue: The First Twenty Years* (London: Pergamon, 1985); Robert L. Rothstein, *Global Bargaining: UNCTAD and the Quest for a New International Economic Order* (Princeton: Princeton University Press, 1979); Branislov Gosovic, *UNCTAD: Compromise and Conflict* (Leiden: Sijthoff, 1972); Diego Cordovez, *UNCTAD and Development Diplomacy: From Conference to Strategy* (London: Journal of World Trade Law, 1970); Kamal Hagras, *United Nations Conference on Trade and Development: A Case Study in UN Diplomacy* (New York: Praeger, 1965); and Thomas G. Weiss, *Multilateral Development Diplomacy in UNCTAD: The Lessons of Group Negotiations, 1964–84* (London: Macmillan, 1986).

17. Georges Balandier and Alfred Sauvy, *Le "Tiers-Monde," sous développement et développement* (Paris: Presse Universitaire de France, 1961).

18. See Joseph S. Nye, "UNCTAD: Poor Nations' Pressure Group," in *The Anatomy of Influence — Decision Making in International Organization,* ed. Robert W. Cox and Harold K. Jacobson (New Haven: Yale University Press, 1973), 334–370.

19. Richard Wright, *The Color Curtain* (Jackson, Miss.: Banner Books, 1956), 13–14.

20. See Olav Stokke, *International Development Assistance* (Bloomington: Indiana University Press, forthcoming).

21. Stephen Browne, *Foreign Aid in Practice* (New York: New York University Press, 1990), 14. Chapters 1 and 2 of this book contain an overview of East-West competition in the aid business.

22. Jan Tinbergen, "What Is Peace Economics?" *Peace Economics, Peace Science, and Public Policy* 1, no. 4 (Summer 1994): 1–2.

23. See, for example, Judith Randel and Tony German, eds., *The Reality of Aid 1997–1998* (London: Earthscan, 1997).

24. Commission on International Development, *Partners in Development* (New York: Praeger, 1969).

25. See Thomas G. Weiss and Anthony Jennings, *More for the Least? Prospects for the Poorest Countries in the Eighties* (Lexington, Mass.: D. C. Heath, 1983).

26. UNDP, *Human Development Report 1992* (New York: Oxford University Press, 1992).

27. OECD, Development Assistance Committee Statistics; available on the Internet at www.oecd.org/dac/htm/dacstats.htm.

3. Employment Creation and Basic Needs

1. Dudley Seers, "The Meaning of Development," *International Development Review* 11, no. 4 (1969): 3.

2. Simon Kuznets, "Economic Growth and Income Inequality," *American Economic Review* 45 (1955): 1–28.

3. See, for example, Sudhir Anand and Ravi Kanbur, "The Kuznets Process and the Inequality-Development Relationship," *Journal of Development Economics* 40, no. 1 (1981): 25–52; and Klaus Deininger and Lyn Squire, "New Ways of Looking at Old Issues: Inequality and Growth," *Journal of Development Economics* 57, no. 2 (1998): 259–287.

4. Amartya Sen, "Development: Which Way Now?" *Economic Journal* 93 (December 1983): 745–762.

5. The ILO World Employment Program played an important role here, together with the Institute of Development Studies at the University of Sussex, which led to Hollis Chenery et al., *Redistribution with Growth: Policies to Improve Income Distribution in Developing Countries in the Context of Economic Growth* (London: Oxford University Press, 1974). See also Alec Cairncross and Mohinder Puri, eds., *Employment, Income Distribution, and Development Strategy: Problems of the Developing Countries: Essays in Honour of Hans W. Singer* (London: Macmillan, 1979).

6. ILO, *Scope, Approach, and Content of Research-Oriented Activities of the World Employment Programme* (Geneva: ILO, 1972).

7. John Fei and Gustav Ranis, *Development of the Labor Surplus Economy: Theory and Policy* (Homewood, Ill.: R. D. Irwin, 1972).

8. For a retrospective view, see Harold Lubell, *The Informal Sector in the 1980s and 1990s* (Paris: OECD, 1991).

9. Hans W. Singer, *Technologies for Basic Needs* (Geneva: ILO, 1977).

10. Mark Blaug, *An Introduction to Economics of Education* (New York: Pergamon Press, 1968).

11. ILO, *Matching Employment Opportunities and Expectations: A Programme of Action*

for Ceylon (Geneva: ILO, 1971); and ILO, *Employment, Incomes, and Equality: A Strategy for Increasing Productive Employment in Kenya* (Geneva: ILO, 1972).

12. Amartya Sen, *Employment, Technology, and Development: A Study Prepared for the ILO within the Framework of the WEP* (Oxford: Clarendon Press, 1975).

13. Arthur C. Pigou, *Unemployment* (London: Williams and Norgate, 1913).

14. Arthur C. Pigou, *Theory of Unemployment* (London: Macmillan, 1933).

15. John Maynard Keynes, *The General Theory of Employment, Interest, and Money* (London: Macmillan, 1936), 289.

16. Ibid., 260.

17. ILO, *Employment, Growth and Basic Needs: A One World Problem* (Geneva: ILO, 1976), also published commercially as *Employment, Growth, and Basic Needs: A One World Problem—The International "Basic Needs Strategy" against Chronic Poverty* (New York: Praeger, 1977). See also Dharam Ghai et al., *The Basic-Needs Approach to Development: Some Issues Regarding Concepts and Methodology* (Geneva: ILO, 1977).

18. Albert H. Maslow, "A Theory of Human Motivation," *Psychological Review* 50, no. 3 (March 1942): 370–396.

19. Dag Hammarskjöld Foundation, *What Now? Another Development* (Uppsala, Sweden: Dag Hammarskjöld Foundation, 1975).

20. Glen Sheehan and Mike Hopkins, *Basic Needs Performance: An Analysis of Some International Data* (Geneva: ILO, 1979).

21. ILO, *Employment, Growth, and Basic Needs.*

22. Paul Streeten et al., *First Things First: Meeting Basic Human Needs in the Developing Countries* (New York: Oxford University Press, 1981). See also the discussion by Devesh Kapur, John P. Lewis, and Richard Webb, *The World Bank: Its First Half Century*, vol. 1: *History* (Washington, D.C.: Brookings Institution, 1997), 215–330.

23. Edward C. Luck, *Mixed Messages: American Politics and International Organizations 1919–1999* (Washington, D.C.: Brookings Institution, 1999).

24. ILO, *Unemployment in Its National and International Aspects, Report of a Conference, Organized by the League of Nations Union of Great Britain, and Held in London, 25–27 March 1924*, Studies and Reports, Series C (Unemployment), no. 9 (Geneva: ILO, 1924).

25. The International Labor Office in collaboration with Professors Ansiaux, Cole, Hahn, and Hersch, *ILO: Unemployment Problems in 1931*, Studies and Reports, Series C (Employment and Unemployment), no. 16 (Geneva: ILO, 1931).

26. Ibid., 29.

27. Ibid., 38.

28. Ibid., 70.

29. Ibid., 72–73.

30. ILO, *Bibliography of Published Research of the World Employment Programme* (Geneva: ILO, 1986).

31. ILO, *Towards Full Employment: A Programme for Columbia* (Geneva: ILO, 1970); and ILO, *Matching Employment Opportunities and Expectations.*

32. ILO, *Employment, Incomes, and Equality.*

33. ILO, *Matching Employment Opportunities and Expectations.*

34. Chenery et al., *Redistribution with Growth.*

35. See, for example, V. Djukanovic and E. P. Mach, eds., *Alternative Approaches to Meeting Basic Health Needs in Developing Countries—A UNICEF/WHO Study* (Geneva: WHO, 1975).

36. Robert McNamara, extract of his speech to the Annual Meeting of the Governors, Nairobi, 1973.

37. Johan Galtung, Peter O'Brien, and Roy Preiswerk, *Self-Reliance, A Strategy for Development* (London: Bogle-L'Ouverture Publications, 1980).

38. Robert E. Riggs and Jack C. Plano, *The United Nations,* 2d ed. (Belmont, Mass.: Wadsworth Publishing Company, 1994), 160.

39. UN, *Economic and Social Consequences of the Arms Race and Military Expenditures* (New York: UN, 1972, 1978, and 1983); UN, *Report on Disarmament and Development* (New York: UN, 1972); UN, *Reduction of the Military Budgets of States Permanent Members of the Security Council of 10 Percent and Utilization of Parts of That Funds Thus Saved to Provide Assistance to Developing Countries,* document A/9770/Rev.1.(New York: UN, 1975).

40. Serge Sur, ed., *Disarmament Agreements and Negotiations: The Economic Dimension* (New York: UN Institute for Disarmament Research, 1991); and Manas Chatterji, Henk Jager, and Annemarie Rima, eds., *The Economics of International Security: Essays in Honour of Jan Tinbergen* (New York: St. Martin's, 1994).

41. UN, *The Relationship between Disarmament and Development, Report of the Secretary-General* (The Thorsson Report) (New York: UN, 1982).

42. Among the unpublished background reports prepared for the Thorsson group were the following: "The Effects of Arms Transfers on Developing Countries"; "Defense Spending, Economic Structure, and Growth"; and "Formalized Studies and Econometric Analyses of the Relationships between Military Expenditure and Economic Development."

43. UN, "Impact of the Arms Race on Economic Growth and Development," in *The Relationship between Disarmament and Development;* and Wassily Leontief and Faye Duchin, *Military Spending: Facts and Figures, Worldwide Implications, and Future Outlook* (New York: Oxford University Press, 1983).

44. John F. Murphy, "Force and Arms," in *The United Nations and International Law,* ed. Christopher C. Joyner (Cambridge: Cambridge University Press, 1997), 122.

45. Data from UNDP, *Human Development Report 2000* (New York: Oxford University Press, 2000), 214, Table 16.

46. The basic-needs strategy and the Kenya report in particular were attacked from the left by those arguing that it was really promoting soft-minded reformism. See, for instance, Colin Leys, *Underdevelopment in Kenya: The Political Economy of Neo Colonialism, 1964–71* (Berkeley: University of California Press, 1975).

4. UN World Conferences and Global Challenges

1. See UN, *The World Conferences: Developing Priorities for the Twenty-first Century* (New York: UN, 1997); and Jacques Fomerand, "UN Conferences: Media Events or Genuine Diplomacy," *Global Governance* 2, no. 3 (September–December 1996): 361–375.

2. See, for example, Barry Commoner, *The Closing Circle: Nature, Man, and Technology* (New York: Knopf, 1971).

3. Boutros Boutros-Ghali, "Secretary General Inaugurates UN Conference on Human Settlements (HABITAT II)," Press Release HAB/IST/3, 3 June 1996.

4. Boutros Boutros-Ghali, "Opening Statement—World Summit for Social Development," Press Conference, 6 March 1995.

5. See Nico Schrijver, *The United Nations and Global Resource Management* (Bloomington: Indiana University Press, forthcoming).

6. We have not edited the language of the time, which is gender-insenstive.

7. Rachel Carson, *Silent Spring* (Boston: Houghton Mifflin, 1962); and Paul R. Ehrlich, *The Population Bomb* (New York: Ballantine, 1968).

8. See *Development and Environment: Report and Working Papers of a Panel of Experts Convened by the Secretary-General of the UN Conference on Human Environment* (New York: UN, 1972).

9. Donella H. Meadows et al., *The Limits to Growth: A Report for the Club of Rome's Project on the Predicament on Mankind* (London: Pan, 1972).

10. Carson's and Ehrlich's works had appeared somewhat earlier, of course, and Fairfield Osborn had written a book in 1948 that is still widely quoted in writings on environmental and conservation issues. See Fairfield Osborn, *Our Plundered Planet* (Boston: Little, Brown, 1948).

11. *Development and Environment*, ix.

12. Patricia Birne, "The UN and the Environment," in *United Nations, Divided World*, 2d ed., ed. Adam Roberts and Benedict Kingsbury (Oxford: Clarendon Press, 1993), 343.

13. See, for example, M. W. Holdgate, M. Kassas, and G. White, eds., *The World Environment 1972–1982: A Report by the United Nations Environment Programme, Natural Resources and the Environment* (Dublin: Tycooly, 1982); and Mostafa K. Tolba and O. A. El-Kholy, *The World Environment 1972–1992: Two Decades of Challenge* (London: Chapman and Hall, 1992).

14. See Sally Morphet, "NGOs and the Environment," in *"The Conscience of the World": The Influence of NGOs in the UN System*, ed. Peter Willets (London: Hurst, 1996), 116–146.

15. Barbara Ward and René Dubos, *Only One Earth: The Care and the Maintenance of a Small Planet* (Harmondsworth: Penguin, 1972).

16. World Commission on Environment and Development (Brundtland Commission), *Our Common Future* (Oxford: Oxford University Press, 1987), ix–x.

17. See Nitin Desai, "Address to the Organizational Session of the Open-ended Working Group of ECOSOC on the Review of Arrangement for Consultation with NGOs," 17 February 1994.

18. *Report on the United Nations Conference on Environment and Development*, vol. 4, document A/CONF.151/26 (New York: UN, 28 September 1992), 74.

19. UN, *Agenda 21: The UN Programme of Action from Rio* (New York: UN, 1997).

20. John Vogler, "Environment and Natural Resources," in *Issues in World Politics*, ed. Brian White, Richard Little, and Michael Smith (New York: St Martin's, 1997), 241.

21. See Robert Wade, "Greening the Bank: The Struggle over the Environment," in *The World Bank: Its Second Half Century*, vol. 2: *Perspectives*, ed. Devesh Kapur, John P. Lewis, and Richard Webb (Washington, D.C.: Brookings Institution, 1997), 611–734.

22. See Jason L. Finkle and Barbara B. Crane, "The Politics of Bucharest: Population, Development, and the New International Economic Order," *Population and Development Review* 1, no.1 (1975): 87–114.

23. "Country Statement by Dr. Karan Singh, Minister of Health and Family Planning, India, August 1974," in UN, *UN World Population Conference, 1974* (New York: UN, 1974), 3.

24. Kaval Gulhati and Lisa M. Bates, "Developing Countries and the International Population Debate: Politics and Pragmatism," in *Population and Development: Old Debates, New Conclusions*, ed. Robert Cassen (Washington, D.C.: Overseas Development Council, 1994), 51.

25. Mohammad Ali Taskhiri (Iran), "Intervention at the International Conference on Population and Development this Morning," document POP/CAI/14, 7th Meeting (AM), 8 September 1994.

26. UN, *Population and Development: Programme of Action Adopted at the International Conference on Population and Development Cairo, 5–13 September 1994*, vol. 1 (New York: UN, 1995).

27. "Plenary POP/572, Press Release, Final Meeting and 14 September 1994 Round-up of Session International Conference on Population and Development Concludes in Cairo, 5–13 September, Adopts Programme of Action Emphasizing Reproductive Rights; Health Needs; Empowering Women; Sustainable Development Pattern."

28. Plenary—3—Press Release POP/CAI/18 10th Meeting (PM), 9 September 1994, Kari Nordheim-Larsen, Minister for Development Cooperation of Norway.

29. Henry A. Kissinger, "A Just Consensus, a Stable Order, a Durable Peace," Address to the 28th session of the General Assembly, 24 September 1973, Department of State Pub. no. 8742, p. 8.

30. See Thomas G. Weiss and Robert S. Jordan, *The World Food Conference and Global Problem Solving* (New York: Praeger, 1976).

31. UN, *Assessment of the World Food Situation: Present and Future*, document E/CONF.65/PREP.16 (New York: UN, 1974).

32. UN, *The World Food Problem: Proposals for National and International Action*, document E/CONF.65/4 (New York: UN, 1974).

33. Daniel P. Moynihan, "A Dangerous Place," *Commentary*, March 1975, and *A Dangerous Place* (Boston: Little, Brown, 1978). For a discussion of these days and Moynihan's role, see Seymour Maxwell Finger, *Your Man at the U.N.* (New York: New York University Press, 1980), chap. 7.

34. See Robert L. Rothstein, *Global Bargaining: UNCTAD and the Quest for a New International Economic Order* (Princeton: Princeton University Press, 1979).

35. Chris Brown, *Understanding International Relations* (New York: St. Martin's, 1997), 194.

36. Independent Commission on International Development Issues, *North-South: A Programme for Survival* (Cambridge, Mass.: MIT Press, 1980).

37. Rosemary Righter, *Utopia Lost— The United Nations and World Order* (New York: Twentieth Century Fund, 1995), 117.

38. Robert W. Cox, "Ideologies and the New International Economic Order: Reflections

on Some Recent Literature," in *Approaches to World Order,* ed. Robert W. Cox and Timothy J. Sinclair (Cambridge: Cambridge University Press, 1996), 377.

39. For a collection of views, see UN Institute for Training and Research, *A New International Economic Order: Selected Documents 1945–1975* (New York: UNITAR, 1976), 2 vols.

40. UNCTAD, *The Third United Nations Conference on the Least Developed Countries: First Meeting of the Intergovernmental Preparatory Committee,* document A/CONF.191/IPC/ 12, 14 July 2000; and Thomas G. Weiss and Anthony Jennings, *More for the Least? Prospects for Poorest Countries in the Eighties* (Lexington, Mass.: D. C. Heath, 1983).

41. UNDP, *Human Development Report 1995* (New York: Oxford University Press, 1995), 10.

42. See Martha Alter Chen, "Gendering World Conferences: The International Women's Movement and the UN," *Third World Quarterly* 16, no. 3 (1995): 477–494; and Jane Connors, "NGOs and the Human Rights of Women at the UN," in Willets, ed., *"The Conscience of the World,"* 147–180.

43. See UN, *From Nairobi to Beijing— Second Review and Appraisal of the Implementation of the Nairobi Forward-looking Strategies for the Advancement of Women: Report of the Secretary General* (New York: UN, 1995); and *Platform for Action and the Beijing Declaration, Fourth World Conference on Women,* Beijing, China, 4–15 September 1995 (New York: UN, 1995).

44. See UN, *Report of the Fourth World Conference on Women, Beijing, 4–15 September 1995,* publication sales no. E.96.IV.13, Resolution 1, Annex II (New York: UN, 1996).

45. UN, *Report of the Secretary-General: Initiation of the Comprehensive Review and Appraisal of the Implementation of the Beijing Platform for Action,* Commission on the Status of Women Acting as the Preparatory Committee for the Special Session of the General Assembly Entitled "Women 2000: Gender Equality, Development and Peace for the Twenty-first Century," second session, 15–19 March 1999.

46. See UN, *Human Settlement: The Environmental Challenge* (New York: UN, 1974).

47. Habitat Conference Secretariat, ed., *Aspects of Human Settlement Planning* (New York: Pergamon Press, 1977).

48. UNDP, *Human Development Report 2000* (New York: Oxford University Press, 2000), chap. 2.

49. UN, *World Conference on Human Rights: The Vienna Declaration and Program of Action* (New York: UN, 1995).

50. UNDP, *Human Development Report 2000,* cover.

51. See Felice D. Gaer, "Reality Check: Human Rights NGOs Confront Governments at the UN," *Third World Quarterly* 16, no. 3 (1995): 389–404.

52. Ellen Dorsey, "The Global Women's Movement," in *The Politics of Global Governance,* ed. Paul F. Diehl (Boulder: Lynne Rienner, 1997), 343.

53. See Philip Alston, ed., *The Best Interests of the Child* (Oxford: Clarendon Press, 1994); and Joel E. Oestreich, "UNICEF and the Implementation of the Convention on the Rights of the Child," *Global Governance* 4, no. 2 (April–June 1998): 183–198.

54. "The Quality Benchmark for the Social Summit, An NGO Statement for the Third Session of the Preparatory Committee of the Social Summit," October 1994.

55. UN, *Declaration on Social Development and Programme of Action of the World Summit for Social Development* (New York: UN, 1995), report of the main committee, additive.

56. "The Copenhagen Alternative Declaration," dated 8 March 1995. Internet document available at www.un.org/events/conferences.htm.

57. See Kofi Annan, *Renewing the United Nations: A Programme for Reform* (New York: UN, 1997).

58. UNDP, *Human Development Report 1999* (New York: Oxford University Press, 1999), 100.

59. Fomerand, "UN Conferences: Media Events or Genuine Diplomacy," 366.

60. See, for example, Peter Patbury, "UNCED and the Globalization of Civil Society," in *United Nations Reform*, ed. Erik Fawcett and Hanna Newcombe (Toronto: Dundurn, 1995), 208.

61. Jonathan A. Fox, "The World Bank Inspection Panel: Lessons from the First Five Years," *Global Governance* 6, no. 3 (July–September 2000): 279–318.

62. UN, World Bank Group, IMF, and OECD, *2000: A Better World for All* (Washington, D.C.: Grundy and Northedge, 2000).

63. See, for example, H. W. Singer and Richard Jolly, eds., *Fifty Years On: The UN and Economic and Social Development*, special issue of *IDS Bulletin* 26, no. 4 (October 1995).

5. Current Orthodoxy, the New Social Question, and Policy Alternatives

1. Albert Hirschman, "The Rise and Decline of Development Economics," in Albert Hirschman, *Essays in Trespassing: Economics to Politics and Beyond* (New York: Cambridge University Press, 1981), 384.

2. David C. Colander, ed., *Neoclassical Political Economy: The Analysis of Rent-Seeking and DUP Activities* (Cambridge: Ballinger, 1984); T. N. Srinivasan, "Neoclassical Political Economy, the State, and Economic Development," *Asian Development Review* 3, no. 2 (1985): 40–45; James M. Buchanan, *Liberty, Market, and State: Political Economy in the 1980s* (New York: New York University Press, 1985); Charles K. Rowley, Robert D. Tollison, and Gordon Tullock, eds., *The Political Economy of Rent-Seeking* (Boston: Kluwer Academic Publishers, 1988); James Buchanan, Robert Tollison, and Gordon Tullock, eds., *Toward a Theory of Rent-Seeking Society* (College Station: Texas A&M University Press, 1980); Deepak Lal, "The Political Economy of Economic Liberalization," *World Bank Economic Review* 1, no.1 (1987): 273–285; and Anne Krueger, "Government Failures in Development," *Journal of Economic Perspectives* 4, no. 3 (1990): 9–24.

3. League of Nations, *International Financial Conference* (London: Harrison and Sons, Ltd., 1920), 3.

4. League of Nations, *Proceedings of the International Financial Conference*, vol. 1 (Geneva: League of Nations, 1920), 12.

5. League of Nations, *Official Journal* 32 (October 1925): 16.

6. Per Jacobsson, "The Theoretical Solution as Seen by the Conference," in *The Economic Consequences of the League*, ed. Arthur Salter (London: Europa Publishing Co., 1927), 53.

7. Francis P. Walters, *A History of the League of Nations* (New York: Oxford University Press, 1952), 426.

8. ILO, *XVI Annual Conference Proceedings* (Geneva: ILO, 1933), 889.

9. League of Nations, *General Programme of the Conference Prepared by Preparatory Commission* (Geneva: League of Nations, 1933).

10. Secretariat of the League of Nations, *Report and Proceedings of the Monetary and Economic Conference* (Geneva: League of Nations, 1933), 7.

11. United States Department of State, Press Release 197 (July 1933), 15.

12. Walters, *A History of the League of Nations*, 520–523.

13. Franklin D. Roosevelt, *The Inaugural Address of Franklin Delano Roosevelt, Thirty-second President of the United States, March 4, 1933* (Washington: U.S. Government Printing Office, 1933).

14. See, for example, John Williamson, ed., *IMF Conditionality* (Cambridge, Mass.: MIT Press, 1983).

15. See Ernest Stern, "World Bank Financing of Structural Adjustment," in Williamson, ed., *IMF Conditionality*, 89; and Vittorio Corbo and Stanley Fischer, "Structural Adjustment, Stabilization and Policy Reform: Domestic and International Finance," in *Handbook of Development Economics*, vol. 3, ed. Jere Behrman and T. N. Srinivasan (New York: Elsevier, 1995), 2846–2923.

16. See, for example, Jagdish Bhagwati, *Foreign Trade Regimes and Economic Development: Anatomy and Consequences of Exchange Control Regimes* (Cambridge: Ballinger, 1978); and Anne Krueger, *Foreign Trade Regimes and Economic Development: Liberalization Attempts and Consequences* (Cambridge: Ballinger, 1978).

17. See Gerry Helleiner, "The IMF, the World Bank, and Africa's Adjustment and External Debt Problems: An Unofficial View," *World Development* 20, no. 6 (June 1992): 779–792.

18. Anne Krueger, "Problems of Liberalization" in *World Economic Growth*, ed. Arnold C. Haberger (San Francisco: Institute for Contemporary Studies, 1984), 403–23; Anne Krueger, *Economic Policy Reform in Developing Countries* (Cambridge: Blackwell, 1992); Max W. Corden, "Protection and Liberalization: A Review of Analytical Issues," *IMF Occasional Papers* 54 (August 1987); Vittorio Corbo, M. Goldstein, and M. Khan, eds., *Growth-oriented Adjustment Programs* (Washington: IMF and the World Bank, 1987); and Michael Roemer and Steven Radelet, "Macroeconomic Reform in Developing Countries," in *Reforming Economic Systems in Developing Countries*, ed. Dwight Perkins and Michael Roemer (Cambridge, Mass.: Harvard Institute for International Development, 1991), 56–80.

19. World Bank, *Accelerated Development in Sub-Saharan Africa: An Agenda for Action* (Washington, D.C.: World Bank, 1981).

20. See John Williamson, ed., *Latin America Adjustment: How Much Has Happened?* (Washington, D.C.: Institute for International Economics, 1990); and John Williamson, "The Washington Consensus Revisited," in *Economic and Social Development into the Twenty-first Century*, ed. Louis Emmerij (Baltimore: Johns Hopkins University Press, 1997), 48–61.

21. Moisés Naim, "Fads and Fashion in Economic Reforms: Washington Consensus or Washington Confusion?" *Third World Quarterly*, 21, no. 3 (June 2000): 505.

22. For a presentation of SAP see, for example, Vittorio Corbo and Stanley Fischer, "Structural Adjustment, Stabilization and Policy Reform: Domestic and International Finance," in Behrman and Srinivasan, eds., *Handbook of Development Economics*, vol. 3, 2845–2923; and Paul Streeten, "Structural Adjustment: A Survey of the Issues and Options," *World Development* 15, no. 2 (1987), pp. 1469–1482.

23. ONU/DASEI, database, 1986.

24. Giovanni A. Cornia, Richard Jolly, and Frances Stewart, eds., *Adjustment with a Human Face* (Oxford: Clarendon Press, 1987).

25. Richard Jolly, "Adjustment with a Human Face," in *Development: Seeds of Change*, no. 4 (1985): 83. The history of UNICEF's role in bringing this change has been documented in a special issue of *World Development* 19, no. 12 (December 1991). See articles by Richard Jolly, Rolph van der Hoeven, Giovanni Andrea Cornia, Gerald Helleiner, and Frances Stewart, each of whom contributed to the evolution of UNICEF's thinking and policy development.

26. World Bank, *World Development Report 1990: Poverty* (New York: Oxford University Press, 1990), 103.

27. IMF, "Forces of Globalization Must Be Embraced," *IMF Survey* 26, no.10 (1997): 154.

28. See a discussion in ILO, *World Employment Report* (Geneva: ILO, 1995).

29. ILO, *Defending Values, Promoting Change: Social Justice in a Global Economy, an ILO Agenda* (Geneva: ILO, 1994), 18.

30. UNRISD, *States in Disarray* (Geneva: UN, 1995).

31. Joseph Stiglitz, "Towards a New Paradigm for Development: Strategies, Policies, and Processes," 1998 Prebisch Lecture (Geneva: UNCTAD, 1998); see also Joseph Stiglitz, "Must Financial Crisis Be This Frequent and This Painful?" Paper presented as the MacKay Lecture, University of Pittsburgh, Pennsylvania, 23 September 1998.

32. This theme has been addressed in a number of reports from Geneva, especially since the Asian financial crisis. See UNCTAD's annual *Trade and Development Report* (New York: UN, various years); and the UN ECE's annual *Economic Survey of Europe* (Geneva: UN, various years).

33. See UNDP, *Human Development Report 2000* (New York: Oxford University Press, 2000), 182, Table 8.

34. Nancy Birdsall, "Life Is Unfair," *Foreign Policy*, no. 111 (Summer 1998): 76–93.

35. UNDP, *Human Development Report 1999* (New York: Oxford University Press, 1999), 39.

36. European Commission, *Employment in Europe* (Brussels: European Commission DGV, 1999), 9.

37. Jiri Vecernik, "Vox Populi—What Do People in Central and Eastern Europe Think of Their Reforms?" World Bank, 1997, www.worldbank.org/html/prddr/trans/janfeb97/art7.htm.

38. Francis Fukuyama, *The End of History and the Last Man* (New York: Free Press, 1992), xiv.

39. Council of Europe, *In From the Margins* (Strasbourg: Council of Europe, 1996), 9.

40. Amartya Sen, *Poverty and Famines: An Essay on Entitlement and Deprivation*

(Oxford: Clarendon Press, 1981); and *Resources, Values, and Development* (Cambridge, Mass.: Harvard University Press, 1984).

41. Amartya Sen, "Assessing Human Development," in UNDP, *Human Development Report 1999*, 23.

42. Paul Streeten, "Human Development: Means and Ends," *American Economic Review* 84, no. 2 (1994): 236.

43. UNDP, *Human Development Report 1999*, 3.

44. Ibid., 38.

45. Ibid., 2.

46. Ibid., 149.

47. UNCTAD, *Trade and Development Report 1997* (New York: UN, 1997).

48. Stiglitz, "Towards a New Paradigm for Development."

49. Joseph Stiglitz, "Distribution, Efficiency, and Voice: Designing the Second Generation of Reforms," Paper presented at the Conference on Asset Distribution, Poverty, and Economic Growth, Brasilia, Brazil, 14 July 1998, available on the Web site of the World Bank; "Towards a New Paradigm for Development"; and "Participation and Development: Perspective from the Comprehensive Development Paradigm," paper presented at the International Conference on Democracy, Market Economy and Development, Seoul, Korea, 27 February 1999, available on the World Bank's Web site.

50. Stiglitz, "Towards a New Paradigm for Development," 10.

51. World Bank, "The Strategic Compact: A Summary Note," available at www.worldbank.org/html/extdr/backgrd/ibrd/comsum/htm.

52. World Bank, *World Development Report 2000* (New York: Oxford University Press, 2000).

53. Michel Camdessus, "Development and Poverty Reduction: A Multilateral Approach," Address at the Tenth UNCTAD, Bangkok, Thailand, 13 February 2000, available on the IMF Web site.

54. Eduardo Animat, Deputy Managing Director of the IMF, "Making Globalization Work for All," Remarks at the German Foundation for International Development, Berlin, 14 March 2000, document available on the IMF Web site.

6. The Socialist Bloc's Collapse

1. Francis Fukuyama, *The End of History and the Last Man* (New York: Free Press, 1992).

2. Olivier Blanchard et al., *Post-Communist Reform: Pain and Progress* (Cambridge, Mass.: MIT Press, 1993).

3. Jeffrey D. Sachs, *Poland's Jump to the Market Economy* (Cambridge, Mass.: MIT Press, 1993); and David Lipton and Jeffrey Sachs, "Creating a Market Economy: The Case of Poland," *Brookings Papers on Economic Activity* 1 (1990), 75–147.

4. Adam Przeworski, *Democracy and the Market: Political and Economic Reforms in Eastern Europe and Latin America* (Cambridge: Cambridge University Press, 1991).

5. See, for example, Richard Portes, ed., *Economic Transformation in Central Europe* (London: CEPR, 1993); and Mathias Dewatripont and Gerard Roland, "The Virtues of Gradualism and Legitimacy in the Transition to a Market Economy," *Economic Journal* 102 (1992): 291–300.

6. Janos Kornai, *The Socialist System: The Political Economy of Communism* (Princeton: Princeton University Press, 1992).

7. Alec Nove, *The Economics of Feasible Socialism Revisited* (London: Harper Collins, 1991).

8. Wlodzimierz Brus and Kazimierz Laski, *From Marx to the Market, Socialism in Search of an Economic System* (Oxford: Clarendon Press, 1989).

9. Michal Illner, "The Changing Quality of Life in a Post-Communist Country: The Case of Czech Republic," *Social Indicator Research* 43 (1996): 141–170.

10. For a discussion of the socialist welfare state, see Gosta Esping-Andersen, *After the Golden Age: The Future of the Welfare State in the New Global Order*, Occasional Paper no. 7 (Geneva: UNRISD, 1994).

11. Janos Kornai, *The Socialist System* (Princeton: Princeton University Press, 1992), 210.

12. Robert Boyer, "Quelles réformes à l'Est? Une approche régulationiste," *Problèmes Economiques*, no. 2374 (1994): 2.

13. See Ajit Bhalla and Frédéric Lapeyre, "Global Integration and Social Exclusion with Special Reference to Poland and Hungary," *European Journal of Development Research* 11, no. 1 (1999): 101–124.

14. See Vaclav Klaus, *Renaissance: The Rebirth of Liberty in the Heart of Europe* (Washington, D.C.: Cato Institute, 1997); Leszek Balcerowicz, *Socialism, Capitalism, Transformation* (Budapest: Central European University Press, 1995); and Olivier Jean Blanchard, Kenneth A. Froot, and Jeffrey D. Sachs, eds., *The Transition in Eastern Europe* (Chicago: University of Chicago Press, 1994).

15. Supplement to *Hospodarske Noviny*, 4 September 1990.

16. Joseph Stiglitz, "Wither Socialism? Ten Years of Transition," Keynote address presented at Annual Bank Conference on Development Economics, Washington, D.C., 28–30 April 1999.

17. Jeffrey D. Sachs, "Consolidating Capitalism," *Foreign Policy* 98 (Spring 1995): 50–64.

18. Janos Kornai, "Reforming the Welfare State in Postsocialist Societies," *World Development* 25, no. 8 (1997): 1183–1186.

19. ECE, "Economic Reform in the East: A Framework for Western Support," in *Economic Survey of Europe 1989–1990* (Geneva: UN, 1990), 5–26.

20. ECE, *Economic Survey of Europe 1990–1991: The Hard Road to the Market Economy* (Geneva: UN, 1991).

21. Ibid., 119.

22. For a discussion see, for example, Béla Greskovits, *The Political Economy of Protest and Patience: East European and Latin American Transformations Compared* (Budapest: Central European University Press, 1998).

23. ECE, *Three Decades of the United Nations Economic Commission for Europe* (New York: UN, 1978), 272.

24. Yves Berthelot, ed., *Perspectives on Development: Views from the Regional Commissions* (Bloomington: Indiana University Press, forthcoming).

25. Janos Kornai, "Transformational Recession: The Main Causes," *Journal of Comparative Economics* 19, no. 1 (August 1994): 39–63.

26. Charles William Maynes, "A New Strategy for Old Foes and New Friends," *World Policy Journal* 17, no. 2 (Summer 2000): 68.

27. Ewa Ruminska Zimny, *Human Poverty in Transition Economies: Regional Overview for HDR 1997*, UNDP Occasional Papers no. 28 (New York: UNDP, 1997), 11.

28. Branko Milanovic, "Income Inequality and Poverty During the Transition: A Survey of Evidence," *MOCT-MOST Economic Policy in Transitional Economies* 6, no. 1 (1996): 131–147.

29. Giovanni Cornia et al., "Policy, Poverty, and Capabilities in the Economies in Transition," *MOCT-MOST Economic Policy in Transitional Economies* 6, no. 1 (1996): 162.

30. UNICEF, *Central and Eastern Europe in Transition: Public Policy and Social Conditions*, Regional Monitoring Report no. 4 (Florence: UNICEF, 1997), 4.

31. UNICEF, *Generation in Jeopardy, Children in Central and Eastern Europe and the Former Soviet Union* (New York: UNICEF, 1999), 10.

32. UNICEF, *Central and Eastern Europe in Transition: Public Policy and Social Conditions*, Regional Monitoring Report no. 1 (Florence: UNICEF, November 1993).

33. UN, "Regional Symposium on Socio-Economic Policies during Macroeconomic Stabilization in Countries with Economies in Transition," New York, 3–14 April 2000, available on the UN Web site, www.un.org.

34. UNDP, *Human Development Report 1999* (Oxford: Oxford University Press, 1999), 151.

35. Jan Culik, "Profound Disillusionment," *Central European Review*, 8 November 1999.

36. Joanna Rohozinska, "Last Week in Poland," *Central European Review*, 20 September 1999.

37. Eurostat, *Eurobarometer* (Brussels: European Commission, 1995).

38. Joanna Rohozinska, "Last Week in Poland," *Central European Review*, 25 October 1999.

39. OECD, *Short-Term Economic Indicators* (Paris: OECD, 1997).

40. Joanna Rohozinska, "Last Week in Poland," *Central European Review*, 4 September 1999.

41. IMF, "Forces of Globalization Must Be Embraced," *IMF Survey* 26, no. 10 (1997): 154.

42. Alison Smale, "After the Fall, Traffic in Flesh, Not Dreams," *New York Times*, 11 June 2000, WK6.

43. Joseph Stiglitz, "Towards a New Paradigm for Development: Strategies, Policies, and Processes," 1998 Prebisch Lecture (Geneva: UNCTAD, 1998), 5.

44. Stiglitz, "Whither Reform? Ten Years of Transition," 20; and Gil Eyal, Ivan Szelényi, and Eleanor Townsley, *Making Capitalism without Capitalists* (London: Verso, 1998).

45. Béla Greskovits, *The Political Economy of Protest and Patience: East European and Latin American Transformations Compared* (New York: Central European Press, 1998), 178.

46. ECE, *Economic Survey of Europe 1995* (Geneva: ECE, 1995), 16.

47. We are grateful to Yves Berthelot for this summary.

48. ECE, *Economic Survey of Europe 2000* (Geneva: ECE, 2000), 1.

7. Widening Global Gaps

1. See Jacques Baudot, ed., *Building a World Community: Globalisation and the Common Good* (Copenhagen: Royal Danish Ministry of Foreign Affairs, 2000).

2. Quoted in the *Washington Post*, 5 July 2000, A12–13.

3. See Leon Gordenker, Roger A. Coate, Christer Jönsson, and Peter Söderholm, *International Cooperation in Response to AIDS* (London: Pinter, 1995).

4. Quoted in the *Washington Post*, 5 July 2000, A12–13.

5. UNDP, *Human Development Report 1999* (New York: Oxford University Press, 1999), 3.

6. Stefan Zweig, *The World of Yesterday, an Autobiography* (New York: Viking Press, 1943).

7. The Gini coefficient is a measure of inequality. It is 1 if inequality is extreme, and 0 if everyone is equal.

8. Branko Milanovic, *True World Income Distribution, 1988 and 1993: First Calculation Based on Household Surveys Alone*, World Bank Paper (Washington, D.C: World Bank, 1999), 27.

9. The quote is taken from Angus Maddison, "Economic Policy and Performance in Capitalist Europe," in *Economic and Social Development into the Twenty-first Century*, ed. Louis Emmerij (Baltimore: Johns Hopkins University Press, 1997), 307.

10. Herbert Frankel's article, "United Nations Primer for Development," appeared in the *Quarterly Journal of Economics* 66, no. 3 (August 1952): 301–326; Arthur Lewis's answer, in "United Nations Primer for Development: Comment," *Quarterly Journal of Economics* 67, no. 2 (May 1953): 267–275.

11. Commission on International Development, *Partners in Development* (New York: Praeger, 1969), 3.

12. UNDP, *Human Development Report 1999* (New York: Oxford University Press, 1999), 2.

13. UNDP, *Human Development Report 1998* (New York: Oxford University Press, 1998).

14. UNRISD, *States in Disarray* (Geneva: UN, 1995).

15. World Bank, *Can Africa Claim the Twenty-first Century?* (Washington, D.C.: World Bank, 2000), 21.

16. This was the tenth in the series and devoted to "Globalization with a Human Face."

17. UNCTAD, *The Least Developed Countries 1999 Report—Overview* (New York: UN, 1999), 3.

18. Ibid., 17.

19. UNCTAD, *Trade and Development Report 1999* (New York: UN, 1999), 103.

20. Ibid., vii.

21. Ibid., 118.

22. UNCTAD, *Trade and Development Report 1997* (New York: UN, 1997).

23. UNCTAD, *Trade and Development Report 1999*, 1.

24. ILO, *World Employment Report 1995* (Geneva: ILO, 1995).

25. UN, *Comprehensive Report on the Implementation of the Outcome of the World Summit for Social Development— Report of the Secretary-General* (New York: UN, 2000), x.

26. UN, *Proposals for Further Initiatives for Social Development, Unedited Final Document as Adopted by the Plenary of the Special Session, 1 July 2000* (Geneva: UN, 2000), 7.

27. Ibid., 1.

28. UN, *Compilation of the Summaries and Proposals for Further Action Provided by the United Nations System* (New York: UN, 2000), 7.

29. UN, World Bank Group, IMF, and OECD, *2000: A Better World for All* (Washington D.C.: IMF/OECD/UN/World Bank, 2000).

30. Michel Camdessus, "Keynote Address," UNCTAD Tenth Session, Bangkok, 13 February 2000, available on Internet at www.unctad-10.org/index_en.htm. In this speech Camdessus stressed the importance of introducing a social and poverty dimension into IMF work. It remains to be seen whether his successor will act on this suggestion.

31. Yilmaz Akyuz, *The Debate on International Financial Architecture: Reforming the Reformers*, UNCTAD Discussion Papers, no.148 (Geneva: UNCTAD, April 2000), 2–3.

32. Moisés Naim, "Fads and Fashion in Economic Reforms: Washington Consensus or Washington Confusion?" *Third World Quarterly* 21, no. 3 (June 2000): 505.

8. Governance, Good Governance, and Global Governance

1. See David A. Kay, *The New Nations in the United Nations 1960–1967* (New York: Columbia University Press, 1970).

2. UN, *Measures for the Economic Development of Under-Developed Countries: Report by a Group of Experts Appointed by the Secretary-General of the United Nations* (New York: UN, 1951), 17.

3. See UNDP (Robert Jackson), *Capacity Study* (New York: UNDP, 1969).

4. Colin Legum, ed., *The First U.N. Development Decade and Its Lessons for the 1970's* (New York: Praeger, 1970), especially Appendix A.

5. See, for example, Gabriel A. Almond and Sidney Verba, *The Civic Culture: Political Attitudes and Democracy in Five Nations* (Princeton: Princeton University Press, 1963); Gabriel A. Almond and James S. Coleman, eds., *The Politics of the Developing Areas* (Princeton: Princeton University Press, 1960); Marion J. Levy Jr., *Modernization and the Structure of Societies: A Setting for International Affairs* (Princeton: Princeton University Press, 1966); and Samuel P. Huntington, *Political Order in Changing Societies* (New Haven: Yale University Press, 1968).

6. An extended discussion can be found in Thomas G. Weiss, "Governance, Good Governance, and Global Governance: Conceptual and Actual Challenges," *Third World Quarterly* 21, no. 5 (October 2000): 795–814.

7. See, for instance, James N. Rosenau and Ernst-Otto Czempiel, eds., *Governance without Government: Order and Change in World Politics* (Cambridge: Cambridge University Press, 1992); Jan Kooiman, ed., *Modern Governance: New Government-Society Interactions* (London: Sage, 1993); Mihaly Simai, *The Future of Global Governance: Managing Risk*

and Change in the International System (Washington, D.C.: U.S. Institute of Peace, 1994); Meghnad Desai and Paul Redfern, eds., *Global Governance: Ethics and Economics of the World Order* (London: Pinter, 1995); Richard Falk, *On Humane Governance* (University Park: Penn State Press, 1995); Paul F. Diehl, ed., *The Politics of Global Governance: International Organizations in an Interdependent World* (Boulder: Lynne Rienner, 1997); Martin Hewson and Timothy J. Sinclair, eds., *Approaches to Global Governance Theory* (Albany, N.Y.: State University of New York, 1999); and Errol E. Harris and James A. Yunker, eds., *Toward Genuine Global Governance: Critical Reflection to Our Global Neighbourhood* (Westport, Conn.: Praeger, 1999).

8. Boutros Boutros-Ghali, *An Agenda for Peace* (New York: UN, 1992), paragraph 17.

9. www.soc.titech.ac.jp/uem/governance.html

10. World Bank, *Governance, The World Bank's Experience* (Washington, D.C.: World Bank, 1994), xiv.

11. OECD, *Participatory Development and Good Governance* (Paris: OECD, 1995), 14.

12. Commission on Global Governance, *Our Global Neighbourhood* (Oxford: Oxford University Press, 1995), 2–3.

13. See www.soc.titech.ac.jp/uem/governance.html.

14. James N. Rosenau, "Governance in the Twenty-first Century," *Global Governance* 1, no. 1 (May–August 1995): 14.

15. UNDP, *Governance for Sustainable Human Development* (New York: UNDP, 1997), 2–3.

16. Kofi Annan, *"We the Peoples": The United Nations in the Twenty-first Century* (New York: UN, 2000), 13.

17. See Eric Helleiner, *States and the Re-emergence of Global Finance: From Bretton Woods to the 1990s* (Ithaca, N.Y.: Cornell University Press, 1994). For a discussion of the importance of international institutions in transmitting ideas that in part sustain the dominant order, see Robert W. Cox with Timothy Sinclair, *Approaches to World Order* (Cambridge: Cambridge University Press, 1996).

18. World Bank, *Accelerated Development in Sub-Saharan Africa: An Agenda for Action* (Washington, D.C.: World Bank, 1981); and *Sub-Saharan Africa: From Crisis to Sustainable Growth* (Washington, D.C.: World Bank, 1989). For African responses, see Goran Hyden, Dele Oluwu, and Hastings Oketh Ogendo, *African Perspectives on Governance* (Trenton, N.J.: Africa World Press, 2000).

19. Enrico Augelli and Craig Murphy, *America's Quest for Supremacy and the Third World* (London: Pinter, 1988), 184.

20. See Nassau Adams, *Worlds Apart: The North-South Divide and the International System* (London: Zed Books, 1997).

21. Samuel P. Huntington, *The Third Wave: Democratization in the Late Twentieth Century* (Oklahoma City: University of Oklahoma Press, 1991).

22. The Union of International Associations in Brussels publishes annually its *Handbook of International Organizations*. For a discussion, see John Boli and George M. Thomas, eds., *Constructing World Culture: International Nongovernmental Organizations since 1875* (Stanford, Calif.: Stanford University Press, 1999).

23. See "NGO Futures: Beyond Aid," Special Issue of *Third World Quarterly* 21, no. 4 (August 2000).

24. See Steve Charnowitz, "Two Centuries of Participation: NGOs and International Governance," *Michigan Journal of International Law* 18, no. 2 (Winter 1997): 183–286.

25. To cite merely a few key sources, see Bertrand Schneider, *The Barefoot Revolution: A Report to the Club of Rome* (London: IT Publications, 1988); David Korten, *Getting to the Twenty-first Century: Voluntary Action and the Global Agenda* (West Hartford, Conn.: Kumarian, 1990); and Paul Wapner, *Environmental Activism and World Civic Politics* (New York: State University of New York Press, 1996). A series of articles and an annotated bibliography is found in Thomas G. Weiss and Leon Gordenker, eds., *NGOs, the UN, and Global Governance* (Boulder: Lynne Rienner, 1996), 227–240. See also UN Non-Governmental Liaison Service, *The United Nations, NGOs, and Global Governance: Challenges for the Twenty-first Century* (Geneva: NGLS, 1996).

26. Bill Seary, "The Early History: From the Congress of Vienna to the San Francisco Conference," in *"The Conscience of the World": The Influence of Non-Governmental Organisations in the U.N. System*, ed. Peter Willetts (London: Hurst, 1996), 17.

27. Terje Tvedt, "Development NGOs—Actors in a New International Social System," draft paper, Centre for Development Studies, University of Bergen, 3 November 1997. See also Colette Chabbott, "Development INGOs," in Boli and Thomas, eds., *Constructing World Culture*, 222–248.

28. Julie Fisher, *The Road from Rio: Sustainable Development and the Nongovernmental Movement in the Third World* (Westport, Conn.: Praeger, 1993).

29. Robin Guthrie, *Civic, Civil, or Servile?* (Geneva: International Standing Conference on Philanthropy, 1994), 7.

30. "NGOs: Sins of the Secular Missionaries," *Economist*, (29 January–4 February 2000): 25–27.

31. Kalevi J. Holsti, *The State, War, and the State of War* (Cambridge: Cambridge University Press, 1996), 189.

32. See, for example, Carnegie Commission on Preventing Deadly Conflict, *Preventing Deadly Conflict* (New York: Carnegie Corporation, 1997).

33. Morten Bøås, "Governance as Multilateral Bank Policy: The Cases of the African Development Bank and the Asian Development Bank," *European Journal of Development Research* 10, no. 2 (1998): 119–120.

34. UNDP, *Human Development Report 2000* (New York: Oxford University Press, 2000).

35. Ibid., iii.

36. See Stephen Marglin and J. Schor, *The Golden Age of Capitalism: Reinterpreting the Post-War Experience* (Oxford: Clarendon Press, 1990).

37. Antonio Gramsci, *Selections from the Prison Notebooks* (London: Lawrence and Wishart, 1971), 377.

38. UNDP, *The Shrinking State: Governance and Human Development in Eastern Europe and the Commonwealth of Independent States* (New York: UNDP, 1997), 1.

39. World Bank, *World Development Report 1997: The State in a Changing World* (New York: Oxford University Press, 1997), 131.

40. See, for example, Joseph Stiglitz, "Redefining the Role of the State: What Should It Do? How Should It Do It? And How Should These Decisions Be Made?" Presented on the Tenth Anniversary of MITI Research Institute, Tokyo, 17 March 1998, available on the World Bank Web site, www.worldbank.org.

41. World Bank, *World Development Report 1997*, 131.

42. See, for example, *Report of the United Nations High Commissioner for Human Rights*, UN document A/54/36, 23 September 1999.

43. The Mahbub ul Haq Human Development Centre, *Human Development in South Asia 1999: The Crisis of Governance* (Oxford: Oxford University Press, 1999), 28. The early papers for this report on humane governance were drafted by Lord Meghnad Desai.

44. Annan, *"We the Peoples,"* 13.

45. Mark W. Zacher, *The United Nations and Global Commerce* (New York: UN, 1999), 5.

46. Mahbub ul Haq, Richard Jolly, Paul Streeten, and Khadija Haq, eds., *The UN and the Bretton Woods Institutions* (London: Macmillan, 1995), 13.

47. Gerry Helleiner, "A New Framework for Global Economic Governance," Speech to the Second Committee of the General Assembly, 15 October 1999, 2.

48. UNDP, *Human Development Report 1999* (New York: Oxford University Press, 1999), 98.

49. Commission on Global Governance, *Our Global Neighbourhood*, xv.

50. UNDP, *Human Development Report 1999*, chap. 5.

51. Commission on Global Governance, *Our Global Neighbourhood*, 4.

52. Commission on Global Governance, *Our Global Neighbourhood*, 335–348 (reprinted with permission).

53. This idea was discussed by the Independent Working Group on the Future of the United Nations, *The United Nations in its Second Half-Century* (New York: Ford Foundation, 1995), 25–38, and by the Commission on Global Governance, *Our Global Neighbourhood*, 135–224.

54. Lawrence S. Finkelstein, "What Is Global Governance?" *Global Governance* 1, no. 3 (September–December 1995): 369.

55. James N. Rosenau, "Toward an Ontology for Global Governance," in Hewson and Sinclair, eds., *Approaches to Global Governance Theory*, 287. See also James N. Rosenau, *The United Nations in a Turbulent World* (Boulder: Lynne Rienner, 1992).

56. Annan, *"We the Peoples,"* 13.

57. For these and other startling statistics, see Erskine Childers with Brian Urquhart, *Renewing the United Nations System* (Uppsala, Sweden: Dag Hammarskjöld Foundation, 1994); these are from pp. 28–29.

58. Rosenau, "Toward an Ontology," 293.

59. Amartya Sen, *Development as Freedom* (New York: Knopf, 1999), 112.

60. For example, see Boutros Boutros-Ghali, "Foreword," in Thomas G. Weiss and Leon Gordenker, eds., *NGOs, the UN, and Global Governance* (Boulder: Lynne Rienner, 1995), 7–12; and Kofi Annan, *Renewing the United Nations: A Programme for Reform* (New York: UN, July 1998) and *"We the Peoples."* See also Thomas G. Weiss, David P. Forsythe, and Roger A. Coate, *The United Nations and Changing World Politics*, 3d ed. (Boulder, Colo.: Westview, 2001), especially chap. 10.

Index

Page numbers in *italics* refer to tables.

About the Authors

Louis Emmerij is Senior Research Fellow at The CUNY Graduate Center, where he is co-director of the United Nations Intellectual History Project. Until 1999 he was special adviser to the president of the Inter-American Development Bank. Before that he had a distinguished career as president of the OECD Development Center, rector of the Institute for Social Studies in the Hague, and director of the ILO's World Employment Program. Among his recent books are *Economic and Social Development into the Twenty-first Century* (Johns Hopkins University Press, 1997), editor; *Limits to Competition* (MIT Press, 1995), coauthor; *Nord-Sud: La Grenade Degoupilée* (First, 1992); *Financial Flows to Latin America* (OECD, 1991), coeditor; *Science, Technology, and Science Education in the Development of the South* (Trieste, 1989); *One World or Several?* (Paris, 1989), editor; and *Development Policies and the Crisis of the 1980s* (OECD, 1987).

Richard Jolly is Senior Research Fellow at The CUNY Graduate Center, where he is co-director of the United Nations Intellectual History Project, and Honorary Professorial Fellow at the University of Sussex. Until mid-2000 he was special adviser to the UNDP administrator and architect of the widely acclaimed *Human Development Report*. Before this, he served for fourteen years as UNICEF's deputy executive director for programs, and prior to that a decade as the director of the Institute of Development Studies at the University of Sussex. Publications to which he has contributed include *Development with a Human Face* (Clarendon, 1997); *The UN and the Bretton Woods Institutions: New Challenges for the Twenty-first Century* (Macmillan, 1995); *Adjustment with a Human Face* (Clarendon, 1987); *Disarmament and World Development* (Pergamon, 1978); and *Planning Education for African Development* (East African Publishing House, 1969).

Thomas G. Weiss is Presidential Professor at The CUNY Graduate Center, where he is director of the Ralph Bunche Institute for International Studies, co-director of the United Nations Intellectual History Project, and editor of *Global Governance*. From 1990 to 1998, as a research professor at Brown University's Watson

Institute for International Studies, he held a number of administrative assign-
ments (director of the Global Security Program, associate dean of the Faculty, associate director), served as executive director of the Academic Council on the UN
System, and co-directed the Humanitarianism and War Project. He has also been
executive director of the International Peace Academy, a member of the UN secretariat, and a consultant to several public and private agencies. His latest books
are *Military-Civilian Interactions: Intervening in Humanitarian Crises* (Rowman
and Littlefield, 1999); *Humanitarian Challenges and Intervention* (Westview, 2000),
2d edition with Cindy Collins; and *The United Nations and Changing World Politics* (Westview, 2001), 3d edition with Roger A. Coate and David P. Forsythe.

About the Project

The United Nations Intellectual History Project was launched in mid-1999 because there is no adequate study of the origins and evolution of the history of ideas cultivated within the UN and of their impact on wider thinking and international action. Although certain aspects of the world organization's economic and social activities have been the subject of books and articles, there is no comprehensive intellectual history of its contributions to setting the past, present, or future international agendas, nor a comprehensive intellectual history for the economic and social fields.

This project is analyzing the evolution of key ideas and concepts about international economic and social development born or nurtured under UN auspices. Their origins are being traced, and the motivations behind them as well as their relevance, influence, and impact are being assessed against the backdrop of the socioeconomic situations of individual countries, the global economy, and major international developments. The project is commissioning studies about the major economic and social ideas or concepts central to UN activity, which will be published by Indiana University Press. It also is conducting fifty to seventy-five in-depth oral history interviews with leading contributors to crucial ideas and concepts within the UN system.

For further information, the interested reader should contact:

United Nations Intellectual History Project
The CUNY Graduate Center
365 Fifth Avenue, Suite 5203
New York, New York 10016-4309
212-817-1920 Tel
212-817-1565 Fax
UNHistory@gc.cuny.edu
www.unhistory.org